Abbé Hulst

Life of Mother Maria Teresa

Foundress of the congregation of the adoration of reparation

Abbé Hulst

Life of Mother Maria Teresa
Foundress of the congregation of the adoration of reparation

ISBN/EAN: 9783742840608

Manufactured in Europe, USA, Canada, Australia, Japa

Cover: Foto ©Andreas Hilbeck / pixelio.de

Manufactured and distributed by brebook publishing software (www.brebook.com)

Abbé Hulst

Life of Mother Maria Teresa

THÉODELINDE DE BOUCHÉ

LIFE

OF

MOTHER MARIA TERESA,

FOUNDRESS

OF THE

Congregation of the Adoration of Reparation.

BY THE

ABBÉ HULST.

TRANSLATED BY LADY HERBERT.

LONDON: BURNS AND OATES,
Portman Street and Paternoster Row.

LONDON:
ROBSON AND SONS, PRINTERS, PANCRAS ROAD, N.W.

PREFACE OF THE TRANSLATOR.

IN giving to the English Catholic public a translation of the Abbé Hulst's beautiful Life of this holy and devoted soul, we can add but few words of our own. Those who wish to find a narrative full of exciting incidents will be disappointed in this book. It is the history of a soul which on earth was hidden from all eyes but God's and her confessors', and which is only revealed to us now through the obedience which compelled her to put in writing the account of the wonderful graces she received. Those, again, who have no sympathy with the supernatural life, who are disposed to criticise every expression of a devotion which leaves the beaten path for ways pointed out to a soul by God Himself, would do well to leave these pages unread. We would dedicate them to the lovers of the Blessed Sacrament, to the adorers of the tabernacle, to the humble followers of the hidden life of Nazareth—to all those who hope and pray to see this beautiful Religious Institute established in our own land, according to the expressed wish of its holy Foundress. None can read the touching expressions of her burning love and zeal for the glory of her Eucharistic Lord without being inflamed with a like spirit, and being encouraged to imitate her, in however slight a degree, in her fervent self-abnegation and the immolation of her whole being to the will of God.

PREFACE OF THE AUTHOR.

It is an old custom in the Church that, when any great crime has been committed which specially outrages the Divine Majesty, the faithful should be summoned before an Exposition of the Blessed Sacrament, and solemn prayers addressed to the Eucharistic Mediator in reparation of the sacrilege.

This thought brought about, three hundred years ago, the institution of the 'Forty Hours'' Adoration. The three days which precede Lent are, for the world in general, the occasion of sin: for the children of God they should be consequently days of expiation, and the Holy Eucharist is proposed to them as the Divine method whereby alone their expiation can be made effective for the salvation of souls.

Later on, the same inspiration gave to the faithful a variety of devotions in honour of the Blessed Sacrament, each and all to be performed in a spirit of reparation and penance. Finally, at a later era, the idea of reparation, always closely united with the worship of the Eucharist, gave rise to the beautiful and touching devotion of *Perpetual Adoration*.

It was in 1848, between the two crises of February and June, that Paris, the main cause and the theatre of our misfortunes, gave birth to this spontaneous fruit of faith. Christian souls, in this hour of anguish, felt that the measure of God's justice was full. Many conceived the idea of opposing perpetual reparation to perpetual outrages; and to prolong, night and day, at the feet of the tabernacle, where the Blessed Sacrament would be exposed, holy watches of adoration and prayer. This pious wish could not fail to find an echo in the heart of Paris's chief pastor, Mgr. Sibour, who had witnessed at Rome the marvellous fruits of this devotion, which is an old one in the Eternal City, and had been the first to introduce it in France in his diocese of Digne. It was then, with a holy eagerness, that, having become Archbishop of Paris, he welcomed the spontaneous impulse of his flock, and transformed it into an association which enabled all the sanctuaries in the capital to share the honour of opening their gates in turn to these religious exercises. From Paris this association spread rapidly through the greater part of the dioceses of France; and the year which gave it birth marks certainly an important era in the history of the renewal of Catholic piety throughout the country.

But it was not enough to call upon the faithful to follow from church to church the privilege of the exposition of the Blessed Sacrament. It was necessary that a devotion so visibly inspired by God should find somewhere a more hidden sanctuary, where, in a still deeper spirit of recollection, souls consecrated by religious profession should make the adoration of reparation not the object of a passing visit, but the principle of a special vocation; not the occupation of an hour, but that of a whole life. Providence intervened to meet this want. About the time when the diocesan work of 'Perpetual Adoration' was begun in Paris, a vigorous branch was being grafted on the venerable stem of Carmel, and souls eager for sacrifice, and burning with love, found a new career opened to their zeal in a religious institute, which is best characterised in the title bestowed upon it, '*L'Adoration Réparatrice.*' Enriched by all the graces of the cloister without its impassable barriers, the new sanctuary was to have a door open to the world, to call in adorers to join their homages to those of the spouses of Jesus Christ, and to become, as it were, the school of the 'Perpetual Adoration.' This creation became, therefore, at once a religious work and one of apostolic zeal, uniting to the merits of retreat an apostolate of example and prayer.

Twenty years have now elapsed. What, in 1848, was only the dream of a soul passionately devoted to the glory of the Eucharist is become a living and a beautiful reality. The Congregation of the '*Adoration of Reparation*' is thoroughly established. Receiving, at first, the sanction of the diocesan authorities, it has obtained from the Holy See the official canonical approbation. It has already four houses in France; and in the four sanctuaries of the work adorers in large numbers succeed one another, day and night, before the monstrance.

This growth, which might seem rapid when glanced at in this manner all at once, has been operated slowly amidst the trials and contradictions which seem to be the portion of all works blessed by God. Born in poverty, the institute has grown without ceasing to be poor, and yet without failing to receive from day to day the bread asked for in the '*Pater.*' The good it has already done, the number of souls whom it has led in the path of fervour, the continual homages it has procured for the Holy Eucharist, the multiplied graces it has obtained for all kinds of persons, the important part which it plays in the increase and development of the devotion to the Blessed Sacrament, finally the love of obscurity which it has known how to keep as a family tradition—all these marks of a work willed by God and animated by His Spirit naturally call the attention of pious souls to the instrument chosen by Providence as its founder. One is induced to ask, 'Who, then, was this soul? What did God do for her? How did He prepare her for her mission? And in what way did He enable her to accomplish it?'

We own without shame that this curiosity was ours. Three or four years before her death it was granted to us to see this holy Foundress; and we did not approach her without feelings of great veneration. Yet we were far indeed from suspecting the treasures of grace which she kept hidden under the cloak of her intense humility. But having been lately charged with the duty of searching among, and collecting from, her papers some thoughts which might be useful to rekindle the zeal of the '*associates*' of the '*Adoration of Reparation,*' we have not only been struck by the elevation of mind and the solidity and unction of spiritual doctrine contained in them; but her own life, the history of her soul, the thoughts which inspired her work, as they were described in these letters and numerous writings, appeared to us the most eloquent conceivable exhortation to the adoration of the Blessed Eucharist; and, at the same time, the most touching commentary on those words which she had made her motto:

'*Love and Self-sacrifice.*'

It is this story of her life which we now offer to the Christian reader. The born enemies of mysticism—those who confound beforehand the abuse of a good thing with the thing itself—will not like this book. But simple souls, who do not limit the Power of God, and who know that its measure is that of His Love, will find in these pages, whatever may be their other demerits, a perfume of grace which emanates from the subject itself, and which rejoices the eye of faith. They will see the workings of that mysterious Providence which chooses, fashions, and governs, according to His will, the instruments of His supernatural designs. They will gather warmth and strength from contact with this great heart. They will feel for her anguish; they will sympathise in her generous ardour and in her noble self-devotion. They will follow, step by step, across all the phases of her trials and suffering, this passionate lover of the Glory of Jesus Christ in the Holy Sacrament of the Altar. From this humble and hidden life they will draw a bright light which may dissipate for many the obscurities of faith. And perhaps then, happy to find themselves in the current of Truth, they will feel secretly an ardent wish which was frequently ours during this work. May these pages, intended for the support and encouragement of faithful souls, fall by chance under the eyes of the unbeliever, fix for a moment his distracted attention, and furnish him with the sweetest and most powerful revelation which can manifest God to the heart of man—the revelation of His unutterable Love!

CONTENTS.

CHAPTER I.
Childhood of Theodelinda.—Religious indifference of her family.—First graces.—The pious and retired life of Theodelinda until the age of twenty-two years 1

CHAPTER II.
Her own account of her life from the time of her departure from Orleans until her mother's death 10

CHAPTER III.
Interior sufferings.—Laborious life.—Works of charity.—Conversion of her father 30

CHAPTER IV.
First thoughts of vocation.—Extraordinary devotion to the Blessed Sacrament.—Vision of the Sacred Face.—Some reflections on the supernatural state 50

CHAPTER V.
Interior life.—Thoughts of vocation.—Dealings with Carmel.—Spiritual connection with Mother Isabella.—Desire for reparation.—Theodelinda settles with her father . . . 69

CHAPTER VI.
Theodelinda's zeal for souls.—Her confessor instructs her in spiritual direction.—Revolution of February.—Forty days' penance.—First idea of the foundation of a community of Réparatrice Sisters 80

CHAPTER VII.
Events of June.—Foundation of the Third Order . . . 91

CHAPTER VIII.

First year of religious life.—Novitiate.—The Foundress's first coöperators separate from her.—Interior and exterior trials.—M. Dubouché generously agrees to his daughter's vocation.—Theodelinda's profession under the name of 'Mary Teresa' 96

CHAPTER IX.

Spiritual joy caused by her profession.—She abandons herself to supernatural action.—Her extraordinary states alarm her directors.—Humiliating examination.—Frightful temptations which ensue.—The Blessed Virgin restores peace to her soul.—Incredible zeal for the sanctification of souls.—She commits her rules to writing.—The institute in danger.—It is saved by the humility of the Foundress and the devotedness of her spiritual daughters 110

CHAPTER X.

The foundation at Lyons.—Fearful trial occasioned by the infidelity of the local Superioress.—More favourable dispositions of the Diocesan Council at Paris.—Astonishing prosperity of the new institute 139

CHAPTER XI.

Mary Teresa devotes herself to the government of her institute.—Characteristics of her direction.—Solidity of her mystical doctrine.—The institute obtains a Laudative Brief from Rome.—Project of a foundation apart from Carmel.—Reasons which determine the choice of the old Ursuline convent.—Laborious life of the community at the time of their installation 163

CHAPTER XII.

Vicissitudes of her interior state.—Journey to Rome.—Political and religious impressions.—Return to France.—The order for men seems on the point of being founded.—Spiritual relations of Mary Teresa with Mgr. Luquet and Brother Francis 187

CHAPTER XIII.

Fire in the chapel at Paris.—Mary Teresa is saved from the flames half burnt.—Her faith and energy amid sufferings.—She gradually withdraws from the government of her houses.—Her dealings with Cardinal Morlot.—Her abdication.—She causes another Superior to be elected . . 211

CHAPTER XIV.

Serious illness.—Foundation at Chalons.—Increasing ardour of Mary Teresa's feelings towards the Holy Eucharist . 225

CHAPTER XV.

Building of the new monastery.—Laying of the foundation-stone of the chapel.—Difficulties raised at Rome concerning the Approbation.—What Mary Teresa suffers on this account.—Interior trials.—Last illness.—Sentiments during her last days.—Her death and burial 237

CHAPTER XVI.

Principal characteristic of the sanctity of Mary Teresa.—A few traits of her virtues: her faith, love of God, poverty, humility, love of suffering.—Her own idea of her foundation.—Conclusion 260

Life of Mother Mary Teresa.

CHAPTER I.
1809-1831.

Childhood of Theodelinda.—Religious indifference of her family.—First graces.—The pious and retired life of Theodelinda until the age of twenty-two years.

PROVIDENCE makes use of various means to attain her ends. Sometimes, to lead a soul on the road to perfection, she surrounds it from the cradle with every care, lesson, and example, in order to show that even the resources of nature are, with her, instruments of grace and means of sanctification; at other times she shows forth the power of her grace by causing a lily to blossom among thorns, and sanctity to germinate amidst indifference and impiety.

It was in this latter way that it pleased God to conduct Theodelinda Dubouché to the goal to which His love had destined her.

Without being impious, her family professed that practical indifference to all religion which satisfies the consciences of so many in these days. Her father, diverted from the faith by the prejudices of the last century; her mother, engrossed in the affairs of this world, and contemning every kind of religious practice; a brother, who had died young after a life of dissipation—all formed from her cradle an *entourage* which threatened to bury her for ever in earthly thoughts and wishes; add to this, a lively disposition, a quick but reflective mind, ardent feelings, and rare artistic talent, and you will be able to form an idea of how, humanly speaking, her mind would be led to the idolatry of all created things, and a contempt of the supernatural.

She was born at Montauban on the 2d May 1809. Her father was from the south of France, her mother was of Italian origin. From her earliest years she betrayed the natural qualities and defects of her southern nature: kindhearted and excitable, proud and irascible, but generous and devoted, she at the same time possessed an amount of perseverance and reflection rarely to be met with in such lively characters. If she had been brought up in a Christian manner, she would have been pious from her childhood; for she was not five years of age when she began to admire everything in nature, and to take a pleasure in thinking of Him who had created all this beauty. Without knowing why, she was always recollected in church, and her mother laughingly called her *the little devotee.* But these good dispositions were not cultivated. She heard God spoken of with coldness or indifference, and no one strove to inspire her with love for Him. Henceforth her reasoning powers gained the mastery over her. She quitted games suitable to her age to listen to the conversation of her elders. She had fits of seriousness too; and, when left alone, instead of playing, she would make a sort of hermitage in the garden, where she could muse at her ease. Her family considered her a little wonder, but whom they loved, esteemed, and even laughed at. It was, however, from this profane circle that God called her, and imprinted on her soul that first mark of faith and love which was never after effaced. Her parents went to church but rarely, and then only for appearance' sake; for the same reason, and to please the village *Curé,* they erected each year in their garden a *reposoir* for the procession on Corpus Christi. Theodelinda relates that her mother, ever ready for amusement, took pleasure in dressing her as an angel, to scatter flowers on the altar of the Blessed Sacrament. She never doubted that the God of the Eucharist had favourably received this simple homage of His future spouse, and shed on her soul at that time the first grace of her vocation. Towards the end of her life she loved to revive in her soul the memory of these divine favours. 'I still remember,' she writes to her confessor, 'what the Blessed Sacrament said to my heart when It visited the *reposoirs* prepared in my mother's garden.'

From that time the Holy Spirit became her master. Before she had reached her seventh year her baby-conscience understood that her parents were not walking in the right path; that, nevertheless, it was her bounden duty to respect them, and that she should devote herself to them out of love for that God whom they did not serve. Her piety was not in any way sentimental; she was animated with the feeling of duty and the firm resolution rather to die than ever to offend God mortally. Thus, without any exterior assistance, that perfect charity infused by baptism developed itself in the heart of a child. Certain faults likewise appeared in her character, and her education did not tend to correct them. She compared herself with those who surrounded her, and, feeling her own superiority, she became difficult to manage. There was a singular amount of reflection, however, even in her childish escapades; when her impertinent repartees had evoked a little bodily punishment, remembering the maxim she had so frequently seen when learning to read—*Kiss the hand which chastises you*—she never failed after correction to kiss her mother's hand. When about ten years of age she was sent to school as a boarder;* but she was of such an independent character that she could only remain there a few months. She had taken for her emblem an open cage, with the motto, '*Liberty makes me faithful.*' Nevertheless these few months of captivity worked an important change in her character. Until then she had but few religious *instincts;* she then received religious instruction, and her soul eagerly imbibed celestial truths. Whilst still young she made her First Communion; but alone, without companions, and under circumstances little calculated to develop her natural piety.

Imagine a child between ten and eleven years of age con-

* At Orleans, where she lived with her parents from 1818 to 1831.

demned to a retreat of three days, without sermons, without religious exercises, without pious books, the direction of her confessor, or help of any kind. God doubtless permitted this strange conduct on the part of her superiors to show that He alone wished to be her Master. Those three days of seclusion and silence, which for other children would have been days of *ennui* and disgust, were spent by Theodelinda in serious meditation. She considered her difficult position with respect to her family; the distance which separated her from them in religious matters; the future struggle she would have to make. She felt that a powerful tie bound her for ever to the Catholic Faith, and that the only means of corresponding to this light was courageously to embrace virtue—such as she understood it—and to isolate herself, by a life of occupation, from the worldly and frivolous circle around her. However, deprived of all counsels or encouragement, timid with God as with her parents, she thought it best to adhere to such religious practices as are strictly binding; consequently, for many years, she only approached the Sacraments at the four principal Feasts; but, as far as possible, she assisted at Mass daily.

Theodelinda left school immediately after making her First Communion, and began at once, with a courage beyond her years, to put in practice the plan she had laid down for herself. Her mother was troubled at seeing her going so often to church, and separating herself from society; but her maternal pride consoled her; seeing her child shutting herself up all day with her pencil or her books, she comforted herself with the thought that she would grow up a clever and superior woman; and so the mother's frivolity took pleasure in the daughter's seriousness.

The maturity of this childish mind was truly singular. Study, nature, and art alone attracted her; and at the same time the reading of history inflamed her heart with a passionate admiration for great actions, and everything which showed great devotion. 'Jeanne d'Arc,' she says, 'Jeanne Hachette, all illustrious women were my heroines; I studied their lives as I should have done the lives of the Saints.' One cannot help asking one's self what enthusiasm would not have been produced in her ardent mind by the knowledge of that supernatural heroism and devotion which casts all human heroism into the shade? But as yet all that was to her an unknown land.

With very little spiritual direction this young soul might then have been made a great saint; for all her good feelings had a religious bent, and the thought of God was never absent from her. But so far from that, she was continually warned against religious influences. Her mother frequently told her that devotion leads to madness; that she must be reasonable, maintain her independence, and allow no person to interfere in her life or direct it, even in the name of God. Example seconded this teaching, and the young communicant of yesterday now knew but one person who practised his religious duties. This was one of her father's clerks, whom she secretly admired because he alone had the courage to go to Mass on Sunday. Although Theodelinda remained faithful to the resolutions which were to separate her from her worldly relations, still it was difficult for her not to imbibe some of the prejudices instilled into her. Full of respect for confession, she nevertheless felt a mistrust of her confessor, and only mentioned at the holy tribunal what seemed to her positively a fault. Thus, alone and unassisted, she might gradually have lost that essential of piety which she had resolved to keep so carefully. But grace was struggling in her soul against family influence. Love preserved her faith. She says that she triumphed over all the assaults made on her convictions by the thought *that Christianity demands* ALL, *and that it is more exacting than the noblest philosophy*. From that time she began to take notice of the sensible favours by which God wished to gain her whole heart to Himself. She says, 'When I was fourteen years old, whilst preparing one day for confession, I felt a kind of ecstasy, which did not last long, but I was so transported with love that I thought I was going mad.' Then, her reasoning nature gaining the upper-hand, she became afraid of this grace. 'Really,' she thought to herself, 'my mother was right; one does indeed lose one's head when one is too devout.' Her confessor dying about this time, she took another, whose direction rendered her still more reserved. He wished to give her a rule of life, and forbade her amusements in which she saw no sin, and in which she joined simply in order not to irritate her mother by a refusal. Her conscience told her she was in the right; she was indignant at the thought of restraint, changed her confessor, and became more distrustful than ever.

She was then sixteen years of age. Study and the love of her parents had until then occupied her life. Her brother's death, which caused the family great sorrow, developed her sensibility in a singular manner. She began to feel an extraordinary desire to love. But God watched over her heart; and if in after years the love of that jealous God bitterly reproached her with feelings which were not wholly His, nevertheless her profound humility could never discover in her past life the slightest dangerous or culpable attachment. Indeed it appears that even then she had resolved to preserve her virginity. She thus explains herself in her account of her life:

'I wished to hide myself under the earth, saying that the love which devoured me was pure. Can any sentiment be pure which is not for God alone? What I mean to say is, that by a mysterious Providence, in the midst of a frivolous and pleasure-loving world, in which I heard day by day the most scandalous stories, or at least those which were the most calculated to make me consider human passions as an indispensable element in life, since *that interior promise I had made to God not to marry*, my mind was, so to speak, unable to understand such things; never did any impure thought or feeling find place in my will, or even in my understanding. I knew, as if by instinct, what I should avoid hearing or reading. I can never explain my feelings. I used to isolate myself completely, entering into a kind of recollection which rendered me deaf and blind when such subjects were discussed. In society or at the opera I enjoyed the splendour of the *fêtes*, the scenery or the music, but I never received any bad impression or had any thought hurtful to my innocence. I was as ignorant as a child of certain sins, and my aversion for everything that might enlighten me in such matters (which St. Paul did not wish should be named) was so strong that, if I happened to hear words or read anything equivocal, I was, and have since always been, covered with a cold perspiration. My horror for everything which was not chaste was so violent and natural that, when studying painting, during my visits to the museums or my dealing with artists, if I happened to see any unbecoming figures, I turned away with the same disgust that the sight of a bad wound would have produced.'

The same great Master who had thus instructed her in the infinite delicacy of Christian purity had already inspired her with that mistrust of prosperity, and that attraction for suffering, which are the safeguards of virtue. Doubtless, as she afterwards accused herself, there was in this feeling a certain amount of human pride—a something naturally brave—which led her to seek trouble rather than avoid it, and to love a struggle for itself; but at least her will became strengthened in these exercises, and prepared her, without her knowledge, for the great sacrifices which God would one day require of her. Whilst still a child, shortly after her First Communion, she continually sought to inflict suffering upon herself, and devoted herself with the greatest ardour to what cost her most. 'To surmount a difficulty,' she says, 'I would have persevered to my last breath; and my mother used to say of me "*that I only liked to do what gave me pain and trouble.*" To strengthen her delicate health, she had been ordered bodily exercises, to which she devoted herself with her usual energy—walking, riding, and braving fatigue of every kind—showing a vigour which seemed to belie her want of physical strength. As she grew older she did not lose her energy; but God gradually taking still further possession of her heart, what was at first only stoical courage soon became a love of the Cross.

Her intellectual tastes continued to develop themselves. Her love of the arts, especially of painting, continued to increase. In order to make progress in it, having no resources at home, she obtained her mother's permission to work at the Museum, and she there passed whole days. On her return home, when she did not go into society to please her mother, she would again shut herself up with her books. She wished to read Pascal, and the *Thoughts* (*Pensées*) of that deep genius filled her mind with fresh food. Whilst her brush was occupied on the canvas her mind travelled with Pascal through an ideal world, and she gladly gave herself up to emotions which brought her nearer to God. She loved to see religion so great, and to think that human intellect was always increased when brought in contact with it. These reflections led her to devote more time to exercises of piety, and encouraged her to ask her mother for more liberty in this matter. For the first time in her life she got leave to follow the Lent Sermons, and found in them the solution of many of the difficulties she had heard raised, and which, without shaking her faith, had often troubled her mind. The love of her Divine Master, which had thus procured for her such valuable help, inspired her with a lively gratitude and an ardent wish to be strengthened in the faith. Her Christian education had been so much neglected that she had never received Confirmation; of her own accord she determined to prepare for it, and she did so with all the gravity and earnestness of a mind already matured. The holy unction bestowed on her the gift of intense faith; she felt herself full of confidence and courage to defend her faith and make it respected. From that time she no longer feared religious discussions, which she often could not avoid, with bad Catholics and with Protestant friends, and her words were so full of holy confidence and trust that they imposed silence even on superior minds.

There was perhaps a little presumption in a young girl thus entering into controversy with people older than herself; but the real good she more than once effected by this means leads us to believe that God was pleased with the honesty of her intentions, and the ardent faith which was inspired by love.

One might have fancied that the reputation she rapidly acquired of being a woman of superior intellect might make her become proud, but the rectitude of her judgment preserved her from such a delusion. She felt herself, she said, like a one-eyed man in the midst of the blind, and desired above all things to merit the esteem which, she thought, she had acquired too cheaply. This entirely human view of our own worth would be enough to make us modest; but, as it is compatible with a great contempt of others, it is still far removed from humility. The truth is, that humility is a secret of Grace, which is gradually revealed only to the disciples of the Cross; and he who believes that he has long loved God above all things, does not yet know how to look upon creatures with the eye of charity. Thus we shall see Theodelinda the more she rises above others by the heroism of her virtues, the more she will make allowance for the defects of others, reserving for herself her clearsighted severity.

CHAPTER II.

1831-1842.

Her own account of her life, from the time of her departure from Orleans until her mother's death.

Up to the time when we shall come to Theodelinda's correspondence, our only guide in her biography is her own account of her life, written in 1852, in obedience to the express command of her confessor. In speaking of her early years we were content with analysing, by abridging, this precious document; but at the point we have now reached we feel that to touch it would be to disfigure it. In fact, we have now to relate how God definitively took possession of her heart; and in presence of those mysteries of grace of which no one knows but he who receives them, we think it right to lay aside our pen, and let her speak who was the object of so many favours.

'At the age of twenty-two my life underwent a change: I was called upon to accompany my father, who then filled an official position in a town in the north,* and who wished me to keep house for him. My mother would not change her residence, so I had to separate from her. I found myself alone and independent in the midst of the world, where I was too well received for my vanity not to be excited. The prefect's wife and daughter were fortunately good Catholics, and as they were likewise women of talent and sense, I began to feel an ardent affection for them. In our familiar intercourse they did me good; but their position obliging them to keep open house, I no longer ceased to frequent *fêtes*, dinners, concerts, and balls.

---

* Mezières. M. Dubouché was named treasurer of the department of Ardennes on the 1st January 1831. Theodelinda joined him during that year.

Seeing me adopted as one of the family, every one paid me attentions and flattered me, whilst the men did all in their power to make themselves agreeable to me. All this, without really seducing me, amused me very much. I became less serious, less prudent; I spent more time over my toilet, and sought to please those around me. A young man thought he had made an impression upon me, and wished to lead me astray. I did not dream of evil. His attentions flattered my imagination, but did not touch my heart: when I was again alone I was troubled and uneasy, and I prayed earnestly to God that I might not offend Him. That merciful Father saw my folly, and took pity on me. He began powerfully to work on my heart. The light of faith no longer sufficing, He wounded my heart as with a sharp arrow. During prayer, I felt at times a sensible feeling of love which enraptured me; I was, as it were, annihilated in that burning furnace, and I let myself be consumed. Now that I was free, I went daily to Mass, during which I was so recollected that one might have thought that I was a saint; but then in the evening I recommenced my worldly life. Nevertheless God, who watched over me, gave me a great grace: He sent me the smallpox, which cut short my worldly career. In His great mercy He did not call me away to judgment in that dreadful moment. What would have become of me? However, I saw death close at hand. Our Lord, who had tried gentle means, now allowed terror to take possession of me. But my heart was not yet won.

'I left that part of the country a few months later. The world of pleasure no longer attracted me; but I was now bewitched with wit and talent. To please me, my parents removed to Paris; I was just twenty-four.* I determined to cultivate my talent for painting, and accordingly worked from eight to ten hours daily in a studio. I eagerly frequented the society of celebrated persons. God, who wished to inspire me with disgust for all things by seeing them near, permitted an elderly man, illustrious by his writings, to take a particular affection for me. He received at his house the most distin-

* 1833.

guished persons in art and literature. On more intimate acquaintance with these remarkable men, however, I found them so full of silly vanity, that my illusions respecting human glory vanished. There were certain women too, poetesses, who might have proved very dangerous to me; but my conscience warned me to avoid them. I continued to devote my time to music and painting; but seriously, and for the love of that beauty, that eternal and celestial harmony, which reflects itself in its works.

'The study of nature led me to an incomprehensible admiration for the Creator of all things, and I became solitary, silent, and studious. My heart had always preserved its lively impressions of divine love; nevertheless my life was at that time made up of contradictions. I went to the opera to hear the music; there I used to recollect myself, and sometimes I was sensibly in the presence of God, utterly forgetful of the place where I was. I went to Mass every morning, and in the evening, on my return from my studio, I again used to go to the church to pray; and yet, in spite of that, I cherished idols, and made a kind of worship of the beautiful.'

It is probable that the 'idols' she speaks of do not simply refer to the frivolities of the world, to which she was not insensible, but that she also alludes to a feeling which possessed her heart for many years. Whilst she was living at Orleans, and was but sixteen years old, the place in the family circle left vacant by her brother's death was filled by a young cousin, whose education was intrusted to the father of Theodelinda. The latter welcomed him as a brother, sent by God Himself, and she devoted herself to him with all a sister's love. Her intentions could not have been more pure: she hoped, by means of their warm friendship, to attract him to virtue and to God. To this end she devoted herself to him; her loving heart eagerly seized this occasion for self-devotion; her whole mind was bent on the care of this soul; and her cousin's affection fully responded to hers. Eight years later, when we find her at Paris, intoxicated with the love of wit and talent, these feelings had not diminished; but those of the young man had become what she did not wish them to be. She strove to content him by persevering in her sisterly affection, but that did not suffice. Now, however perfect was Theodelinda's devotedness, it did not go so far as to denaturalise her feelings. She had always had a great repugnance for marriage; so in despair at his persistence, she proposed to her cousin that he should marry one of her friends. But this proposal on her part disgusted him beyond measure: henceforth he estranged himself from her altogether, and, alas! from virtue also.

Such was the *idolatry* with which, years after, the jealousy of Divine Love reproached her with so much bitterness. She says, '*My affection for my cousin prevented grace from obtaining supreme dominion over me.*' We must respect the exacting rigour of a love whose sole object is offended by the slightest comparison. And whilst recognising the justice of these reproaches we may be allowed to add: Happy are the souls capable of loving thus, even a created object; to love it with such ardour and such purity! Such souls do indeed merit that God should draw them to Himself, and teach them to love but Him and all things in Him.

But we will return to our narrative. On her arrival at Paris, Theodelinda sought a confessor, and she unfortunately addressed herself to one who, by a severity which appeared to her indiscreet, wounded that soul so jealous of its independence. But we will let her continue her own account of her spiritual life.

'Repulsed by the severity of my first confessor, I went in search of another, and chose the mildest I could find. I succeeded above all my expectations. When I accused myself, he excused me. He used even to speak of the Saints, and say, "Courage! God wishes you to be a saint." His simple goodness touched my heart. I inwardly laughed at his mistake, for I felt that I was not even a Christian. O, yes! God in His grace made me understand that virtue and not sensible devotion sanctifies. This good priest was far too indulgent. God doubtless permitted it to be so on account of my weakness, which as yet could endure no yoke. The great latitude allowed me by my confessor made me more circumspect than severity would have done, though, on the other hand, I feel that if I had been restrained God would have given me grace to bear it. My faith was great, and rather than give up approaching the Sacraments, I would have suffered martyrdom. The Divine Master, who has left us the liberty of the children of God, who cries, "Father, Father," in our hearts, did not wish that I should be compelled to serve Him. I began to feel a longing for more frequent communion, but I did not think myself worthy. Until the age of twenty-five I continued to approach the divine table only four times a year, as I had done since my First Communion. God doubtless pardoned me this infatuation of false humility which made me fear to cause it to be said "that devout persons were no better than any one else;" for He showered down on me His graces and lights. Everything spoke to me of Him, even what might have caused my ruin. I had a painting-master who possessed great talent. We were closely united by an affection which always remained good, simple, and pure. Nevertheless he was not a Christian; if he had been he would have been a saint, for God had gifted this soul with the noblest qualities I ever met with in a single heart. We passed many long hours together; he took a pleasure in developing my talents and judgment. We conversed on every possible subject, but he so respected my innocence and my principles that during the eight years our intimacy lasted he never uttered a word which might wound my feelings. However, we sometimes entered into religious discussions, and he loved to embarrass me, making use, as objections, of the sophisms of those who pretend to have faith. Instead of silencing me, this gave me greater strength; no sermon ever made so much impression on me as did his clever mocking pleasantry on pharisaical Christians and sensual devotees. I wished that I were really a saint, in order to show him that it was possible to be a disciple of that Jesus whose doctrine seemed to him to be too perfect for this world, and nothing more than a beautiful dream. Nevertheless, in his enthusiastic affection for me, on account of some little good I did to the young girls who, like myself, came to take lessons in painting, and also seeing that I showed some little affection for my good parents, he sometimes said to me, "If there are still saints in this world you will be one." If I had been what he supposed, I should have obtained his conversion, whilst as it was I had the misfortune of seeing him die without the Sacraments, although I did not leave his bedside for a fortnight. He used to say to me, "My dear child, I hope in the goodness of God." During his last night on earth I said the prayers for the agonising by his side; he prayed with his lips; he surrendered his soul to God whilst kissing my crucifix. God has His secrets of mercy; but the fate of this beloved soul still weighs sorrowfully on my heart.

'I have just said that I already had done some good, that is true; but I had no other merit than that of our Lord, who made use of me as He did of Balaam's ass. No one unacquainted with the artistic world can understand what good as well as evil young girls who frequent these painting-studios are capable of effecting. My influence with my master influenced us all, at least exteriorly; and with regard to some, I was the instrument of their return to a reasonable and Christian mode of life. They loved me and looked upon me as a mother, confiding in me and revealing to me all their little miseries. I had the good fortune to be useful to them in many ways. Since then several have consecrated themselves to the service of God; but if I had then corresponded with God's grace I might have helped them to avoid many troubles. They always followed my example; which sometimes, instead of aiding, retarded the progress of these souls, who were open to every good impression. Whilst speaking of this, I may as well mention that a little later, imitating the Roman artists, I formed an association of St. Luke. Every year, on that saint's feast-day, I assembled the members at the Mass said for our intention, and nearly all received communion. At one time we numbered seventeen. Then we breakfasted at my house. I read the Gospel aloud, and the day passed pleasantly. In the evening I went with them to pay a visit to the Blessed Sacrament. When I recall this to mind I look upon it as a prelude to what God demanded of me later. From that time I began to understand souls and to direct them; but having no mission I was doubtless inspired by a natural desire to command. Often, in my fright at being thought superior, I see my condemnation in these circumstances which have always raised me above others. I feel that I stand in need of being humbled, trodden under foot, despised; when shall I suffer the purgatory necessary to efface this life of pride and independence?

'Further, I am troubled at the thought of having spoken to you of God's graces towards me without confessing the sins I committed when they were most superabundant. When I say that I was loved, one would think that I was amiable and sweet-tempered; but, on the contrary, I can say with truth, that up to the age of twenty-six or twenty-seven I know no character more detestable than mine was. Every one had to give way to my will; I never yielded to any one unless it pleased me to do so. I made many sacrifices, it is true; but never any that did not suit my whims. My freedom of action was inconceivable. Confiding in my good reputation and my wish to help others, I lived an eccentric life of my own, utterly at variance with custom or the requirements of my position. I wished to see and know everything. My imagination and my heart wanted that eternal food which can alone satisfy their longing for love and light. Feeling that man was created to acquire knowledge, I thought that nothing that could increase that knowledge or develop my talents without sin should be forbidden me. Hence I committed a thousand imprudent actions which might have caused my damnation had not God Himself preserved me.

'At this time I had great confidence, both as regards soul and body, in the holy angels. When travelling I exposed myself to great dangers in order to see the beauties of nature, and whilst I was tempting God I depended on my guardian angel to watch over my bodily life. In my inordinate affections, in my eager curiosity, in my extravagant enthusiasm, I always hoped that he would check me at the right time. My faith in the presence of the angels was very great. Even as a child I had always believed in them, and in every danger to which I was exposed, by a simple internal aspiration, I invoked their assistance, and thus peace came to my soul. This belief was so natural to me that it never entered my mind to question it or to seek proofs of its truth. I called upon the angels for everything, even for greater skill in painting; for I believed that what is called the inspiration of genius is communicated to the soul through their agency. Since then I have heard with delight an eloquent preacher confirm this idea; but whilst quite young I had adopted the idea, and this it was, I think, which served to spiritualise my passionate love for study and the fine arts, and to transform my natural admiration of beauty and harmony into a means of grace. As soon as any exterior thing touched me, I retired within myself to consider its connection with the immaterial principle. And I think I may say with truth that it was this interior power which elevated my soul, far more than vanity, and which led me to love learning and to seek what was not ordinary in my pursuits.

'The first extraordinary and prolonged grace I received was on my return from the Louvre, where I had admired the energy and strong feeling of faith depicted in the Spanish paintings. I had remained a whole day before several. I remember principally a *Saint Francis of Assisi*, and a female martyr. I had often experienced, when painting and during prayer, very violent ecstasies; but they had passed away like lightning. Besides, as I had always resisted these impressions, which I could not understand, they had never obtained the mastery over my will; but this time the real battle of love began. I was twenty-six years of age, and almost crushed at that time by my quarrel with my cousin. In spite of myself, I sought in prayer consolation for a sorrow which I at the same time regarded in a somewhat romantic light. God, seeing that faith alone would not make me a Christian, sent a love stronger than the death of the foolish passions which tyrannised over me. In the evening of the day when I had meditated for so long on the real faith and holiness of these Spanish pictures, whilst saying my night prayers, I was, as it were, dumbfoundered; an ardent fire of divine love sprang up in my heart; and ever since that night all the rage of hell has been unable to quench this flame, although the smoke and dust of this world have often prevented it from bearing fruit. The remembrance of that night will never be effaced from my memory. I prayed, I loved, I adored God in a manner that I should before have thought impossible. I was intoxicated with happiness, and nevertheless the astonishment I felt at what was passing within me caused me to feel very sad. I feared that I was becoming mad; and then again in my rapture I allowed myself to be carried away without resisting.'

It is probably to this portion of her life that a few pages belong which we find among her papers, bearing the simple title *Studio*. The reader will be pleased with a short extract:

'My heart overflows, grace superabounds; my heart can no longer contain all the great sentiments which fill it. O, my God, what mystery of love art Thou working in me? O, pardon sinners, for they do not know Thee. If Thou but once raised the veil which hides Thy splendour from them, all would be at Thy feet. But, O Lord, what can our being reply to Thy love? Thy love burns and consumes me; my soul is so raised above itself that I lose the feeling of my own identity; I am, as it were, plunged in a lake of fire and light, and yet I have not sufficient love; no, no, increase my love still more! Why dost Thou pursue me, O Lord? Am I not a mere nothing, a sinner? What then is this new life which penetrates me and which I feel does not belong to me? Thou punishest the least fault that I commit; Thou desirest to reign supreme in my heart; to conquer my slightest resistance, to turn my attention from myself, Thou rainest down upon me I know not what fire which attracts me so powerfully to Thee that life is almost extinct. Nevertheless can I say that in these moments of agony I feel as if a victim to Thy anger? O, no; it is rather a marytrdom of love.'

Decidedly God had conquered. The reasoning Theodelinda was a captive to that mystical love which those belonging to another slavery look upon as a dream, but which is revealed to the soul animated by it as a powerful and imperious reality.

But let us leave Theodelinda to relate the fresh graces which transformed her life.

'I remained in this state for several days. When alone, especially at night, I prostrated myself on the ground and adored. I could not bring myself to open my mind to any one. I was troubled and uneasy; but I felt myself drawn to do great good, and my resistance was truly culpable. About this time my talent for painting spread abroad. I received an order for a painting for a church. The subject was the martyrdom of St. Philomena. In the hope of overcoming my grief and the *insouciance* caused by the violent *attrait* which drew me to God, I set to work with incredible ardour, and, in order to have more leisure, I lived a still more solitary life. Jesus was already saying to my poor soul, "I will lead her into solitude, and there I will speak to her heart." The work of God, instead of diminishing, continued to increase. I chanced to buy the *Manuel du Chrétien*, in which I found the Gospels, which I had never before read *in toto;* the Psalms, with which I was unacquainted; and the Epistles, of which I was completely ignorant. This book acted like fresh fuel to the fire; when I read certain Psalms—such as "The hart panteth," &c., "How amiable are Thy tabernacles," &c.—and, above all, in the Gospel, the discourse after the Last Supper, I was penetrated with an indescribable feeling. I remained as if paralysed, kissing instinctively these sublime pages. But meditation on the martyrdom of the saint I was painting was, perhaps, a still greater source of light and love; when I thought how that young girl had preferred death to marriage, I felt my heart melt with the desire of, like her, giving myself to my God, and, palette in hand, I became rapt in God. Nevertheless my conscience suffered greatly, for I feared I was labouring under a deception. After many interior struggles, I resolved to consult a priest whom I knew to be very enlightened and very good, but who was not my confessor. Never had I experienced such dreadful torture. A woman about to reveal her dishonour could not have felt greater shame. What was not my amazement when, instead of annihilating me, as I expected, he said,

"Do you not think that to correspond with such extraordinary graces you should become a nun? They require of you perfection, to attain which you should communicate frequently. *God loves you,* and wishes that you should belong entirely to Him." I was stunned, and felt sure that either the priest or myself had lost our senses. I become a nun! I communicate often! Of all that had been said, I could only think of those words, *God loves you;* they consumed me like fire.

'A few days later, on the Feast of Corpus Christi, I was assisting at High Mass in the Church of St. Sulpice, when, as I was looking at the Sacred Host, a dart of love issued from it, and seemed like a sharp arrow to pierce my heart with sorrow for not having communicated. I had never experienced such heartrending sorrow, which was not, however, unmixed with love. I knelt down and wept bitterly. For a whole hour I conversed with our Lord, who wished me to approach Him oftener than four times a year, whilst I pleaded, by way of excuse, my faults, my temper, my pride, &c.; He spoke to me of His love and conquered. I promised to correct myself, and to merit by my efforts to unite myself oftener to Him. I began to feel an ardent love for the sacred humanity of our Lord. The thought of my unworthiness to communicate led me to meditate much on the mystery of the Redemption. I now only thought of Jesus as my Saviour, and I began to feel that the Sacrament of Penance was so great a benefit, on account of the communication we then receive of the merits of Jesus Christ, that my repugnance to it ceased. I went to confession oftener. This greatly pleased my kind director, who encouraged me, and persuaded me to communicate oftener; but I scarcely knew what I should do. However, I found him so indulgent, and, on the other hand, my love for our Lord increased so much, that I entered the confessional in spite of myself. Soon I went every week, and sometimes I even communicated oftener. I felt at the same time great joy and great sorrow. I found heaven and purgatory side by side in this mixture of love and fear.

'I made great efforts to correct myself, and, above all, to become good. When taking possession of my heart, our Lord at the same time gave me a great compassion for His suffering members. I visited a poor invalid in the hospital, and received admirable lights concerning the sacred humanity of our Lord. One day, after seeing a poor woman whose face was covered with cancers, I repaired to the hospital chapel, and was there rapt in ecstasy whilst contemplating the reparation made for sin by the Passion of our Saviour. I began to feel a great zeal for souls; I wished to do good, and I became more and more devoted to my family. God made use of this natural inclination to induce me to make a strange retreat.* My nephew was ill, and I took him to the seaside for sea-bathing. Alone with him in a peninsula in Brittany, completely solitary and free, I sat for many hours each day on the beach meditating on God in presence of that beautiful reflection of His immensity; then I passed my evenings before the tabernacle in the village church. There I became acquainted with a *Curé*, remarkable for his learning and sanctity, who did me a great deal of good. I spent in this spot six happy weeks in union with God.

'From this time I separated myself in a visible manner from the world. I could think only of our Lord, and such thoughts inspired me with a wish to become better. I had no book on the spiritual life; my painting-master, who belonged to a Jansenist family, had often spoken to me of Nicole. I read his works, and took an interest in them. I admired his severe morality, which, however, only augmented my fears concerning Holy Communion. I wept much over confession, and my confessor did his best to console me; but his indulgence only alarmed me. I feared to fall a victim to dreadful delusions. Then I desired to obey as ardently as I had before feared to do so; but I dared not follow his counsel, because it appeared to me to be too mild. In spite of my filial gratitude for his kindness, I decided on leaving him, and placing myself under the spiritual direction of a *Curé* who had the reputation of being a

---

* Here, as in other places, the order of incidents is not correctly followed. The sojourn at Croisic belongs to the year 1837, and precedes by one year the narrative of the picture of St. Philomena and the graces connected with it.

very enlightened man, and who is in fact a saint.* After examining me, he said, "My child, the Holy Spirit is with you; you should devote yourself entirely to God; you should be in the world as a living sacrifice, devoted to your relations, a true sister of charity in the midst of your family." These words were as an oracle from God Himself. I left the studio of my master, whom I loved so well, to live with my mother, who was very seriously ill. I began to fear for her salvation, to obtain which I would have made any sacrifice. For four years I tended her day and night; I dressed her wounds with fresh ardour; my life became a real martyrdom.

'Until then I had gone to church constantly without her finding it out, because as I was accustomed to go out every day, I went to church without her knowledge. When she understood that I belonged to God, the devil excited in her a kind of despair; she repeatedly reproached me; she was jealous of my confessor, nay, even of my devotions; nothing could satisfy her. My terrible temper often occasioned me frightful interior struggles; but in order to be able to communicate, I became gentle, at least exteriorly. My mother was strongminded and sensitive, but as these characteristics had never been called forth save in worldly concerns or human sorrows, they caused her to give way to terrible fits of violence. Besides, although she was kind and made me her idol, she also caused me great suffering, and my ardent desire for her conversion made me fear so much to give her reason to say "that I was less good and amiable since I had become more devout," that I can scarcely describe the state of constraint to which the devil reduced me. Shortly after choosing my new director, I began to experience the same fear as with the former one, passing from an excessive independence to an exaggerated obedience; I always felt that my actions, however good they might be, sprang from pride and self-will.

'These troubles proceeded doubtless from a too great desire for perfection. But not being well-versed in the spiritual life, I did not perceive this, and when my confessor told me "that

* In 1838.

the most subtile pride is that of our own perfection," I thought myself lost; and yet a devouring fire excited me, particularly after Communion, to perfection and good works. I thought I sinned when I sorrowed for having missed Communion or desired to approach oftener to the holy table. When I visited the poor, I feared that I was seeking my own satisfaction. Nevertheless my confessor permitted it, and had even, for that purpose, placed me under the direction of a Sister of Charity. I had never before known a nun; my respect for her was very great, and I consulted her like a child.

'My first act done in obedience to her was blessed: I cannot think of this grace without emotion. An old woman, a great sinner, was dying and would not receive the Sacraments. The sister sent me to her bedside; I felt very awkward, not knowing what I should do. I evinced so much love for this poor soul that she took a fancy to me and was at last touched by my filial affection. She died a holy death. In her last moments she said to me, "If I go to heaven, your mother will also go there." I have always attributed, in a great measure, my dear mother's conversion to the prayers of this poor woman.

'Our Lord spoilt me from the commencement. I cannot tell you how many graces I received at the sick-beds of the poor, especially at the moment of their departure from this world. I instructed them with great care. What made most impression on them was to see me decorate their rooms as a *reposoir* to receive our Lord. I used to adorn them with lace, flowers, and a great number of candles. All this excited their faith, while it filled my heart with joy.

'But my charity created astonishment. Although I kept as quiet as possible, my confessor heard of my conduct, and prudently fearing that I was seeking to make myself extraordinary, often humbled me. My fervour, my tears, even my exactitude in visiting the Blessed Sacrament daily—all were fresh motives for suspicion. O, what great reason he had to fear my pride! His wise guidance was one of the greatest of our Lord's graces to me. However, as I was really acting in good faith, with all the simplicity of a strong and irresistible love, I suffered tortures, not understanding how I should act. When I happened to speak of my ecstasies of love it was still worse; for I was advised to be so cautious that I dared scarcely venture to pray. The Psalms and the *Imitation* appeared too exciting for me. They were so indeed; for a single sentence of the Gospel was sufficient to send me into raptures. For many years I spent my nights in unceasing prayer. I rose every morning at two o'clock to prostrate myself on the ground; I communicated only twice a week. On the eve of those happy days I was almost mad with joy. On those days that I did not receive Communion, when I saw the tabernacle opened without being able to approach, I experienced the sensible suffering of neglected love. These fervent feelings have continued to increase, only they have sometimes been united to feelings of despair, especially on the days of confession, which was to me a punishment. I regarded it in the same light as the Last Judgment, and was always expecting my condemnation. This emotion prevented my speaking, so that my holy and worthy director did not know the real state of my feelings, although my desire for him to do so was so great that it amounted to a positive scruple. God permitted this in order to purify me from past sin, and to deaden nature, which was still strong within me. But, alas, I corresponded so badly with that grace that this death is not yet achieved, and I still suffer agonies. Since my conversion, with the exception of two different times, making in all about four years, my life has been a continued alternation of celestial beatitude and terrible storms.

'During these months of interior trial I often offered my tears and my mortal anguish for the soul of my poor mother. God in His goodness then cast a look of mercy on my family. Two years before my mother's death the doctors believed her to be in danger, and gave me warning of the fact. I had no longer any hope. The kind Sister of Charity joined with me in a novena to St. Joseph; then on the feast-day* she herself went to see my mother, and spoke to her of the Sacraments. To all appearances she was not badly received. I was not present;

* The 19th March 1840, as we learn from a letter of Theodelinda to General C.

but on my return a scene took place which could only have been caused by the presence of Satan in a soul. She accused me of everything—even of her death; indeed, her anger was so violent that she might have died in consequence. I had just received the God of all mildness, and He gave me calm. I knelt down by her bedside, asked her pardon, kissed her hand, and retired to seek refuge at the feet of Jesus my Saviour. My emotion had been so great, my grief so heartfelt, that I fainted away in the church. But God had only wished to try my faith. On my return I found my dear invalid calm. She said to me, "Since you desire it, go and bring the *Curé.*"

'My dear mother's conversion was entire and perfect. She prepared for the Sacraments with the willingness and simplicity of a child. Separated from God for fifty years, she had forgotten everything. I was appointed to teach her the Catechism. Though very ill, she had the full use of her reason. What a happy time to my filial heart was that when I introduced the light of faith into that dear soul, so worthy to be loved for her admirable natural gifts.'

The joy which then overflowed Theodelinda's heart poured itself into that of a generous and holy friend, General C., who had long joined in her earnest desires and zealous endeavours for her mother's conversion. She wrote thus to him on the 12th May 1840 :

'I should indeed be ungrateful did I not hasten to announce to you the miracle of love which God has worked in our favour, and to thank you as the instrument He has made use of to give me the only consolation possible in these days of sorrow—but an infinite consolation; for now I no longer fear a few days' separation; the soul of my beloved mother is now united to the principle of life and immortality.'

Contrary to every expectation, Mme. Dubouché recovered from this crisis, and regained a kind of strength. After receiving her Saviour as viaticum she recovered so far as to communicate in the church. But soon she relapsed, and for two years was a victim to great sufferings. She had two cancers, and half her body was paralysed.

During this struggle Theodelinda was her guiding angel. Those who accuse devotion of crushing natural affection do not know what strength a habit of Christian self-denial adds to the resources of filial piety. When her mother was very ill, Theodelinda left all to be at her side; but when her health improved a little she set to work to help her in another manner. 'Shall I mention,' she writes, 'my poor painting? You regret it, as if it were a thing of the past; and you are right. If now I take up my pencil it is without hope, without pleasure, without ambition. My only motive for doing so is not to be a burden to my parents, who now require every possible comfort. During the two months that my mother has been able to do without me I have painted several portraits, and I likewise gave a few lessons at home; but when it is necessary I shall leave all. Providence gives me the means of preserving to my mother her lovely room—overlooking a garden—and the maid who is so useful to us. Sufficient for the day is the evil thereof.'

If her attention to her mother and her labour for her comfort occupied her whole time, her heart nevertheless preserved its liberty to give itself to God with an incomprehensible love. Would that we could here quote all those burning words of love which we find in the scattered sheets on which she noted down her feelings. Sometimes it is the sad wail of anguish and humiliation, at others the song of thanksgiving, always, however, the dart of love. We quote almost haphazard from her notebook:

'What shall I say, O God, in this abyss to which the sight of my miseries reduces me? Love alone can raise me up. O, my heart! my heart! what will become of thee? Everything crumbles and vanishes around and within me. Thou art about to find only a void; yes, a void. To this I am journeying. A void must be made before arriving at the source of all life. But this void terrifies me. I shudder! I do not wish it. My God, take the life of my body, but leave me that of my soul. But what ingratitude! what a revolt to oppose God! Ah, I detest myself! Like Adam, I wish to hide myself. When I hear the voice of our Lord I shall take to flight. Why then did I tremble at the threat of being deprived of Communion? O, it is because nature revolts in vain; I love my God more than myself. Yes, I seek in vain to persuade myself to the contrary: I love God more than myself. If I must die, I shall die; but I must belong to Him.'

And again: 'Yes, I wish to suffer; but, O God, I require Thy pardon. If anything could separate me from Thee despair would take possession of my heart. But, Lord, how dreadful are those words which I repeat daily: *Forgive me as I forgive*. O, listen not to me when I say them with a heart full of bitterness, contempt, and malice; when I implore Thy mercy, and at the same time complain of my neighbour—no, my God, I will not say those words; and yet it was Thou who gave them to me. O God! my God! it is not the words, but my heart which requires to be changed. Lamb of God, who takest away my sins, make me to love every one, so that I may be able to ask for Thy love. Didst Thou not suffer unjustly? Why then should I not suffer with the appearance of injustice? But, Lord, perhaps the interior of my heart is not really as wicked as the surface; perhaps I love those who cause me to suffer; perhaps this bitter feeling is simply a temptation. O, try my heart and my reins; judge me mercifully, and drive far from me, for the future, these frightful temptations. Those are the most cruel which tend to destroy love within me. I acknowledge that there are others more humiliating, and perhaps more dangerous; but there is not one more painful to a heart to which Thou hast given a spark of that divine love the possession of which forms the felicity of the blessed, and the privation of which I feel to be the torture of the damned. This fearful struggle almost drives me mad. Thou knowest that not a single portion of my being is respected by the enemy. O, cast on me a look of pity. I can no longer endure the trial; it is too great. I no longer say that I can do any thing of myself; I hate myself—I despise and deny myself. Well, that is sufficient. O Lord, take possession of me. Formerly my pride forbade me; but now I can have none. O, my beloved! Thou hearkenest to my voice, Thou comest to me in the midst of the darkness which surrounds me; Thou walkest on the waters to save my bark, and Thou sayest to me, "Be not afraid, my child; it is I, thy Master, thy Father, thy Redeemer." Thou wilt enter this poor bark, rescue it from all danger, and cause me soon to be brought ashore. O, let it be *soon*, I entreat of Thee; for my heart and my soul thirst after Thee, O my Lord!'

Such were the outpourings of her soul. At her mother's bedside she was a tender nurse, prodigal of care, consolation, and smiles; then when she was free for an instant she repaired to the tabernacle, there to seek a Confidant in her anguish and a Witness of her love. And her heart, eager for love, was consumed with the fear of not loving sufficiently either God or her mother; a sure proof that she loved both the one and the other.

At length the end came for the poor invalid, who had been purified by intense sufferings, borne with perfect resignation. The hour of her deliverance had come.* Theodelinda assisted at her mother's last struggles, firmly persuaded that her purgatory was ended even before she expired. 'When she had breathed her last,' she writes, ' I felt so great a joy, seeing, as it were, heaven opened, that I could not shed a tear.' But grief soon recovered its rights over the loving heart of Theodelinda. On the 20th January 1842 she wrote thus to General C.: 'The admirable resignation of my poor martyr had raised my courage; the expression of bliss on her beautiful face deprived me of even natural sorrow; for one moment I think God allowed me to share her recompense; but I assure you that the grace was soon withdrawn, and I am now plunged in extreme grief. Everything recalls her to my mind, and in everything I find her dead. My father, in his kindness, thought he would console me by giving me an independent fortune and absolute authority over his household. I know not what to do with it all. I feel as if they were robbing her of rights which she still possesses; for she always appears present to my mind; day and night she reposes on my breast, as in the last days of her illness. My excellent friend, I reveal to you my weakness; do not judge me too

* Mme. Dubouché died on the 4th January 1842.

severely. I do not think I shall ever really be the same again. Some part of me went from me when she uttered her last cry.'

We give in full these expressions of her filial grief; not to make a merit of these natural feelings, but to show what was the warmth of her heart, and the immense difference that exists between a soul that is detached and one that is insensible.

CHAPTER III.
1842-1845.

Interior sufferings.—Laborious life.—Works of charity.—Conversion of her father.

OF the two souls so long separated from her by a real abyss one was conquered, and Theodelinda's whole thoughts were now centred on her father; for her sister, touched by divine grace, had already returned to God. But this new conquest required fresh tears. Theodelinda had to purchase by suffering all the souls she loved. Like another Monica, she begot them in sorrow, and thus became the mother of those to whom she owed her life.

Even during the lifetime of Mme. Dubouché, Theodelinda, anxious for her father's salvation, communicated her fears and her hopes to a soul worthy to understand them. 'He possesses,' she would say, 'the pride of learning, which may stifle every good seed; and yet I must hope through all. For how many false ideas has he not lost during the last few years! What respect, nay, even pleasure, he showed at my mother's conversion!' It was not then mere natural tenderness, but an ardent zeal for the salvation of his soul which led Theodelinda to devote herself to her father. Immediately after his wife's death M. Dubouché, clasping his daughter in his arms, begged her to promise not to leave him during his lifetime. She promised; and, according to her testimony, God engaged to prevent that promise, however imprudent it might be, from being detrimental to her future vocation.

Grace does not stifle the feelings of the heart, but it raises them and directs them to God. The profound grief into which Theodelinda had fallen after her mother's death, far from diminishing her courage, only rendered the gift of her life to

God more perfect. 'On the very night of her death,' she writes, 'I cut off my hair, in order to bury something belonging to me with her whom I loved, and I promised God to consecrate myself entirely to His service.' This promise was not a vain one. We find in a letter written in the same year the account of the manner in which she lived: 'I make every effort to prevent others suffering from my grief, and I think that I may say with truth that I have really sought to forget myself. God has blessed my good will. I feel a divine energy which is exterior to me, but which acts within me, and which has influenced my entire life. From five o'clock in the morning until night I leave myself no time to think except at prayer, and those thoughts are the spring of my life. I still work at my painting, without feeling any relish for it; but, never mind, labour is a law of penance. I give lessons to about ten girls who come to my house; I am in some sort their mother; for I look after them in many ways. Finally, my father, sister, and some poor persons whom the *Curé* recommended to my care, occupy the rest of my time, so that I always find the days too short for the duties I have to fulfil, though I wish my task were over; for I do my duty in the spirit of obedience, without esteeming myself henceforth of any use.'

It was a few months after her mother's death, during a retreat that she made at the house of the Sisters of Charity in the country, that she laid out for herself this new rule of life. But let us leave to her, in her own autobiography, the narrative of the graces and trials she received:

'During those days of solitude I reviewed my whole life. God prepared me for my general confession by inspiring me with sentiments of true contrition. I spent part of the days completely alone before the Blessed Sacrament, which was reserved in the little chapel. I gave way to the effusion of my love for our Lord, who overwhelmed me with His graces. He solaced me in my repentance, and then Himself dried my tears by ineffable consolations. I went to Paris to make my confession, after which my confessor told me to thank God for His mercies; that after receiving such favours I should rest assured that He wished to possess me entirely. I was always very reserved with him, and, feeling then greatly moved, I did not tell him of the graces which I had received during the retreat; but I joyfully treasured up these words: *God wishes to possess me entirely;* and returning to the foot of the tabernacle, prostrated on the altar steps, I did indeed become entirely lost in God. I had begun my retreat in union with Mary and the Apostles in the upper chamber to prepare myself for the Feast of Pentecost. I imagined myself in that holy assembly, and, almost in spite of myself, I pronounced the vows of perpetual chastity. The following morning, after Communion, I renewed that vow. God redoubled His favours. When I returned to myself, after Holy Communion, I was cold as marble. I know not what change God had wrought in my soul; but, in spite of the remorse caused me by this vow, made without any other permission than these words, "*God wishes to possess you entirely,*" I nevertheless believe that our Lord, seeing that I did not intend to disobey, and that I had been led away by my feelings, received me from that day as His poor spouse. When the retreat was over I was asked what I had done. I found it impossible to answer, and I was scolded for my reticence. However, I gave my superiors a written account; but they forgot to read it, and returned it to me, to my great mortification. I then burnt it, believing that pride had urged me to write it. From time to time my interior trials became a real hell. I fought against God; I wished to give up prayer, though I never did so. I had permission to read St. Teresa, whose life made such an impression on me (my tears never ceased flowing whilst I read this book, which so plainly depicted my own feelings) that I was forbidden to read it; and I was told that it was strange that any one should have authorised me to do so. I was terrified when I thought that it was presumption on my part to imagine that God gave me the same graces as to that saint. I believed myself to be the prey of the devil and a reprobate. My confessor was at this time giving from the pulpit admirable sermons on the spiritual life. He cried out against the Pharisees, and I imagined myself to be a whitened sepulchre; but when I revealed my fears to him, he only laughed at me. His clever irony touched me to the quick. One day a friend of mine announced the visit of a very distinguished man, who, I had reason to believe, wished to ask my hand in marriage; and although I had refused several other candidates, this one being a very advantageous offer, I consulted my confessor as to how I should refuse him. He replied: "Well, why should you refuse him?" This pained me; and I said tremblingly, "But, father, my vow of chastity!" "What vow?" I then related what I had done. He rebuked me, saying, "Your vow is null, since you made it without permission." Never had I experienced such bitter grief. It seemed as if God Himself were repulsing me, that I was lost; and thinking really that my confessor deemed me fit only for marriage, and that it was my excessive pride which led me to deviate from the usual path, I returned to him and said: "If you wish, father, I will marry; but I think it will kill me." He laughed at my simplicity, but nevertheless he took pity on me, saying that he did not wish to force me to marry, and that I had his full permission to give myself to God.

'These are only a few instances out of a thousand; for I was continually agitated by strange feelings which the devil made use of to try and discourage me. If I had not been possessed by a dumb devil, I should probably have been better able to make myself understood, and have been in consequence treated less severely. I was principally tormented by my desires for Communion. Once when asking for an extra Communion, I received a humiliation. I thought I was truly humble when I replied: "Well, father, do not give it to me, if I am not worthy." Perhaps there was a little self-love in this answer; at least I was told so, and the refusal was persisted in. On leaving the confessional I felt great sorrow, and I heard our Lord thus tenderly reproach me: "You have lost a Communion through your own fault." I wept during a whole hour, and then, urged by an irresistible love, I reëntered the confessional and begged my confessor to grant me the Communion. But he was inexorable. On leaving him, I promised our Lord never again to miss Communion through my own fault; and since then, in spite of every trouble and difficulty, I have never willingly missed Communion. This I regard as a great grace, and one which has sustained me during long periods of discouragement and sorrow.'

We will here interrupt Theodelinda's narrative in order to answer a question which the reader has doubtless more than once made to himself since its commencement. Of what use is spiritual direction if it can thus torture generous souls, if it makes them distrust themselves to such a point that even their virtues become a source of suffering? Assuredly spiritual direction shares the fate of all things which are, on one side, human; it has its inconveniences and its dangers. St. Teresa frequently declares that before she found a real director she suffered greatly, and lost much time on her road to perfection. We do not hesitate to say the same of Theodelinda. But even this proves the utility of direction, since, when we do not find it what it ought to be, we are subjected to a trial which greatly retards our advance in virtue. With regard to this, it is scarcely possible to say whether the absence of direction or a mistaken direction be the most detrimental. Theodelinda endured both trials, and perhaps if she had had to make her choice she would have chosen the latter. At a time when the prejudices of her education and the independence of her character led her to observe, with her confessor, an absolute silence on all subjects which were not matter for absolution she acknowledges that she lost a great number of graces because she did not know how to correspond with them, and let the most precious favours lie barren in her soul. Who can say what progress she might not have made in sanctity if she had not waited until the age of twenty-five to approach the Sacraments oftener than four times a year, at a time, too, when our Lord was bestowing on her the most striking proofs of His love! It is equally true that the mistrustful prudence and undue severity of her first director proved dangerous trials to her soul, and might, had she been less faithful, have been the means of discouraging her altogether. Nevertheless even Theodelinda herself acknowledges that he was an enlightened and virtuous man, but he encouraged in her a reserve which was hurtful to her, however useful and even necessary it might have been with others.

Much has been said, and certainly nothing too severe can be said, of those exalted devotees the extent of whose piety consists in a certain tenderness of heart, a sensitive temperament, and a lively imagination. It is but right that dreams and enthusiasm of this sort should undergo severe criticism; and when once the frivolous character of such persons is discovered they should be treated with coldness, even with irony: to act thus is the sign of an enlightened direction. But when this rigour becomes a general principle in the guidance of souls; when all that is not ordinary is without distinction treated as exaltation and madness; when every generous impulse and every action prompted by divine grace is suspected by the director, in spite of continued proofs of humility, obedience, and solid virtue,—such conduct we do not hesitate to call an indiscreet prudence which sometimes amounts to a cruel abuse of authority and absolute injustice. The soul thus repulsed in all her aspirations, opposed in all her inspirations, terrified by the phantom of illusion and subtle pride with which she is continually reproached, finds herself obliged to flee from God and to dread His gifts; at the same time, haunted by divine grace, wavering between the two abysses of infidelity to God or disobedience to His minister, bowed down by this sad perplexity, she seeks refuge in a state of universal and sorrowful abstinence, in which she vainly throws away her mental powers and her strength of will.

However, God who knows how to draw good from evil, gives to the most generous of His servants the grace to resist this trial, and even to derive from it in the end a certain spiritual benefit. Their faith is tried in these struggles of obedience, their love is strengthened, their humility, especially, increases in the severe school of rebuffs and mortifications to which they are subjected. It was in this sense that Theodelinda said of the director who caused her to suffer so much, that to him, after God, she was indebted for the little solid virtue she thought she had acquired. But however real this profit may have been, it was certainly much less than would have resulted from a firm mild guidance, equally distinct from softness or severity; in a word, large-minded, just, and true, as everything is which God inspires.

But let us leave Theodelinda herself to relate how she escaped from these difficulties:

'However, God, seeing that I was not sufficiently strong to endure this state much longer, brought about my visit to Belgium,* where I had placed my nephew at one of the Jesuit colleges. In my fear of seeking for consolation I should have thought it a sin to consult any other confessor than my own, and I so arranged as not to require to go to confession to the Jesuits, whom I thought too indulgent. But God knows how to bring about His ends. It was Holy Week: on Good Friday whilst I was in the chapel I felt great remorse for a fault I had committed, and I thought that I should not be able to communicate on Easter Sunday. So great was the anguish caused by this thought that I forgot my repugnance. Confessions were being heard, and I entered a confessional. Although I tried to confine myself to the accusation of my fault, my expressions of real discouragement led the father, or rather the Angel of Gethsemane, to give consolation to my poor soul. I left greatly calmed; that night I could not sleep; what I had heard had given me a new idea of mercy. I longed to see this priest† again, but I did not know his name, and I had only seen his back. I said to my nephew: "He is bald and holy." He understood, and I was able to see him again. No soul leaving Purgatory could feel a sweeter sensation than I did when I heard that father say to me: "But Jesus is not displeased with your wish to communicate; your fears are nothing else than Jansenism; from the depth of the tabernacle the love of our Lord's Heart incessantly calls you. He desires you even more than you desire Him. Obey your confessor, but love and desire without scruple." This language, so new to me, transported me out of myself; that night God favoured me with an ecstasy (this had not occurred for a long time). I saw heaven, and it

---

* In the spring of 1844.

† The Rev. F. Arsenius Lefèvre, not the same as the religious of that name so well known in Paris.

seemed as if all the beatitudes were given to me. The next day the good father placed on my chair a small pamphlet containing admirable advice in the true sweet spirit of the Gospel. On leaving the college he told me to go in peace. I asked his permission to write to him, but he would not allow it. I was calm for six months; but then my fears returned so violently that I again made the journey to Belgium: this time purposely to see my good father. He was exceedingly kind. He advised me to make a retreat, and every day in the parlour he gave me an instruction taken from St. Gertrude. It is impossible to describe the happiness I felt during these heavenly discourses. This father has ever since proved my devoted spiritual friend, and most useful to my soul. For many years he wrote to me frequently; this was one of God's greatest graces.'

At the conclusion of this retreat at Brugelette, Theodelinda received permission to change her confessor. Nevertheless, strengthened by the direction she had just received, she did not immediately profit by the latitude allowed her, and for nine months more she continued to confess every week to the same *Curé;* avoiding, however, every conversation concerning her interior life, and confining herself to receiving with faith the Sacrament of Penance. Confession then ceased to be a martyrdom to her; she could humble herself for her faults without perpetually doubting the mercy of God. Everything became simplified to her soul, and for the first time her spiritual life took a free untrammeled flight. The concentration of her soul in God became natural to her; from the commencement of her meditation, whatever care she had taken to prepare it, she always found herself engaged in passive prayer without any effort on her own part. Half an hour before Mass in the morning, and another hour in the afternoon before the Blessed Sacrament, did not satisfy her ardent longings; and if the law of labour and the calls of charity had not drawn her from her converse with God, she would have continued it during a great part of the day.

The Saints never separate prayer from the love of penance. Theodelinda had not waited until now courageously to embrace this practice: the Friday fast, the periodical use of a rough hair-shirt, sleeping on a board, rising at five in the morning in spite of the fatigue caused by a multitude of home-duties,—all these exercises of a penitential life, far from appearing burdensome to her, only excited in her that holy joy of spirit which triumphs over the affliction of the flesh. However, the interior struggles which had so long tortured her, her uneasiness for her father's soul, her solicitude for her nephew's education, and a variety of other causes combined, so diminished her strength and preyed upon her nerves that her director was obliged to interfere to moderate her zeal for penance: he did so with the discretion of a man of God who, whilst sparing the health, does not pretend to pamper nature, and who, distinguishing between practices hurtful to the body and those which are not dangerous, encourages the latter, and knows how to substitute others for the former.

On this condition only is it permitted to prefer interior mortification to that of the senses. Those who make use of the former in order to neglect the latter show clearly that they understand neither the one nor the other. The life of a Christian bent on perfection is a war to the death against self-love; when it turns its arms against the flesh it takes for its limit the preservation of the body, which it only permits to live in order to work. In the soul, on the contrary, there is nothing to dread; pride, self-seeking, excessive sensibility, should be unmercifully uprooted; but this destruction is by far the most difficult, and those only seriously work to obtain it who have already raised themselves, by the mortification of the senses, above the weaknesses of sensuality.

To complete the description of Theodelinda's life, we have only to reproduce the rule of life which she laid down for herself during her retreat at Brugelette; for she was strictly faithful to it, and never broke her rules, except now and then to exceed them. In the paper we have before us, drawn up with great prudence by her new director, we see that she took 'for the spirit of her rule the holy liberty of the Heart of Jesus; that is, to renounce without pain one good for a still greater good, and to do all from love and not from fear.'

She fixed certain hours for her exercises of piety, including in her rule the two persons who were in her service. Profiting by their good dispositions, she instructed them in the method of meditation, and made her spiritual reading with them every day. Charity and the forgetfulness of self regulated at every hour her dealings with her neighbour. We shall speak of this more at length when describing her good works; we will at present simply say a few words, to show to what a degree of interior detachment this soul, so ardent and yet so enthusiastic, had already attained. 'God has deprived me,' she says, ' of the last friend for whom I had any natural affection. I will courageously fight against this weakness of heart, which makes all my feelings so sensitive. But if I do not wish for the future to bind myself to any creature, it is only in order to love them more in the Divine Heart.'

Further on her painting is another occasion for detachment. Speaking of her physical weakness, which at that time paralysed her talent, she adds : 'When I have more virtue and love God will perhaps restore my strength to me. I will try to acquire them; I feel that I can do so, and that by the grace of God I only desire it for His greater glory. I have exhibited my pictures several times, but it was a matter of indifference to me. Once, however, my works were refused, and I felt great mortification; another time they were praised in the newspapers, and I felt too great pleasure. But that is a long time since; last year it did not seem to make any impression on me. I wish to do that which would best tend to crush my pride. I have resolved no longer to avoid humiliations, and perhaps for an artist of ordinary talent there is more chance of meeting with them by exhibiting than by not doing so. I will do what God wills: all for Him for ever !'

A letter written a few months later to her director reveals to us the holy delicacy of her soul. 'Lately, finding that I was better and more calm, I resolved to pay more serious attention to painting. On setting to work, I felt a delight which alarmed me; I thought that I was about to reattach myself to the world, and I felt much troubled, thinking that it would be better to give it all up than to expose myself to this danger. Certainly of all my earthly affections, the love of my art has remained the most powerful within me; and I cannot be sure, when I am doing a thing which pleases me, whether I am not seeking myself. But to avoid all these perplexities, which wear out my strength, I have promised God that, if you will tell me once again, in a positive manner, that it is His will that *I should be an artist*, I will banish from my soul all fears concerning this my vocation.' It appears that her confessor replied in the affirmative, and it was about this time that the pious artist's talent became fully developed.

Theodelinda's first journey to Brugelette took place in the Holy Week of 1844, but it was not until the summer of 1845 that she finally left her confessor. A letter which she wrote on Wednesday in Holy Week speaks of this change as imminent; another, on the 25th July, speaks of it as recently accomplished. The motives which finally led her to take this step were not so much of her own creating as of that of the venerable priest himself, who declared that he could not understand her. Besides, for several months both confessor and penitent had avoided any explanation, and maintained a reserve which was embarrassing to both. The confessor whom she next chose (the Abbé B.) soon inspired her with confidence and veneration; nevertheless, finding the guidance sufficient which she received from Brugelette, she at first confined herself to the simple confession of her faults. But the man of God, whilst respecting her silence, discovered the state of her soul, and gave her advice which coincided with her wants. Gradually he took upon himself her spiritual education, instructing her in the principles of that interior life which she already practised under the inspiration of grace. Her love of meditation became stronger and stronger. In order to be less disturbed, she resorted by preference to small deserted chapels, and there poured forth her soul to God with ineffable consolation.

These spiritual joys were, however, tempered by violent physical suffering. Continual fits of neuralgia would have completely destroyed her health had she not learnt to find comfort in the love of the Cross. The Stations of the Cross had become to her the remedy for all her sufferings. 'One day,' she says, 'whilst making the Stations, I felt greatly consoled in the thought that my beloved Saviour was comforted during His sad journey not only by Veronica, but by myself each time that I suffered for love of Him. This inspired me, with a great joy, and a true desire for my sufferings to increase. It was also whilst making the Stations of the Cross that I experienced the first movement of supernatural love for the Blessed Virgin. Until now I had honoured rather than loved her. At the Station where Jesus meets Mary, I saw that she alone loved Jesus as He deserves to be loved, and I felt deep gratitude to the Blessed Virgin. I then received great lights concerning the Immaculate Conception, so that now I would prefer having my heart plucked out rather than consent to doubt that such was her privilege.'*

Neither her love for meditation nor the state of depression to which her physical sufferings had reduced her made her forget her works of zeal and charity. Those who only knew Theodelinda as a Religious, and who were unacquainted with the secrets of her interior life, perhaps thought that hers was an exclusively contemplative nature, and one little suited for active work; and, in fact, terrible and lengthened trials had then so destroyed her natural energy, that she appeared to have no predilection save for contemplation and prayer. But this death was in her the triumph of grace; her letters and memoranda reveal her inward struggles; often and often does she complain of that devouring activity which destroys the strength of her soul. This is a complaint which the world does not understand, for it asks, How can activity, when used in a good cause, be a subject of reproach? Nevertheless, they who are well versed in the mysteries of supernatural life well know the cause for this complaint. God wishes to act alone in souls that He has called to the perfection of His love; besides, His grace seconds

---

* These words are taken from her autobiography, written two years before the definition of the dogma of the Immaculate Conception.

and assists nature, and sometimes even supplies it in some sort, replacing the exercise of natural powers by a superior action, on the whole more simple and more energetic. The soul thus under the action of God has no greater enemy than her own activity, which, being sometimes in opposition to the divine operations, creates in her strange struggles and painful agonies.

What is called Quietism was erroneous, and only merited the censures of the Church, insomuch as it proposed this passive state as the goal we should try to reach by voluntarily rejecting the use of our natural faculties, and by even renouncing free will in the exercise of all such Christian virtues as suppose personal efforts. To neglect the ordinary means which God makes use of for our sanctification, to contemn the essentially gratuitous character of the divine favours, which can in some cases raise us above these means; to yearn after, with a kind of ambitious presumption, what it belongs to God alone to give to such as serve Him in the simplicity of their hearts; in fine, to consider as the normal and permanent state of Christian perfection what can only be in this world a rare privilege and a fugitive ray from the world to come;—such is doubtless a perilous illusion and a baneful temerity far removed from the humble fidelity of a soul who, amidst the fiercest struggles and the efforts she makes to respond with the love of her Creator, finds herself surprised by the all-powerful action of a superior grace, which takes her out of herself, and which sometimes suspends, and always lessens, natural activity, to substitute for it that of God.

Theodelinda was called to this sublime destiny. However, as if to render the victory of His grace the more incontestable, it appears that God wished to prepare her for this vocation by means which, to all appearance, would have removed her from it —an ardent, active, anxious character, and an indefatigable zeal in works of mercy. It is even probable that she would never have thought of leaving this path if, little by little, Providence, to draw her from it, had not made use of those powerful means which betray the divine action; sometimes by sending severe interior pains, which troubled her even whilst performing good works by the terrible thought that she was lost; sometimes through the severity and distrust of her confessor; at others from physical suffering and the sickness which became habitual to her shortly after her mother's death. The more these obstacles multiplied to shackle or suspend her exterior activity, so much the more did grace attract her and strengthen her in the exercises of a contemplative life: meditation gradually became her sole strength and repose. Thus she was compelled to recognise her vocation and to follow it; but at the outset she had no idea of it, and her soul, open to every good impression, followed as ardently the love of charity as that of prayer. We have already seen her engaged in works which would have repulsed a less courageous soul; but when, under different guidance, her soul dilated itself in holy joy and confidence, her zeal increased in the exercise of exterior charity.

Her small fortune did not suffice for her liberality; and being assured of a sufficient competence for her own existence, she worked unceasingly to gain the bread of others.* 'If you cannot send me money,' she writes to one of her friends, 'find me work—copies of paintings for chapels, copies of family portraits, indeed anything. I undertake all; the more troublesome it is, the more it will pay for heaven. I am now working at a painting which amuses me; but it is only lost time—for such work is not the labour which man has to accomplish by the sweat of his brow; and truly the time which we do not employ in *ransoming* ourselves is lost.'

The same letter tells us that the work for which she was thus obliged to beg was to pay for the education of two little girls whom she had adopted. These poor little children had lost their mother, and their father, to get rid of them, had taken them to the *Enfants trouvés*, from whence, however, their grandmother had taken them on the same day. Unfortunately this poor woman possessed no other quality than kind-heartedness, and

---

* It was at this time that she gave over the interesting work of composing pictures to devote herself to the less gratifying task of copying models and portrait-painting.

brought up her grandchildren badly; herself a great drunkard, she accustomed them to drink, sent them to beg in the barracks or steal in the market-place. Theodelinda one day met the eldest, who was then twelve years old; struck with her beauty she kept her in mind, and met her several other times. But one day, on her return from Mass, she again saw her begging, and felt an ardent desire to wean her from such bad habits; she took her home with her, gave her shoes and stockings, and leading her to her oratory, made her pray beside her. Then the poor child related the sad story of her life, after which Theodelinda could not make up her mind to abandon her; she begged and worked in order to be able to place her and her little sister at school. But a fresh obstacle arose: the father, who had abandoned his children, determined to reclaim them, as if he could not bear that they should be religiously brought up. Theodelinda, who had now become their true mother, begged that he would renounce his claim to them; but in vain. Prayer achieved what charity had begun. On the first day of the Month of Mary, Theodelinda led her dear children to the altar of our Lady, and begged that she would adopt them. The following day, without any one knowing his motive, the father came of himself to sign the act of renunciation. However, their charitable guardian had not arrived at the end of her troubles. For a long time the elder of these children caused her great anxiety. For prudential reasons she had sent them to a school at a distance from Paris; but the child was disgusted with the *ennui* of her life, and resisted every sort of kindness. Theodelinda was obliged to remove her, and place her at a convent at Versailles, where she received an education greatly superior to her position. Theodelinda was at length recompensed for the sacrifices she had made. Ardently desiring the salvation and perfection of this soul, she never ceased praying for that intention, and she was heard as she deserved to be. The street-child became an angel of the sanctuary; a religious vocation was bestowed upon her as the price of the tears of her adopted mother; and when the time came that she was to give herself to God by vows, Theodelinda, beside herself with delight, wrote thus to her confessor: 'Her superiors cannot find words in which to express their satisfaction with this young spouse of Jesus Christ; and for myself, had I ever doubted that our Lord mercifully looks down on my misery, I should now believe it, seeing that my prayers have been answered even beyond my expectations. Yes, this beautiful and so unhoped-for vocation (for every one that knows her is astonished) gives me more confidence in the protection of God than all the interior consolations I have received.'

At other times it pleased God to exercise her charity and her patience without granting her any success. Imitating the example of several of the Saints, she had lodged in her own house an old blind woman who was utterly destitute, and upon whom she lavished the most tender care, reading to her and treating her as if she were her mother. But it was impossible to please her: by a strange reversal of the order of things, the *protégée* tyrannised over her mistress and complained on every possible occasion. Theodelinda accepted this penance as a precious trial; she bore it for two years, and never willingly deprived herself of what she considered a grace. But it was the old woman who at length left her. We find the following remarks concerning her in a letter to one of her friends: 'You remember my delight on taking Mme. G—. Well, I have not done what I should have done; for this poor old woman grew tired of me and left me yesterday. I did all in my power to persuade her to remain; but God did not grant me this grace, of which I was doubtless unworthy. This has caused me great grief; but humiliation is of even more value than good works. Pray to God that I may profit by this lesson, and entreat of Him not to abandon the soul of this poor woman, who left my house with a heart very uncharitably disposed towards me. Her great age will, I hope, atone for her faults. She has gone to live with a coal-merchant in the Rue du Petit-Bac,' &c.

This wicked old woman was immediately replaced by another pensioner, for Theodelinda was not discouraged by the hard trial she had undergone with the first. But this time she was rewarded for her charity; the old woman she had received was a very holy person; and a little later Theodelinda loved to style her 'her benefactress:' it was to her prayers that she attributed the conversion of her father, of whom she had the charge. She did not rest satisfied with this domestic work of charity; she used also to visit the poor at their own houses, and to tend them in the hospitals. At the time we write of, she was accustomed to visit thirty-five families; those who know what these visits of charity are—how much time, fatigue, and trouble are required to ascend all those stairs, to listen to so many complaints, to witness so many miseries without being able to assist them save with words of sympathy—will have some trouble in understanding how a person with delicate health and continual suffering could have found time and strength to add this duty to her artistic labours, to long prayers, and assiduous attention to her father. Rising at five in the morning, she allowed herself no rest till evening. She divided her mornings between her oratory, the church, and her studio; the afternoon was devoted to works of charity and to prayer; the evening to her father, with whom she always played a game of piquet, seeking, in spite of her fatigue, to enliven the old man's evenings by her merry ways and amusing conversation.

Her visits to the poor and the sick were not mere visits; often she waited on them herself, and renewed, unknown to any one, the heroic characteristics of the Saints. One day, her confessor, who knew her zeal, gave her the address of a poor woman, formerly a *cantinière* in the army, who was suffering from a frightful disease; her face and whole body were covered with horrible wounds; it was necessary to prepare the way for the visit of a priest, and to dispose this unhappy woman to be reconciled to God before her death. It appears that this was a difficult task, for her soul was even in a worse state than her body. 'Never,' says Theodelinda, 'had I seen humanity brought so low: her life made me understand why the Son of God made Himself like unto a leper.' There it was that our Lord determined to reveal Himself to her by charity. From the first He led her to feel a particular pity for this unfortunate woman: nearly every day she went to bind up her wounds; the operation lasted for a whole hour, and caused the sufferer to scream with pain: at this time Theodelinda was so united to our Lord that she saw Him alone in her, and she was sometimes beside herself with joy. To please the poor patient, she had given up using pincers when dressing her wounds, and did everything with her fingers. The doctor one day, surprising her in the act, scolded her severely because of the risk of infection. In obedience to her confessor, whom the doctor had spoken to in his alarm for her safety, she wished to use the pincers; immediately fear, disgust, and an invincible repugnance succeeded to her joy; the invalid on her side complained and screamed out. Theodelinda, ashamed of having listened to such human prudence, abandoned this precaution which seemed to displease our Lord, and she instantly recovered her peace and happiness.

Soon her charity bore fruit; it gave rise to gratitude, then affection, and at length confidence; the conversion of the poor woman was entire, and she died a holy death three months later.

Seeing her apostolic zeal, her new confessor determined to give her a new commission. He sent to her several persons to receive advice on spiritual matters; two of them he placed under obedience to her; and he at the same time instructed her in the principles of the direction of souls, which proved of great service to her later in life. This holy priest was thus unknowingly preparing her for the functions of spiritual mother, which she was one day to exercise with so much fruit. But neither confessor nor penitent had at that time any ulterior views.

One can easily imagine what this holy soul suffered in the midst of her charitable works to see her father so far removed from God. However, the Holy Spirit had instructed her in that discretion which knows when to be silent and when to speak; that patience which is willing to wait; that faith which trusts in prayer and which hopes against all hope. 'I think I see some progress,' she wrote to her friend, Clemence C——; 'he now rarely makes religious objections; and when he does, he listens to what I say in reply. But I only began to do him any good when I became convinced that reasoning did him more harm than good, and that praying by his side in the evening caused a grace to descend into his soul which will, I trust, end by triumphing over every difficulty; for grace is the power of God Himself.'

This longed-for grace at length arrived, and in such a manner as again to astonish her who so ardently sighed after it. Their great love for each other caused the father and daughter to live in perfect union. One day, however, their peace was troubled by a storm, the result of which was the old man's conversion. Their conversation had turned upon religious subjects, and M. Dubouché made a remark which wounded his daughter's faith; the latter replied sharply, and her father appeared displeased. Theodelinda was in despair; she reproached herself with having injured this cherished soul. Casting herself on her knees and emboldened by her anguish, she kissed her father's hand, and exclaimed almost beside herself: 'How do you think that I, who love you so much, should be able to bear to be separated from you for all eternity? What your poor child is now saying to you, your mother too would have said.' The mention of his mother's name touched the old man's heart; he began to pace the room in an extremely agitated manner. 'It is true,' he said suddenly; 'your grandmother was pious and holy; as long as I remained with her, I had faith.' A solemn silence succeeded to this moving dialogue. It was late; Theodelinda retired to her room, and spent the night in prayer. There are many kinds of prayer, but there is only one to which the promises of the Gospel are attached. Theodelinda's prayer that night was of this kind; she prayed with the certainty of being heard, I had almost said with authority. The following day she told her confessor what had passed, and begged him to call and see her father. He came and was well received; nevertheless the victory was still far from being complete; the spirit of man was wrestling with the Spirit of God. The poor father said to his daughter with a bitter smile which betrayed a desire and a regret: 'They wish to convert me; but it is too late, I can no longer have faith.' But prayer had begun the change, and prayer was to accomplish it. The Feast of the Immaculate

Conception was at hand. On the 25th November 1845, the Feast of St. Katherine, actuated by an irresistible impulse, M. Dubouché sought the priest; and this time no longer to raise objections, but to make his confession with tears. On his return home he pressed his daughter to his heart, saying: 'How happy I am! My child, this is the happiest day of my life. I have regained my faith.'

She verified as a daughter that promise of St. Ambrose to a mother: '*Non peribit filius tot lacrymarum,*—He shall not perish, for he is the child of many tears.'

All whom Theodelinda had loved were through her means to return to God: she had already conquered the souls of her mother, her sister, and her father; about this time God also granted her that of her young relation to whom she had formerly offered so devoted and pure an affection. She had long ceased to think of him, but about this time he was attacked with consumption; she heard of it, and all her old ardent affection for him revived. Almost frightened at finding in her soul so strong a feeling, she asked the advice of her confessor, who, seeing plainly that God Himself was the author of it, encouraged her to recommence her long-discontinued prayers for his soul. No one was less prepared than this young man for the grace which, unknown to himself, a devoted friend was begging for him. Married to a Protestant, surrounded by impious companions, imbued with socialist principles, he thought himself far indeed from all religion, whilst he was in reality close to it. His young wife, more Christian than himself, though not a Catholic, of her own accord called in a priest; faith returned to this soul, and with faith the most heroic feelings of resignation and sacrifice. His death was not only consoling, but admirable; he expired in a sort of ecstasy, making aloud, with hands and eyes raised to heaven, an act of aspiration after eternal happiness.

Thus God made known to His spouse that He accepted her offering, and in return for the gift she had voluntarily made of herself, He placed at her disposal the wonderful resources of His power and His grace.

CHAPTER IV.

1845, 1846.

First thoughts of vocation.—Extraordinary devotion to the Blessed Sacrament.—Vision of the Sacred Face.—Some reflections on the supernatural state.

WE now approach the decisive epoch in Theodelinda's life. The two years which elapsed between the conversion of her father and the revolution of 1848 were those in which the action of God was the most visible, and in which her soul made the most sensible progress. It was also during this period that her religious vocation became fully developed.

Then it was that, free from all anxiety respecting her father, she gave herself up without reserve to the attractions of the interior life. She was permitted to communicate daily, and the price which, until the end of her life, she set upon this grace shows that she was in a fit state to receive it. At first she was so timid in profiting by it that she no longer ventured to go to her parish-church, for fear of being remarked. She often changed churches, and preferred the least frequented convent-chapels. Humility doubtless inspired her with this timidity; nevertheless she reproached herself later, and not without reason, with a want of simplicity. But whatever had been her previous anxiety, once in possession of her divine Spouse she forgot all other objects to give herself to Him. Her union with Jesus Christ was then so intimate that no event of the day could disturb it; and the return of night, bringing with it the cessation of the temporal cares which filled her day, again plunged her, without effort, into meditation on God's presence within her. 'My soul,' she writes, 'habitually filled with the impression of the Divine Presence, now mingles in the business of life only with great disgust.' Nevertheless she worked on with the same activity;

but physical sufferings, as well as natural inclinations, rendered work a real torture to her. She constantly suffered from neuralgia, which, far from preventing her from praying and loving, only united her more and more closely to God. This state of suffering was not destined to be a temporary trial, it was henceforth unceasing; and if there was any change, it was the feeling of joy which God granted her in the midst of her sufferings, but which gave place later, during many years, 'to a mortal anguish without any consolation.' Six years after she recalled to mind, when speaking to her confessor, the great consolations which accompanied her first trials; but she added immediately, 'Now, when I feel this agony approaching, I shudder. If I abandon myself to it, I feel at ease; but if I seek the slightest comfort, my body and soul become greatly agitated: all the care that is taken of me causes me to suffer terribly. I feel an ardent desire for solitude, so as to be able to assume the only attitude which comforts me, viz. to extend my arms in the form of a cross.'

If the reader be astonished at this state of mind, he cannot be more so than Theodelinda herself, who always dreaded being the victim of some delusion. 'There are times,' she writes, 'when my life appears to be like a story; the demon of irony, who has haunted me since my conversion, torments my soul at this very moment; and yet, if I am not suffering from delusion, I know that I do not lie when I say that all this, and a great deal more, takes place within me. O God, what tears one must shed in order to love Thee! And how powerful is Thy love in thus preventing mind and heart from giving way under such dreadful trials!' Sometimes, while writing this account of her interior life, though imposed on her by obedience, she was forced to stop. 'I need courage to go on,' she exclaimed; 'everything appears like a dream, a fable. I should like to destroy all I have written. My state is terrible. Father, I am greatly troubled; I wish to be simple and obedient; I should feel still greater trouble in disobeying you; yet I ardently wish before I die to see all that I have written destroyed. This is, perhaps, again self-seeking and false humility; I do not know.'

It is necessary to understand to what a degree (naturally as well as from humility) this soul was averse to extraordinary guidance; for at this period of her life we shall see her enter further than ever into those mysterious paths which she so much dreaded, and into which she was drawn by an irresistible force. Whilst we recognise in her state many of those peculiarities which strike us in the lives of several celebrated Saints (amongst others of St. Catherine of Sienna and St. Jane Frances Chantal), we must remember that she had then read but few books on mysticism, and still fewer of the *Lives of the Saints*; and that, even had she known them, the idea of imitating anything more than their solid and every-day virtues was that furthest from her mind.

The course of events brings us to the spring of 1846. The remarkable incident we are about to relate belongs to this period; but it is connected with a former one, which took place in August 1845. One cannot be separated from the other. The following is Theodelinda's account of both:

'I had been told that the relic of the holy crown was to be exposed in the Church of Notre Dame. I eagerly hastened there the following morning. I found that I had been wrongly informed; but I remained for several hours in prayer, feeling supremely happy. On my return, in spite of the noise of the streets, I preserved so strong an impression of the presence of God, that on my arrival home I shut myself up in my oratory, and was there rapt in ecstasy in an unprecedented manner. Nevertheless I did not lose my senses; for I spoke aloud to our Lord in a delirium of love more burning than fever; and as I lovingly reproached Him with having disappointed my expectations of seeing His crown, I thought I heard these words in the very depths of my heart: "Every morning My blood flows into yours; take your heart's blood—for it is Mine —and saturate with it this little crown" (my crucifix had a very small crown of thorns). I could not have resisted. I took my penknife and made an incision, marking with blood not only the thorns, but also the stigmata of Christ. The following Lent (1846) I gladly learned that this time I should really venerate the precious relic, as it was to be exposed in Notre Dame during the whole of Holy Week. I resolved to communicate daily at the altar where Mass was said before the reliquary. On Monday in Holy Week I felt happy, but nothing extraordinary occurred. On Tuesday I was more fervent, but nothing supernatural took place within me, save a feeling of great recollection, and in Communion much faith in and love of the real Presence. Whilst making my thanksgiving, I felt that I possessed something within me greater than any relics, even those of the Passion. Prolonging my prayer, I became sad, and thought to myself: "The sacred species are destroyed within me; the Blessed Sacrament is not on this altar, and yet the Blessed Sacrament *is more than all else.*" Then I felt an eager desire to kneel before the tabernacle. Before doing so I looked again at the reliquary, and on the ground of red velvet beside the holy crown I distinctly saw a Host, which seemed to be unsupported—there was no monstrance. I thought I was labouring under a delusion; I buried my face in my hands, whilst my heart beat violently. I looked again; my sight was perfectly clear, and yet the Host was still there, immovable. I was terrified, thinking that it was an hallucination. I prostrated, recited the *Miserere* and an Act of Contrition, at the same time begging God would pardon me if I deserved to be deceived by the devil. I shed tears; for I feared also that I was wanting in faith. I said to our Lord, "My Beloved, if it be the Blessed Sacrament, I adore Thee in it." Love, fear, a firm conviction that *our Lord can do everything*, an inexpressible confusion when thinking of my own unworthiness—all these various feelings contended in my soul. After some time I again looked up, and still seeing this sign of the Holy Eucharist, I tried to distract my mind from dwelling upon it. For this purpose I walked round the church; but on my return I still saw the holy Host exposed in the very same place, where some years later the devotion of the "Quarant' Ore" was to be begun. I went up to a priest, and asked him what the white thing was that I saw close to the holy crown. He did not understand me, for he saw nothing. Worn out with emotion and fatigue, I retired, and did not dare return, so impressed was I by this miracle. My heart, already so powerfully drawn towards the Holy Eucharist, was from that time still more closely united to the tabernacle.'

Perhaps some one now will ask, Did not such graces destroy her simplicity? We shall find the answer to this question in a letter written a few days later to her friend Clemence C. This is all that she says concerning the great spiritual graces which had been vouchsafed to her, though one would think that the intimacy existing between these two souls would have permitted more unrestrained confidence: 'One day during Holy Week I went on a pilgrimage to Notre Dame to honour the holy Crown of Thorns. I earnestly prayed, through these holy relics of our Redemption, for the salvation of all the souls united to us.' The letter then goes on to give news of her father and nephew, expressions of affection, and projects of a visit to the seaside for bathing. The supernatural and the miraculous were overflowing within her, and yet her most intimate friends knew nothing of it. Exaltation and illusions inspire very different conduct in those who are led away by them.

It was in the midst of these alternate trials and favours that Theodelinda was called upon to decide a new and momentous question. Until then one only vocation had been present to her soul—it was that interior calling to perfection to which she had so generously responded; another more special vocation was now to mould her whole future life. The cloister and the world, contemplation and action, were now about to dispute their possession of her: counsellors were not wanting, but their advice differed, and even had it agreed, there was another to be consulted—that Counsellor whose soft whispers find an echo in our hearts which the least interior tumult drowns. Those who witnessed Theodelinda's devoted care of her father said to her: 'Your duty is to remain with the old man.' Those who were in the secret of her good works, the Sisters of Charity who met her in her visits of mercy, said: 'Go on doing good to those around you.' The admirers of her artistic talent advised her to glorify God by her painting, and to teach artists to serve Him.

Her confessor and the enlightened director who wrote to her from Brugelette tried to draw her mind from all thoughts of the future, and to engross it entirely with the wish of honouring God by her present fidelity. But there is a secret trouble produced in some souls by the Holy Spirit, and this trouble cannot be soothed. All Theodelinda's letters at this period bear the impress of a submissive anxiety which no advice could calm.

She was in this state of mind, suffering and agitated, when she left Paris with her nephew to pass six weeks in Normandy at the seaside.

The education of her nephew was a source of great uneasiness to her. She had been obliged to take him from the college of Brugelette, where he was not making progress; she had persuaded her sister to give over to her all her maternal authority; and she exercised her rights over the child with a firmness, a tenderness, and a perseverance which nothing could weary, and the good effects of which were soon manifest. Theodelinda did not fear to add to her daily work the incessant watchfulness necessary for the cultivation of a delicate and difficult character. In order not to lose the fruit already gained, she courageously refused his mother permission to see her son during the vacation: she took him with her to Normandy, where, notwithstanding the solitude which must have proved disagreeable to a young man, and the continual watchfulness of his severe guardian, the ever-increasing affection and docility of her pupil testify to the wisdom and vigour of the training he then received.

It is one of the characteristics of great minds to know how to multiply themselves and to live at the same time several lives, one only of which is known to lookers-on. Theodelinda possessed this power in an eminent degree; and what is still more astonishing is to see such numerous forms of human activity in a soul already so absorbed in God. The education of her nephew, the care of her father, works of charity, painting, —all these duties would easily have filled more than one existence; add to this, prolonged meditation, moral trials, and constant bodily suffering, and one would think that no physical strength could long have borne such over-work and over-strain.

Such, however, was her life, as we learn from her letters. Let us follow her to the seaside, where nine years before she had been for the first time. Then the melancholy disposition of her soul had found relief in the contemplation of the immensity of the ocean. Now she does not stand in need of this assistance to raise her soul to God. Jesus in her heart was far dearer to her, and her life was becoming a perpetual prayer. During the day she intrusted her nephew to the care of the village *Curé*, while her brush was depicting on canvas the image of the Immaculate Mary; but her soul was not more detached from God before her easel than before the tabernacle—she remained for hours beside herself lost in contemplation.

Such a retreat did not tend to diminish her growing desire for solitude. She returned to Paris, her health not improved, her sufferings as great as ever; but a violent impulse was leading her to quit the world. Exterior labour fatigued her, she did not fear to suffer; but the interior life having become supreme, the outward one became to her a perfect martyrdom: she wished to hide herself, to obey, to be forgotten. She asked her confessor's permission to enter religion. 'You may do so without committing sin,' he replied; 'but you would do better to remain in the world a little longer for the sake of your father and nephew.' Then she sought another means of hiding herself from the world. She knew in Normandy a community of Hospital Sisters; she thought it would be so nice to live near their house with her father, when she could be the servant of the sisters; she would tend the sick, she would be unknown. She made the journey; but was dissuaded from her project. Among other advice there was one which she received with joy and surprise from the Superioress: '*Perpetual adoration will suit you better than our life.*' Then she returned to Paris, her mind more tormented than ever. Her hour had not yet come, but it was close at hand. Before finally recognising her religious vocation, Theodelinda was for another year to purify herself in desire, labour, and suffering. Hers was not one of those delicate souls which are cast down under contradictions and become inactive when disappointed. No sooner had she returned to Paris, in October 1846, than she courageously recommenced her duties. 'I am working like a day-labourer,' she writes to Clemence C—. 'I have a gigantic portrait to finish. I have to rise before the sun and write to my friends late in the evening, so they must excuse me if I am brief.' Her nephew still occupied her thoughts; but his progress consoled her, and she felt that she had not had her trouble for nothing. Her good father did not decrease in piety. 'He is,' she would say, 'the most fervent of us all. He told me the other day that he did not understand how one can pray without meditating. If he follows out this idea, his progress will be very great.' All her letters written at this period are energetic, and breathe a sweet bright gaiety. Excusing herself for involuntarily neglecting her correspondence, she says: 'I wish every criminal's conscience were as clear as mine on that point.' Later on, thanking a person for rendering her a service of which she had given up all hopes, she writes: 'I had made the sacrifice of it; but one likes sacrifices which terminate in the same way as Abraham's.' There seems to be something joyous in all she says; nevertheless, the cause of her anguish was still the same, though unbounded confidence filled her soul to the exclusion of all over-anxiety. At the same time, her object of attraction became more special. Something in her heart spoke to her of Carmel; she mentioned this desire in a letter to her director. The Feast of St. Teresa brought with it an unaccustomed joy to her soul, and the life of St. Peter of Alcantara, which she read for the first time, delighted her. Winter was coming on, the days were short. The Carmelite chapel in the Rue de Vaugirard was far from her home. I know not what it was that led her to go there to pray; but the chapel closed at five o'clock. Theodelinda was not discouraged. She wrote to the Prioress, who was unknown to her, asked and obtained admission, and there, alone, every day during the winter she prolonged her prayer before the Blessed Sacrament, and received special graces which closely united her to the spirit of Carmel. Thus was she preparing in silence for the accomplishment of the designs of God.

Never, perhaps, was the devotion of this soul to the Blessed

Sacrament more lively and more ardent. 'I feel,' she writes to her director, 'that if such were the will of God, I should wish to live here on earth for centuries, so as to adore Him in His Sacramental Love. I have such lively faith in the real Presence that even when I suffer most this divine Presence is palpably near to me. I have often imagined the feelings of those who lived in close friendship with our Lord on earth; but I never envied them; for now at least that Divine Body is impassible. Sometimes this thought has transported me with joy during the whole time of meditation: "You no longer suffer, my Love; it is I that suffer for You."'

It was more especially during her solitary prayers before the tabernacle that she experienced the holy violence of Divine Love. She sometimes visited a Community of Sisters of Charity, who, not having a regular chapel, kept the Blessed Sacrament in a very small oratory. 'There,' she says, 'I shut myself up alone, and was free to weep, to prostrate, to speak. O, in one way I prefer seeing Him exposed—surrounded by adorers. He is my God! But what consolation there is in these intimate visits, unrestrained by any witness! There I forgot all the world; I no longer thought of scandalising people nor of edifying them. I often said, "O Lord, I love Thee here for Thine own sake alone."'

It is most probably to this year of her life that the following anecdote belongs, which reveals to us the simple warmth of her feelings. One Holy Thursday, being in the Chapel of the Sepulchre of her parish, she said to herself rather fretfully: 'All these people do not come here for Thee, my Beloved! They crowd in to see the decorations and the lights.' An ardent desire then occurred to her that all these lights should burn for Jesus alone. Immediately she rose, bought several pounds' worth of candles, and retired to her oratory, where she made a splendid illumination *for Jesus alone.* 'It was folly,' she said; 'but did not a Saint once say to our Lord: "Thou wert more madly in love than I am!"' Our Lord showed that He accepted her good will. She had scarcely knelt down, when she no longer beheld chapel, tabernacle, nor lights; her eyes could only see a Heart immense as the world; and within her she felt a bliss which, overcoming her physical strength, left her senseless for three hours.

Such were her feelings during the year 1846, 1847. She was passing through one of those periods of ineffable sweetness with which God recompenses the great sacrifices of a life generously given to Him, and prepares the soul for fresh struggles. She often thought she heard a voice saying to her: 'I have chosen you to be a queen and to gain souls.' A letter addressed to F. Lefèvre, on the 2d February 1847, admirably expresses her feelings. She still fears illusion, but 'the danger of excessive confidence,' she says, 'has replaced the temptation to doubt and despair.' She was attracted to God by a continual and violent yearning which made her sigh in the prison of her body. In the same letter we find several interesting details. It appears that at this time she had already begun a spiritual correspondence with the Prioress of the Carmelites in the Rue d'Enfer. She had revealed to her her yearnings towards Carmel, and her wish to join at once the Third Order. But the Prioress, as well as her confessor, the Abbé B—, persuaded her not to do so. The latter, by the discreet wisdom of his conduct, gained every day greater ascendency over his penitent, to whom the distant direction of Father Lefèvre, though always precious, became less necessary. The extraordinary states of mind through which she often passed at length obliged her to unburden herself freely to her confessor, as she felt the necessity of having her own feelings explained and her line of conduct confirmed. The man of God taught her how to act in these various phases; he *simplified* them for her, as it were, and preserved her from the anxiety which paralyses the workings of God's grace in a soul. Attentively directing, but not crushing, the movement which led her upwards, he only dissuaded her from entering the Third Order to encourage her to make a still more heroic resolution: the vow of doing always what should seem to her to be most perfect.

What is most admirable in souls who take such resolutions is not, perhaps, so much the courage of the will as the maturity of mind necessary to preserve fidelity from all scruples. St. Teresa, St. Andrew of Avellino, Abbé Olier, and many other Saints have made this vow; so that by permitting it when he judged his penitent capable of heroism, the Abbé B— showed that he had a clear knowledge of her soul. She made it for a certain period, and renewed it several times until her death. The result was a more intimate and confiding union with Him whom she was constantly to invoke and call upon for assistance. 'Formerly,' she writes, 'I looked upon Jesus as my judge; now I can scarcely tell you the friendship that exists between us. I consult Him at every turn, and He answers me, during the day, during the night, in the streets, in the midst of the world—everywhere!'

Such favours led her to seek still greater retirement, and to do so, she was under the necessity of changing her daily routine. She gave over receiving pupils in her studio, and she would have wished to replace her portrait-painting by paintings for churches. By doing this she would have been able to work alone, and prolong her prayer at the same time. She also thought of reducing her expenses and housekeeping, but the consideration due to her old father obliged her to give up all ideas of this sort. 'I still continue my portraits,' she writes; 'I am still surrounded by my fine ladies, with all their vanity and luxury. I am leading a singular life; but may God be praised! I banish *ennui* and sadness, in order that the world may not think that the child of God is cross or gloomy.' However, she was free to carry on her works of charity to whatever extent she pleased; but without renouncing them altogether, she gave up seeking for them, confining herself to those that came in her way, 'in order,' she says, '*to avoid the great illusions sometimes produced by zeal.*' The truth is that grace was gradually withdrawing her from her former activity to dispose her to become in her turn a centre and focus of the contemplative life.

At each step she took in this path she received the most powerful encouragement from God. Now she obtained a decisive grace, which may be considered as the origin of her mission. From the *vision of the Holy Face* sprang the *Congregation of the ' Œuvre Réparatrice.'*

Until then, however sensible had been the impressions she had constantly received of the Divine Presence in her soul, however intimate had been her union with the Sacred Humanity of our Saviour, she had never represented it to herself under any visible form. Careful not to anticipate the action of grace, she would have blushed to give way to any imaginary fancies on the subject, rejoicing as she did in the hidden God. If all the advocates of the contemplative life were to imitate her reserve, there would be fewer illusions to deplore, and mysticism would not be received with that mistrust and unjust contempt to which real abuses give a semblance of truth. Although her thoughts were ever fixed on Jesus Christ, still Theodelinda would never reproduce His image, either in imagination or on canvas; no picture of Christ, however well executed, came up to her ideal; she found the type either too vulgar or two *recherché*. Morales, the Spanish painter, alone satisfied her with regard to the expression. As to herself, when conversing with our Lord, she compared herself to a blind man who could feel the impression of the sun's rays, without seeing the luminous globe from whence they emanate. Such were her feelings, and she thought of nothing beyond, when a powerful grace raised her to a more perfect intimacy with her Divine Spouse.

It was the Thursday after Sexagesima Sunday (February 1846), whilst assisting at Benediction at the parish-church, she was seized with one of those violent headaches to which she was subject, and which deprived her of the use of her faculties. Not being able to think or pray, she contented herself with adoring our Saviour crowned with thorns, to whom she sensibly united herself in her suffering in the spirit of expiation for the sins committed during the Carnival. She remained for a long time in this state, and on coming to herself she felt ill and thoroughly worn out. That night she saw in a dream a bust of Christ. Whilst she was admiring it it became animated; she saw before her a living face divinely beautiful. It was

Christ in His Passion, covered with blood, and His face and mouth wounded. He bent over her with ineffable sweetness, and let fall on her lips two drops of blood which had issued from His own. She then awoke in a state of ecstasy, which lasted for the remainder of the night. Until then she had only had a dream, and there was nothing wonderful in it. Accustomed as she was to view things reasonably, she would not have attached any importance to it. What was there astonishing in a dream representing to her the object which was continually present to her mind? What was there surprising in this representation exciting in her an ardour which was ever on the increase? The next morning she resumed her ordinary occupations with great calmness; but during Mass, after Communion, she saw reproduced within herself the same picture she had seen in her dream. This time she was wide awake and perfectly recollected; never before had she seen anything similar to it. She had not sought it; she was surprised, but she could not doubt the evidence of her own senses. This sight penetrated her with confusion and love. After some time the vision disappeared. That same night, Friday of the Carnival, she was making the Stations of the Cross, when to her surprise, at the sixth Station, she again beheld the representation. She fell into an ecstasy, and begged our Lord to impress His holy image on her, as formerly He did on Veronica's handkerchief; immediately what she had seen in her dream was renewed in her mind : the same movement on the part of the picture, the same drops of blood deposited on her lips, the same words, but this time more distinctly uttered : '*Thou art My well-beloved ; I have chosen thee ; I give thee these two drops of blood from My lips for sinners.*' Theodelinda heard these words, but did not clearly understand them ; it never entered her mind to regard these words of her Master as a prelude to an ulterior vocation and a life specially consecrated to reparation for sinners ; only she was impressed with the profound conviction that God required something of her, and wished to make an instrument of her in some unknown work. After this mysterious communication, our Saviour did not disappear as He had formerly done. The Sacred Face was still there, interiorly visible, the permanent object of her intellectual sight—a sight which is not that of the eyes. Theodelinda's prayer seems to have been heard; the image of Christ was so impressed on her soul that she could no longer pray or think without seeing it. Several days passed in this way. Uneasy, agitated, fearing some illusion, frightened at seeing that, in spite of her daily occupations, nothing could efface this object from her view, she at last decided to overcome her repugnance and speak on the subject to her confessor. He, however, hesitated to pronounce as to the nature of the phenomenon; but feeling reassured by the humble and discreet dispositions of his penitent, he told her to be calm, not to let her thoughts run on this picture, and if she were deceived, to turn the illusion into grace by conforming herself lovingly to the adorable will of her Lord. Theodelinda followed this line of conduct, and it appears that nothing further was said respecting this event, the consequences of which were, however, visible at a later date in the foundation of her great work.

Assuredly in all that we have just related there is nothing that surpasses or even equals the wonderful facts which we read of in the lives of the most celebrated Saints whose names and doctrines are venerated by all Christians. Nevertheless, the human mind is so formed, that what it admits in the past it suspects in the present. Those who firmly believe in the miracles of St. Francis of Assisi, for example, regard a contemporary miracle as an impossibility; they accept the revelations of St. Catherine of Sienna, but they at once set down the supernatural phases of a soul who has lived in our midst as delusions produced by the over-excited imagination of a devotee. I do not wish to be the advocate of hallucinations which are sometimes unreal, though often genuine; but it is absolutely necessary to define the meaning of terms in order to spare one's self that ridiculous panic which seizes on certain people at the bare mention of visions or extasies. A little philosophy can do no harm to any one; and true mysticism requires it, in spite of the distrust with which it is generally looked upon.

What, then, is imagination? Is it, as some melancholy souls pretend, a deceptive faculty, the natural enemy of common sense, the mother of illusions and foolish dreams? In such a view of the case, I see many reproaches and epithets, but no definition. Now I wish for a definition, and I begin thus: the imagination is a faculty which enables the soul to represent to itself, in the absence of sensible objects, the image of those which it has previously seen by means of her exterior senses; or objects analogous to those that it has perceived. Each time that any cause whatsoever excites within me this mysterious remembrance which reawakens the vision of the absent object, the image is reproduced within me, although the sense of sight is not affected. I have in my mind the same representation as if the object were still before my eyes, only my reason, if it be in a healthy state, will abstain from pronouncing on the exterior reality of a body corresponding to this image. This is a phenomenon of the imagination.

Hence it stands to reason that the imagination takes part in all our intellectual operations. It is one of the laws of the human mind here below not to able to grasp things save by giving them a form which can be seized upon by the senses. The most metaphysical conceptions have need of language which is like a primary covering; and in language, the most abstract conceptions are those which appeal the oftenest to metaphor, that is, to a comparison borrowed from sensible objects. Now where are all these sensible forms to be found, which the understanding unceasingly calls to her aid in order to conceive, judge, or reason upon a matter, save in the treasury of the imagination?

How, then, can imagination deserve the reproaches of which it is so frequently the object? In reality the imagination is never wrong, it never deceives, for it does but show forms; but the understanding is sometimes compromised by a too precipitate judgment—if, for want of examination, it rashly pronounces on the reality of the objects of which it conceives the image.

Let us now return to the supernatural phenomena whence we have gone astray.

Has the imagination a legitimate part in meditation? Yes, certainly; for to meditate is, under the action of grace, to exercise one's mind on objects called into existence by faith. Now these objects are of two kinds, one of which, by its nature, escapes the senses; for instance, all that relates to God, to His perfections, to His eternal kingdom, to the life to to come. To think of these things it is necessary to have recourse to sensible images, to metaphors which speak to us of the throne of God, of the sword of His justice, of the thunder of His vengeance, of the light of His countenance, of the fire of His love, &c. To conceive these things without forms would be to leave the terrestrial state, to enter into the direct vision of glory; and it is the property of the highest, most supernatural, and most manifestly Divine communications occasionally to raise certain souls to a simple and purely intellectual view of these objects. The second kind embraces everything connected with the mystery of the Incarnation. God so well knew the human nature of man that, in order to draw him to Himself, *He was made flesh.* From that time one can no longer think of the Incarnate Word, of His mysteries, His various conditions on earth, without having recourse to those sensible representations which are so conformable to the nature of the subject. With regard to the glorious state of our Saviour, experience furnishes us with no example; we appeal to suppositions, to analogy, and we form an arbitrary image of the risen Christ, borrowed from what physical nature proposes to us as being most subtle and most luminous. In all this there is nothing which is not legitimate, reasonable, and necessary. If we wish to think of God and of His Christ, we can only do so in this manner.

But let us not forget it: prayer and meditation are not a mere exercise of our natural faculties; they are likewise supernatural actions. That is to say, our powers act conformably to their nature, but under the combined action of two motors, one subordinate to the other—the human will and the Spirit of God. I begin to meditate on the Passion of our Saviour: my memory recalls the circumstances of that sad scene; my imagination represents them; my sensibility is awakened; my understanding tries to conceive the greatness, the justice, goodness of God, the enormity of sin, the necessity for penance; finally, my will becomes inflamed with the desire of resolving to respond to my Saviour's love. Such is the mechanism of my faculties. But where is the source of the movement? In my will, which wished me to apply my mind to all these things? Yes, doubtless; but my will is not alone, and I should grieve to think that it were so. If I felt for an instant that God was not listening to me when I pray; that He was not within my heart attracting it to Himself, and forming within me those ineffable yearnings which mount to His throne, crying, Father, Father, Father! I would immediately renounce a barren exercise which would truly merit the contempt with which the unbeliever treats *'the lazy ascetic, the contemplative, sanctimonious idiot.'* One must have faith not to regard meditation in a ridiculous light. But when one believes, it is necessary to believe to the end. It is then God who assists me, supports and *inspires* me in the varied acts of which my meditation is composed. Even in the lowest stage of the mystic life, even in that common form of prayer called meditation, there is the combined action of the human mind and the Divine spirit of *inspiration* and *imagination*. The higher the soul ascends on the mystic ladder, the more does the spiritual part increase whilst restraining the natural, the prayer of perfect souls becomes simplified, the exercise of their human faculties more rare, their activity abates, for their souls live less in themselves than in God. But could this coöperation of human activity become absolutely null? I do not think so. That such a state is possible at intervals under the miraculous action of an extraordinary grace which suspends the natural life to that point when death would naturally follow, it does not belong to me to affirm or to deny. At any rate these are sublime states which it is not necessary for us to consider. Nevertheless, to divide the mystics into two classes—one composed of imperfect souls, who do everything by prayer, and in whom God does nothing; the other of perfect ones in whom God operates alone without any effort on their part—this would be most grossly contradicting common sense, theology, and experience.

Let us suppose a soul already well versed in the contemplative life; she has a vision, she hears a voice and is rapt in ecstasy. One person will say, 'She is a Saint; she has seen our Lord; God has spoken to her.' Another will say, 'She is mad; she imagines she has seen and heard; she is the victim of an hallucination.' Which is right? which is wrong? I cannot decide until I have examined the fact; but on both sides I find a great confusion of ideas and expressions. You who regard it as a miracle, and say, 'She has seen Christ, God has spoken to her,'—do you mean to say that her imagination had no share in what she experienced? How do you know that it was not by means of the imagination that Christ revealed Himself to her or made Himself heard by her, supernaturally placing in her imagination the representation which she beheld? If God really did this, the vision was a true one: this does not imply, necessarily at least, that Jesus Christ was corporally present to her eyes, or that He affected this person's senses with a visual or auditive impression. And, after all, of what consequence is it? Since we have to deal with an effect produced interiorly, the exterior cause is as difficult as it is useless to penetrate. Did not St. Paul say to the Corinthians that he was rapt even to the third heaven, but whether in the body or out of the body he knew not? And you who accuse her of madness, what do you mean? That this person's imagination has been over-excited? That proves nothing, either for or against the reality of the vision. That she has produced *of herself, by a purely human exaltation*, this phantom which she then contemplated in the mirror of her imagination? This is the sole question we have to answer, the precise point of the problem; but it is one that cannot be solved by words any more than by prejudice or reluctance. Do you pretend to limit the power of God? Do you deny that He can set our faculties to work as powerfully as any human cause could do? If you believe in God, your reply is certain. But, then, everything is reduced to an experimental discernment; there are rules of prudence laid down by the wisdom of the Fathers and the masters of the supernatural life; there is that great Gospel maxim, 'You shall know the tree by its fruits;' there are certain axioms reduced to rule by experience; namely, that supernatural states should be undergone and not sought after, welcomed with reserve, submitted to through obedience, and tried by contradictions; that they should produce in the soul a still greater humility, a more generous devotion, a more perfect application to her duties. If these wonderful phenomena can bear this long and severe trial, then I should say, 'God is the Author of them;' if on a single point they give way before the examination, I should say, 'The devil deceives this soul, or she deceives herself; it is not God, but the tempter, who has placed in her imagination what she there sees.' Such is the answer which the wisdom of the Gospel, the vigilant guardian of true mysticism, will always oppose to the vain credulity of some and the unjust condemnation of others.

CHAPTER V.

1846, 1847.

Interior life.—Thoughts of vocation.—Dealings with Carmel.—Spiritual intercourse with Mother Isabella.—Desire of Reparation.—Theodelinda settles with her father near the Carmelites of the Rue d'Enfer.

WE left Theodelinda under the impression produced in her soul by the vision of the Divine Face. The problem of her vocation was presenting itself to her in a very pressing manner. The delays proposed to her by her spiritual guides could not satisfy her; she now only felt repugnance for the good works in which she engaged; only one satisfied her wishes, because the good of souls was its object: it was a lay work for repentant girls. A similar institution had succeeded at Bordeaux. A Sister of Charity, in whom Theodelinda reposed great confidence, urged her to undertake it at Paris, assuring her that she had all the qualities necessary to develop it. Sometimes the idea of this spiritual charity roused her zeal: at one time she seriously thought of devoting herself to it; but, either because she received no encouragement to do so from her directors, or because an interior voice called her to a life entirely devoted to prayer, she soon renounced this project. It became more and more apparent to her that the cloister was the goal to which so many trials had been leading her. For a long time the life and writings of St. Gertrude had become her inseparable companions: often and often do we find in her letters the remembrance of that Saint and traces of the influence that her example exercised on Theodelinda's soul. At the time of which we speak, she was also beginning to entertain for St. Teresa other feelings than mere admiration of her virtues: she felt herself united to that Mother of Mount Carmel;

she lived in her company, and became imbued with her spirit. We have seen that, in the beginning of the year 1847, she had entered into correspondence with Mother Isabella of St. Paul, Prioress of the Carmelites of the Rue d'Enfer. Her frequent visits to the chapel in the Rue de Vaugirard would have rendered a connection with the Superioress of that house more natural; but she herself tells us that in visiting Mother Isabella (with whom she was not acquainted) for the first time, she was obeying a secret order received in prayer. These two souls, so worthy of understanding each other, soon became deeply attached. Theodelinda's affection was always of an ardent and devoted character; but the Prioress united to great personal merit the authority of a long religious life and experience in the guidance of souls. Theodelinda, encouraged by her confessor, placed herself entirely under the direction of this Mother; nevertheless, a remnant of her reluctance to disclose her strange supernatural state again constrained her in her communications. But Mother Isabella, who was fully assured as to the maturity of her judgment and the uprightness of her conduct, testified great confidence in her. One day she handed her a manuscript containing the revelations that Sister Saint-Peter, a Carmelite at Tours, was receiving at that time, and begged that she would read them and give her her opinion of them. Theodelinda began this MS. with all her natural prejudices against whatever was extraordinary in devotion. But soon the striking analogy she discovered between these communications and those which she herself received during prayer excited her interest and filled her with emotion; her heart had already begun to beat, when she read these words: '*The sensible sign of this devotion will be My Face, covered with ignominy and crowned with thorns.*' All that she had undergone in the church of Notre Dame was now renewed within her; she could not hide her feelings from the Prioress. She was obliged to relate her vision of the Sacred Face, and to reveal at the same time that inward Voice urging her to reproduce in painting the image ever present to her soul. Mother Isabella sent her to her confessor, who ordered her to undertake the painting.

She had never worked without a model, and she knew not how to begin; nevertheless, she set to work with great faith. She had chosen a Friday, and had so arranged as that she should be alone. On her knees before the canvas, scarcely had she taken up her brush when she was thrown into an ecstasy: the vision was renewed within her; she painted the portrait. Sometimes the violence of Divine Love deprived her of the strength to work; at others, an astonishing activity caused her to use her brush with a facility and rapidity hitherto unknown to her. She devoted four Fridays to the task, and great was her joy when she found that there was a *resemblance*. 'Many artistic faults will be found in it,' she wrote to F. Lefêvre; 'but for me it is the recollection of a great grace. This canvas reminds me of an unfinished sketch which recalls a masterpiece to my mind, or of a rough painting which resembles a a beloved friend.' Fearing to become too sensibly attached to this material picture, she gave it as a present to her confessor, who, on receiving it, said to her, 'God has willed that you should make it larger than life; later it will be placed in a chapel, but we must wait for God's time.' It was indeed so; for it was round this painting that the first Associates of the Reparation assembled at a later period; but at that time Theodelinda was ignorant of the future; she had executed her commission, and thought no more of it.

Nevertheless, in spite of her abandonment to the will of God and her indifference as to the future, it is easy to follow in her soul the progress of the thought of Reparation. All that does not remind her of it, no longer touches her; all that recalls that thought moves her extremely; and the internal vision of that outraged face of our Saviour rules her supernatural life. The revelations of Sister Saint-Peter, which had made so lively an impression on her, had given rise to the formation of an association of prayers for the reparation of blasphemy and the profanation of the Sunday. Theodelinda entered joyfully into the practices of a devotion which responded so thoroughly to her own feelings. She would willingly have spent the whole day in the exercise of this interior reparation. This desire was with her the natural fruit of a love which was constantly consuming her. Her letters to F. Lefêvre reveal its presence: 'The glory of our King occupies me entirely. I say to Him from my inmost soul, "O Jesus, love the Saints more than me, for they deserve it; cast a look of preference on all my brethren, for it is but just; but, I beg of You, allow me to love You more than any one else in this world!" Father, is this prayer presumptuous?' In the preceding chapter we spoke of the ineffable sweetness God bestowed on her in return for her generosity; these graces lasted during the greater part of the year. Although mingled with occasional trials, they ceased not for several months to sustain her soul and make every sacrifice appear light. But her letters during the last weeks of that year show us that the cross was reassuming its rights, that interior cross a thousand times heavier than any exterior afflictions. But then she had gathered strength for the struggle, and we shall see her courageously endure trials of every kind, which never ceased until her death.

In August 1847 her faith was proved by a very sensible loss. We have seen how the Abbé B——, who had at first been simply her confessor, had acquired over her soul an authority produced by his wise and prudent direction; to his counsels she was indebted for that vow of perfection which had given her so much joy and strength. God deprived her of this guide, to whom, since her father's conversion, gratitude had bound her by so close a tie. Abbé B—— left Paris. Theodelinda accepted this privation with perfect resignation as regarded herself, but with an anxiety mingled with confidence for the cherished soul of her father.

At this time she was alone in Paris. M. Dubouché was spending two months in Brittany with his grandson, who had just completed his studies, and whose success had worthily rewarded the perseverance of his aunt. Theodelinda thanked God for this solitude, which enabled her to devote herself entirely to her principal attraction.

Her letters reveal the use she made of this liberty. She

continued her good works and her painting, whilst she became more and more detached from all things on earth, but not less active nor less overwhelmed with work. 'In vain I work with all my might,' she wrote to Clémence C——. 'I cannot succeed in doing anything. But the path of prayer is always the surest.' In the evening, after her work was over, she spent two hours before the Blessed Sacrament, her soul overwhelmed with ardent desires for the glory of God. 'Every one has his cross,' she wrote, speaking of a person whom she honoured for her virtue; 'this holy soul has dryness of spirit; I have my unfulfilled longings.' Her vow of perfection created in her a strange anxiety; the reason was that she found it too simple and easy. She had heard pious persons and holy nuns speak of this vow as a sublime and difficult thing; doubtless she was mistaken, and did not hear aright, for to her it added nothing to the ordinary dispositions of her heart. 'With or without a vow,' she wrote to F. Lefèvre, 'I do not know what my life would be if I did not always seek to do God's will; the will of God is His own good pleasure, what He loves the most. I feel that I could suffer death if the Heart of Jesus could be consoled by it even for a single instant.' So united was she to Jesus Christ that her weak and worn-out body seemed to receive from this union sufficient energy to accomplish whatever actions were pleasing to God. With regard to her soul, 'it is,' she writes, 'entirely freed from all selfish desires, and has renounced all projects for the future.' The greatest misfortunes and the lowest degree of humiliation appear to her desirable, and trials have already several times shown that her will corresponded to the grace given her. Her heart seemed to be continually penetrated and inflamed; a kind of sadness and a sensible palpitation of heart unceasingly reminded her of the presence of her Beloved, who now very rarely left her. 'Divine love sometimes raised her to a state which she says she does not know, because she is not certain whether it is precisely that which is mentioned in the *Lives of the Saints*. If she doubts, it is not because she is unworthy of it; she is no more astonished at the beatific union than at the Eucharistic union. The gifts of God are entirely gratuitous; she does not think that they are proportionate to her fidelity;* but prolonged and extraordinary graces are often in her case the prelude to a great trial or a great undertaking. As to her active life, it is well occupied and for God's honour alone. She cannot do anything uselessly; she would not read about, look at, or listen voluntarily to anything not having God for its object. In the street she forgets herself to converse with God; the sight of a child reminds her of the child Jesus, a sick man of Jesus fainting. When working at her painting, she no longer fears the temptation to become attached to it, for such an attachment is no longer possible to her.'

She was, however, obliged to seek another confessor. In her perplexity Theodelinda had recourse to Mother Isabella, who advised her to choose Father Bertholon, a Marist, and a man of candid and simple piety and of great virtue. But she desired to find in him the elevated spirit of the director she had lost. Nothing in the minute direction and the artless simplicity of this holy man seemed to accord with what she felt to be the wants of her soul. Theodelinda believed that God desired her to sacrifice this feeling to the advice of her spiritual mother. She prayed long, and it seemed that such was God's will. From that moment she no longer hesitated; and, in order more fully to enter this path of self-abandonment, she resolved to make a retreat under that father's direction at the Carmelite Convent. The time was a favourable one, as she was still alone. She did not delay in profiting by this opportunity, and began her retreat in the month of September. She obtained the reward of her fidelity by receiving the grace candidly to reveal her inmost soul, so that F. Bertholon should understand her spiritual condition, and pacify all her fears with respect to her past life. After these communica-

---

* There is here question of the gifts that console, and not of those which sanctify: the former are often the encouragement of the weak; the latter the reward of fidelity.

tions she received abundant favours from heaven. Without being able distinctly to follow the exercises of the retreat, she was almost continually absorbed in a passive state of union with God, which gained the mastery over all her faculties, and did not even allow her to sleep.

Then it was that St. Teresa adopted her for her daughter. There is preserved in the monastry of the Rue d'Enfer a choir-mantle which belonged to this great Saint. Mother Isabella confided this precious garment to the *retraitante* during her time of prayer. That hour, she says, was delightful. At the end of the hour she was obliged to return the relic; but the impressions of grace were strengthened, and seemed to be to Theodelinda the revelation of the spirit of Carmel. She received a clear insight into the motives of the holy reformer; and the abundant lights with which she was then favoured served her afterwards as a guide to surmount the obstacles she encountered when directing her new institute towards its aim, which appeared to her to be similar to that of St. Teresa. Whenever, yielding to external pressure, she resolved to deviate from that aim, her soul was filled with sorrow; and when it was necessary, she received supernatural warnings to return to her former intentions. This happened to her in a very striking manner, one day that her still infant foundation was on the point of being neglected for other projects. A vision, evidently inspired by the remembrance of that holy hour spent under St. Teresa's mantle, showed her during Mass the foundress of Carmel, calling her again to take refuge beneath her mantle; but at the same time the Blessed Virgin likewise appeared, and covered her with hers. When, later on, she related this grace to her confessor she added: 'This vision of Mary and Teresa simultaneously clothing me with their mantles has given me such a conviction of our vocation as can never be effaced, in spite of the petty persecutions of such as oppose it. *The death of Carmel united to the simple and ordinary life of Nazareth*, such is the summary of my wishes: St. Teresa for everything relating to interior life; but for outward observances, Nazareth appears to me to be a model better suited to our age, to our country, and our habits.* God seems to me to desire that the spirit of St. Teresa should no longer be so restricted and, as it were, inaccessible to people in general; and as Jesus leaves His tabernacle to distribute His Life more abundantly, so He wishes to draw from the tomb the love of His beloved Saint to gain the love and adoration of a still greater number of souls. He desires that this fire which He had given her should burn before His Blessed Sacrament.'

We cannot enter into a detailed account of all the trials and graces which Theodelinda received during her retreat at Carmel; but it is of importance to mention the first revelation which led to her vocation of Reparation. The manuscript which we have before us, whilst revealing the impressions of her retreat, clearly shows us that she had sown in tears to reap in joy. 'Lord, Lord, depart from me a little; for if Thou makest me so happy, I shall not be able to leave this place.' Such was her song of departure. From that time she no longer doubted her vocation; she believed herself called to be a Carmelite: obedience obliged her to return to the world, but it was but a question of time; her resolution was taken, and God would provide for its execution. Her confidence soon appeared justified by the event. Towards the end of October Abbé B— returned to Paris, and took up his abode in the Court of the Carmelites in the Rue d'Enfer. M. Dubouché resolved to follow his example, and Theodelinda was filled with happiness at the prospect of a life more retired than ever, sanctified by the vicinity of Carmel, and which should serve as a kind of exterior novitiate previous to her entering the cloister.

This project, conceived towards the end of October 1847,

* These words are explained by the predominant thought of her duty as foundress. All Theodelinda's manuscripts are a sure guarantee that she never dreamt of disparaging, even indirectly, that austere and hidden life which the Carmelites have perpetuated in our midst. Destined to form a new institute, she must necessarily have seen, as in a vision, an order relatively preferable for souls sharing her peculiar vocation. But to attribute to herself any superiority, or even to insinuate that Carmel was an old form better replaced by another, was far indeed from her thoughts. Otherwise why should she have felt so much sorrow in renouncing her vocation to Carmel, as we shall see in the sequel?

was not put into execution until the month of January 1848. During the interval of three months Theodelinda endured many trials; externally, owing to family troubles, a vexatious law-suit which, as she complains to her friend Clémence, she was not able to avoid in that *comfortable manner* which the Gospel advises: 'Give your tunic to him who takes your cloak,' obedience and the interest of others leading her to follow a different path;* interiorly, from great torments and anguish, much uneasiness respecting her past life—her confessions, which she feared had not been sincere; her repentance, which she deemed insufficient. She spent the whole of December in this cruel anguish; physical sufferings and an increasing weakness added to the tortures of her mind. But for this she easily consoled herself, as she was only too happy to bear the cross of Jesus, and she was pleased to think that it was God's design, by rendering her powerless, to draw her from her active life: this confirmed her in her resolution to quit the world. One of the characteristics of souls acting under the influence of Divine grace is never to lose courage amidst suffering. Though bowed down with so many sorrows, Theodelinda still preserved in her superior part that peace which God alone can give; and far from refusing the chalice, she saw in her sufferings a motive for redoubling her mortifications. 'I think,' she says, 'that I allow my nature too much comfort; that is what makes it live.' To feel nature *alive* when they have done all in their power to crush it is in fact one of the greatest torments of the Saints. In saying this, Theodelinda proved herself to be a true disciple of St. Teresa, who used to say that those alone courageously bear imposed suffering who know how to embrace it willingly. But one comfort which she allowed herself without remorse was the devotion of the Stations of the Cross. In it she gained peace for her soul and repose for her suffering body; she became

---

* Nevertheless, when the time came, she could not bring herself to plead, and agreed with her sister to allow another of the family to carry on the action alone. She suffered considerably in consequence, as she thus deprived herself for a long time of an annuity due to her, being only too happy to be able to practise the Gospel maxims even at that cost.

penetrated with the happiness of suffering, and united herself closely to the Blessed Virgin, begging her with tears to console the Heart of Jesus for the faults of His unworthy spouse.

The festival of Christmas shed on her afflicted soul a ray of joy; she shed many tears before the Crib, but she also experienced there abundant consolation. She became still more powerfully attracted to obedience. Her vow of perfection was no longer sufficient for her; she felt urged to make one of obedience which would serve as a prelude to her entering the religious life; this was truly a supernatural impulse in a soul so jealous of her independence. Even at the time that she was writing to F. Lefèvre to communicate to him her desire, she felt within herself the most violent repugnance to every kind of authority; and both the simplicity of her confessor and the austerity of her Carmelite Mother proved great trials to her. We see from a letter written at a later date that grace gained the victory, and that she made this vow of obedience, not to her confessor, as she had at first intended doing, but to Mother Isabella. God recompensed the fidelity of His spouse, not by those feelings of sweetness which are the nourishment of children and of the weak, but by that largeness of heart which is fed by the good pleasure of God, according to the words of our Saviour: '*My food is to do the will of My Father.*' '*Abandonment, abandonment,*' such is the watchword which she addressed to her friend Clémence with her New Year's wishes. 'O, how sweet it is to live in this Furnace of Love, to drink at this Fountain! I tell you everything, for I feel urged to do so; I have so frequently revealed to you my sufferings, that it is but right that you should know my joys: they will increase in proportion as I draw nearer to that life which is heaven on earth.' It is thus that she speaks of the religious life, and, according to her determination at that time, of the life of Carmel. She was gradually approaching the day when, to use her own words, she would *sit down in the antechamber*, waiting for the door to be opened. It was towards the end of January or the beginning of February 1843, that she and her father left their apartments in the Rue de Sèvres, to become tenants of the Carmelites of the Rue d'Enfer. An attack of illness, fortunately not followed by serious consequences, warned the old man to think more than ever of his salvation; at the same time his decaying strength made him appreciate the advantage of a more peaceful and retired life; moreover, there, where his dear child was, had he not all he wanted? Had not this heart which was so devoted to him the secret of guessing his every wish, of charming his solitude and drawing him to God? It was then very willingly and with great joy that M. Dubouché consented to this change of dwelling, as he afterwards did, with the greatest generosity, to a more complete sacrifice. Thus God led His new spouse by the hand, broke all her earthly ties, and led her, unknown to herself, to the accomplishment of His mysterious designs. Seated under the shadow of Carmel, Theodelinda thought she had but to take one step to cross the threshold of that venerable cloister; and it was in this spot that those events occurred which revealed to her her true vocation, and gave rise to the Congregation of Reparation.

CHAPTER VI.
1848.

Theodelinda's zeal for souls.—Her confessor instructs her in spiritual direction.—Revolution of February.—Forty days' penance.—First idea of the foundation of a community of Sisters of Reparation.

THEODELINDA'S first act in her new abode was, unknown to her, the commencement of her foundation. Her yearning for a still closer retreat had not extinguished in her the zeal of charity. She would have wished to think only of God, and nevertheless serve souls. We have seen how many various projects had presented themselves to her mind, how many various counsels she had received. Now again God alone was to instruct her. Shortly before leaving her house in the Rue de Sèvres, she had conceived the idea of assembling round her, in her new abode, several young persons to whom she would serve as a guide, either to preserve them from the dangers of the world or to prepare them for the religious life. She had communicated her scheme to F. Lefêvre, and the necessity of support and direction in this enterprise was one of her motives in desiring to make the vow of obedience. On New Year's day 1848, whilst offering to our Lord in Holy Communion that year which was to decide her future life, she felt more strongly than ever the impulse of grace, and conceived the design of adding to her humble lodgings several rooms which should serve as a home for young girls out of situations. She put her project into execution immediately on her arrival in the Rue d'Enfer. Mother Isabella joyfully seconded her, and it was she who sent to Theodelinda her *first children*. Her confessor procured her others, so that in the month of February she had already seven under her direction. 'It is impossible,' she says, 'to express my fear and at the same time my joy during these first trials of spiritual direction. My heart burned with charity for the sanctification of souls; and I know of no trial which gave me such a knowledge of my own nothingness as this duty imposed on me by obedience at the commencement of my new career.'

The rare talents which Theodelinda possessed for the government of souls soon revealed themselves; the most remarkable was a wonderful facility in penetrating the secret dispositions of the persons under her care. It was not long before she had occasion to exercise this gift. During her retreat in the previous September, she had met at the Carmelite Convent in the Rue d'Enfer a young girl who was living in the monastery, and who manifested signs of a religious vocation. She had attracted her attention by her great beauty, and F. Bertholon, her confessor, spoke of her as a saint. The Prioress did not, however, share this confidence; troubled by the extraordinary proceedings of this young girl, who had taken a vow of obedience to her, she had begged Theodelinda to take particular notice of her actions, and to try her. In spite of the recommendations of Mother Isabella, the young person could not overcome her dislike to a mistress who, she said, only inspired her with fear. She seldom visited her, and then was never open with her. On her side, Theodelinda, in spite of her ardent charity, felt an aversion towards her which she could not understand: when she saw her communicate, she wept and would have desired to prevent her. This strange feeling, which nothing in the young girl's conduct justified, became a real torture to Theodelinda. She accused herself with tears of severity of judgment; but if she easily succeeded in distrusting herself and considering herself blind and culpable, she could not, nevertheless, get rid of the fatal conviction which was really embittering her life; and this entirely new species of trouble had formed not a small part of her sufferings during the last weeks of her abode at the Rue de Sèvres. Whilst she was still living there, she was one day informed that this young girl had had a great misfortune; she had been suddenly struck with blindness. At the same time an idea flashed across Theodelinda's mind: 'It is only a sham; she wishes to be thought *miraculous.*' She hastened to visit the sufferer, found in her all the signs of blindness, but remained equally unable either to justify her suspicions or to set them aside. Her opinion was asked, and she frankly owned her distrust. This created great astonishment, and, to convince her, she was invited to assist at the visit of the doctor, who, after trying many experiments, declared the young girl to be stone-blind. But Theodelinda was not yet convinced. Then to her mental sufferings were added the severe censures of her confessor. Her health could not bear so many trials; sleep fled from her eyes, she could not eat, and her poor body was made to suffer horrible torments in addition to the anguish of her soul. But all this was a consolation to her, as she was thus able to offer something to Jesus Christ in reparation for the hypocrisy of this unhappy person. This latter, *still blind,* and still, as it was supposed, living in the odour of sanctity, expressed a wish to repair to Argenteuil and implore her cure of the *holy tunic.* But before setting out on the pilgrimage, it was determined that she should, accompanied by Theodelinda, consult a very celebrated physician.* His declaration confirmed the general opinion; but Theodelinda had, on her side, acquired the certainty of the correctness of her opinion. Whilst waiting in the drawing-room with the girl she had looked her steadily in the face. For a long time the young girl did not flinch beneath her gaze, but at length she could bear it no longer and she lowered her eyes, blushing deeply. Theodelinda accompanied her home without any remark, carrying with her the certificate attesting her blindness and the certain proof of her fraud. The following day the young girl was *miraculously cured at Argenteuil.* Father Bertholon severely humbled Theodelinda for her proud obstinacy. The humble girl accepted all in silence; but her trouble became extreme. She was tempted with doubts of the faith, of miracles, of confessors, and her own in particular.

* M. Récamier.

She disclosed them all with sincerity. She was told to treat these thoughts as involuntary temptations, and to seek refuge in prayer. Nevertheless, Father Bertholon at length became uneasy himself; he made a more rigorous examination, and at length discovered the sacrilegious hypocrisy of the miserable creature in whom everything was found to be false—virtue, blindness, and cure. No sooner had she owned her fault than Theodelinda felt her merciful charity reawakened within her. She endeavoured with compassionate kindness to assist her in her repentance, and she engaged her to make a retreat in preparation for her general confession. But the whole affair had greatly lessened her confidence in Father Bertholon. She had admired his charity in his delusion and his humility in acknowledging it, but she had lost her confidence. This, however, God restored to her in a supernatural manner, and by an interior warning led her to confide in him more than ever. She did so with docility; and immediately all her sufferings were at an end.

We have inserted here this remarkable circumstance, the exact date of which is unknown, and which might have happened some time previous to Theodelinda's removal to the court of the Carmelites; but nothing could better show to what a degree God had endowed her with the qualifications necessary for the direction of souls, and how real was the vocation which would henceforth require of her the duties of a *spiritual mother*.

Scarcely had she begun her new life under the shadow of the cloister when the Revolution broke out. It was from this social commotion that sprang the Congregation of Reparation.

In the small house in the Rue d'Enfer could be heard the distant echo of the cannons of February. Theodelinda spent the 24th and 25th of that month in earnest prayer, calmly offering herself to the Divine Justice; for the thought of religion gained the ascendency over all other feelings during those stormy days. The spiritual joy caused by her removal to Carmel had produced in her soul such a disposition to self-abandonment that all her thoughts were bent on union with

God and placing herself entirely in His hands, to do with her what He pleased; if He chastised, she adored His rigour; if He pardoned, she offered herself to Him as a victim. She remembered the revelations of Sister Saint-Peter; she saw in the shock which was threatening Europe, not the consequences of such or such political error, but the necessary sequel to the apostasy of the Christian world. From that time one idea alone filled her heart, that of reparation; whether God would finally show justice or mercy was of little consequence. Whilst waiting for punishment or pardon, it behoved all faithful souls to anticipate expiation. This sentiment can be inspired by God alone; for man, left to himself, quickly forgets the rights of God to think only of his own interests. To pray, groan, and humble oneself when the thunder is rolling and there is a chance of diverting God's anger, is all very well; but to repair the outraged honour of our Saviour when the danger was passed, to do penance when one is no longer afraid, is a thing never thought of by people in general.

Initiated by the Holy Spirit into the secrets of disinterested love, Theodelinda had no difficulty in rising above this selfishness; and the brighter was the light of faith which made her see the Divine justice in the misfortunes of France, the more sincere was her desire to place in the first rank the reparation due to God's honour. She soon found means to associate other souls with herself in these sentiments of religious expiation.

Since the time that, through obedience, she had painted the Sacred Face as she had seen it in the vision, she had often heartily desired to see the picture of that adorable Face exposed in a sanctuary for the veneration of penitent souls. She had even once expressed this desire to her superiors, but received no encouragement in it. But after the shock that society had just received, the thought of reparation had become more general. Towards the end of Lent, Theodelinda felt herself urged to lay her scheme once more before Mother Isabella. This latter had also conceived the same plan, and ordered her to repair to the Superior of the Monastery, Abbé Gaume, and ask his permission to celebrate in the Carmelite chapel penitential exercises of devotion for the space of forty days, she herself undertaking to endeavour to obtain associates. The permission was immediately granted; and three days later, Passion Sunday, 9th April 1848, the devotions commenced. Abbé B— had placed on a small altar the precious painting which Theodelinda had given to him; each day a Mass was celebrated before this picture of the Holy Face *for the reparation of its injuries.* Theodelinda's idea was to assemble forty persons, each of whom should consecrate one entire day to exercises of reparation; instead of forty she found two hundred and fifty, who applied themselves to these practices with admirable eagerness and devotion.

We find amongst her papers the original of the 'Invito Sacro,' which procured her so many adherents, and, later on, more than one vocation to her community: 'A devotion of forty days is about to be made, in reparation for the outrages offered to our Lord during His Passion, and which are daily renewed by sinners. This little association of prayer should be animated by the spirit of sacrifice; it requires a great conformity of soul to the thought of repairing the injuries of our Saviour. *No personal consideration should be brought to it, but only the desire of seeing the justice of God appeased, our Lord Jesus Christ glorified, and our brethren saved.* The object of this quarantaine is to offer to God souls generously united to the Heart of the Saviour of mankind, a Heart burning with desire for reparation to be made to His Father, and with love for the unfortunate creatures who are under the weight of His displeasure. They must make an entire oblation of themselves, an unreserved abandonment of their goods, of their rest, and, if necessary, of their life. To find strength for this sacrifice it is necessary to receive the Divine Victim in Communion at the Mass, which each associate will cause to be said once at the altar of the Sacred Face of our Saviour. Being thus *one* with our Lord, they will then offer up their actions of each day in the spirit of reparation. They will make a visit to the Blessed Sacrament, to honour Jesus as Victim, and obtain, through meditation on the Passion, on the ignominies of the Pretorium and the Cross, the true spirit of this quarantaine. The visit will be ended by the recital of the prayers of the Association of Reparation, the cross and medal of which they will wear.'

Evidently, in taking, with the consent of her superiors, the initiative in this devotion, Theodelinda was only obeying an inspiration of zeal to spend, in the manner most agreeable to God, the time which was still to elapse before crossing the threshold of the convent. Now more than ever she deemed herself a Carmelite; and the idea of a new foundation was entirely foreign to the inspiration of these pious exercises. What, then, was her surprise when, on the feast of the Compassion of our Lady, having been to confession, to commence by this act of penance *her day of reparation*, she heard Father Bertholon ask her a question which to her seemed no longer doubtful. Let us here leave Theodelinda to relate in her autobiography what passed at that time. ' " Well," said her confessor to her, after giving her absolution, " do you give yourself entirely to God ?" My heartfelt reply was, " O yes, Father." " But if God wished you to renounce your vocation, would you do so ?" This question came upon me like a clap of thunder. Never, never shall I forget what I then felt. I had had so much suffering before being able to decide on my future life. I was fully convinced that I should be irrevocably doing God's will in enclosing myself behind those venerated gratings. I was so eagerly yearning after that celestial repose of contemplation. I should have feared less to sacrifice my life than to feel a doubt arise in my weary soul, so thirsting for solitude. I could not answer, my sobs were stifling me; for those words, which I might have regarded as the expression of an impossible supposition, since I had then no other idea than of a quarantaine,—those words appeared to me to be the command of God. The father, seeing me hesitate, resumed. " Then, my child, you will not give *all* to God ?' I answered eagerly, " Yes, father, *all, even my vocation*." I left the confessional, and the offering that I made of myself at Mass was entire.'

I will here quote other words to the same effect, written by her ten years after the foundation of her congregation, when she had experienced all the anguish of such a maternity. 'One of the greatest and most astonishing acts of faith that can be made amidst the darkness of exile is to found a religious order.' And I cannot help admiring, in the touching scene I have just related, the commencement of that heroic act which snatched her from the peaceful haven she was about to enter, to cast her alone, uncertain and trembling, into an unknown sea strewn with quicksands.

The wonderful success of the quarantaine inspired many persons with the desire to see this union of prayer perpetuated by means of an association. In all this Theodelinda avoided putting herself forward, being content to sigh after the thing itself, leaving Providence to find the means of bringing it about; but she was forced to yield to the entreaties of others, and solicit the necessary permission from the Superior for the execution of this design. M. Gaume approved highly of the association; but being persuaded that Theodelinda possessed the spirit of the devotion more thoroughly than any other person, he desired that she should herself seek the Archbishop of Paris, and beg his approbation of the association. It required nothing less than a command from her superior to determine Theodelinda to undertake this mission. Mgr. Affré welcomed her as a father; the idea of reparation could not but be welcomed by him who was so soon to become its heroic victim. He assured Mlle. Dubouché that this was a work which he had long desired, and that he wished to make Notre Dame the centre of it. He added, 'Only collect sufficient names, and I will issue a pastoral announcing the association.' The humble girl set to work towards the end of May; in less than a month she had procured two thousand associates. The list was about to be taken to the Archbishop, when it pleased God to give to the work, not the pontiff's sanction, but the consecration of his blood.

Whilst Theodelinda was engaged in these occupations, which would have absorbed any other life than hers, in what state was her interior life? Her letters describe it, and reveal to us the wonderful workings of grace in this faithful soul. The first three months that she spent in the Rue d'Enfer were perhaps the happiest of her life, although exterior crosses were not wanting: the anxiety of a removal, rendered more tiresome by want of money; uneasiness for her family during those troublous times; the hitherto unknown care of her spiritual daughters; then the anxiety caused by the events which we have just related; finally, her broken health, and the increasing infirmities of a body which was unable to bear so much fatigue and emotion—all this more than sufficed to make her feel that sting of trial which invariably torments those privileged souls admitted to the honour of divine familiarity, even in the midst of the greatest spiritual joys. But what appears to us overwhelming is but a light burden to those souls whom God has touched. 'For some time past,' she wrote to Father Lefèvre, 'my union with God has become more intimate, more simple, more delicious than ever; the longing desires proceeding from it cause my body continual suffering and a weakness which renders work absolutely impossible. But all this is of use; one likes all this; one even likes at times to be, as it were, swallowed up by one's present miseries or past sins. It is so sweet to weep with Magdalen at the feet of Jesus. One really feels that grace superabounds where sin had abounded. One loves to owe all to Him who is our all. My God, my God! what, then, is man that Thou shouldst thus remember him? I am at times positively annihilated under the weight of my happiness.'

Such great graces were, however, preparing the faithful servant of God for great struggles. The unexpected revelation of a new vocation, which had stolen from her the peaceful horizon of Carmel, soon replunged her into that ocean of bitterness from which she never after emerged, save during short and rare intervals.

The impression produced on her mind by the words of Father Bertholon did not wear away. A few days later, on Holy Thursday, during prayer, she felt a more lively desire than ever to see the honour of God repaired and Christians saved by means of penance. She ardently prayed to God for souls who should understand the thought of reparation; she prayed particularly that Paris might produce a Saint to begin this expiation. Great was her faith when she made this prayer, and it seemed to her that God had heard it; but how? This was a question she could not answer; for she would not, for an instant, have entertained the thought that she was herself that elect of grace; nevertheless she could not banish from her mind her firm conviction that God had chosen her for some particular work. During this conflict between inspiration and humility, she suffered strange agonies, fearing to be the plaything of the devil and the dupe of her pride. Mother Isabella had given her the *Life of Blessed Margaret Mary* to read. The narrative of the communications of God to that holy soul, she said, astounded her because they were so similar to what she herself experienced; she trembled to think that our Lord might grant her the same favours; she still found great difficulty, and but imperfectly conquered her repugnance, to disclose her feelings to her confessor or the Prioress. Was there in this excessive timidity of soul a lingering of self-love? Was there remains of human respect in this reserve? Did she fear, in revealing her gifts, to meet with doubt or contempt? God alone knows; for we cannot interpret literally the reproaches with which she overwhelmed herself at a later period for this want of simplicity. She may, however, in some degree have been wanting in that difficult virtue which renders the disciples of Jesus Christ like unto little children. But may we not attribute this excess of discretion partly to her natural character? And should we not admire the ways of Providence, who chose to raise to the most sublime communications with Himself a soul who by habit and natural inclination was most diffident of everything extraordinary?

However that may be, if the humble postulant of Carmel sinned through a want of candour, it was not that she had not made great efforts to correct her imperfection on this point. The confessor to whom, through obedience, she had abandoned her soul with so generous a sacrifice of her own inclinations, seemed expressly destined by God to triumph over her resistance. '*He required in his direction*,' she says, '*such minute details that he made me simple almost by force.*' Theodelinda obeyed, but not without a struggle. Confession again became to her what it had been at the time of her conversion, a real torture; she would sometimes remain the whole morning at the door of the confessional without daring to enter; then, at last victorious over herself, she confided to Father Bertholon all her secrets without even hiding from him that anguish of heart which she felt towards him. The holy man bore all with such humility and charity that his penitent's dispositions immediately changed, and she felt as a little child beside its father. Thus she suddenly passed from an excess of distrust to unlimited confidence; from unfounded doubts respecting the truth of her vocation and of her inclination, to a tranquil certitude which forbade any doubts. But these vicissitudes in her spiritual life became in their turn a subject for anxious doubts. How could a soul thus tormented be called to guide others? How could so uncertain a mind be called to trace out a new road? Would it not be better then to avoid all thoughts which might divert her from her first vocation, and still regard the gates of Carmel as the entrance to the Promised Land where her soul was at length to find rest? Actuated by these thoughts, she more than ever feared to impart to Mother Isabella the view (which became daily clearer) which God had given her of her mission. Whilst, urged by an irresistible force, she was, without knowing it, laying the foundations of her new institute, she appeared to the Prioress as the most resolute of her postulants. And what she led this mother to believe, she also tried to persuade herself of; whilst in her and around her the movement of grace and the course of events were urging her on in another direction. The evil result of this divided life was that, when it became necessary to manifest this change of vocation, she appeared to be wanting in constancy and fidelity; and what was simply a necessary act of obedience to the call of God was regarded by many as a kind of apostasy.

CHAPTER VII.
1848.
Events of June.—Foundation of the Third Order.

THE reader must not be wearied by the proximity of dates; but there are incidents which strike the least attentive mind, and which, in some cases, render visible the intervention of Providence to those who are convinced of the part which God takes in the events of this world. The troubles of February had given rise to that movement of faith which had awakened in a great many souls new desires for reparation and penance. What had been at first merely a small group of pious persons momentarily united for fleeting exercises became organised, through the impulse of one among them, into a numerous association and a durable congregation; and the time that this pious work was to be accomplished was precisely the solemn moment when the crisis of June was filling all hearts with consternation. The gloomy series of *the four days* began with the Octave of the Feast of Corpus Christi.* Whilst Frenchmen were cutting each other's throats in the streets, the new Associates of the Reparation were praying before the monstrance. Strange contrast, and one that may serve as an answer to those who deny or dispute the utility of the contemplative orders. The Carmelite chapel had become a powerful centre of attraction to all who were animated by the idea of reparation; and the humble monastery, which in the time of public peace seemed to many to occupy a useless place in that city of business and pleasure, suddenly recovered its importance in that same great town, which had become for a time the bloody arena in which the two

* That year Corpus Christi fell on Thursday the 22d; the 23d was the first of the *days of June*.

halves of the people met in homicidal struggle. Here was the murderous conflict between human passions and contrary interests; there the touching harmony of penance and prayer, provoking on the part of God, in the name of the Eucharistic Mediation, that union of Justice and Clemency whence proceeds the salvation of mankind.

In this remarkable movement which drew people to the foot of the altar, Theodelinda took an active and considerable part. In a heart like hers, wholly bent on God, there was now no room for fear. She could therefore devote all the resources of her intellect to the cause of reparation. Unceasingly prostrated before our Saviour, she never left Him except to seek for fresh adorers. Whilst in other places they dared not expose the Blessed Sacrament, she had obtained permission to prolong the exposition during the Octave until eleven o'clock at night, and twice even through the entire night. Across streets transformed by the barricades into battle-fields, courageous women repaired to the privileged sanctuary. Theodelinda multiplied herself to be of service to them; her house was theirs; she found means to provide all with shelter, many with food also; nothing discouraged her; a divine strength supported her in a sensible manner. It was not enough for her to pray and cause others to pray; she felt called also to attend to those around her who were in affliction or alarm. She met a soldier's wife trembling for the safety of her husband, who was exposed to great peril. This woman had been long estranged from God. 'If you pray with faith,' she said to her, 'I promise you your husband will not be wounded.' Then she persuaded her to go to confession. Three days later the soldier returned safe and sound.

It was in the midst of this holy activity that Theodelinda learnt the news of the heroic death of Mgr. Affré, which awakened in her at once a sensible sorrow and a firm hope. She did not doubt that he was the Saint she had asked of God; the Saint who was to water with his blood the seed recently committed to the earth. She says, 'I went to venerate his body, which had been exposed for three days, with a feeling of extraordinary faith and devotion. I communicated in the *chapelle ardente*, and, when kissing his feet, I begged him to keep the promise he had made me, and establish at Paris the Confraternity for Reparation.' It is impossible not to think that the martyr of charity heard this simple prayer. And was not the humble girl right in afterwards attributing to this blessing of the *good Pastor* the success of an enterprise which had met with so many trials and contradictions?

Nevertheless the fratricidal struggle was coming to an end; the wounded and the dead were lying in the bloody streets; a gloomy silence succeeded the tumultuous strife; and the last day of the Octave of Corpus Christi ended peacefully at Carmel amidst prayer and thanksgiving. The fervent adorers had obtained permission to have the Exposition of the Blessed Sacrament for the night following the expiration of the Octave. It appeared that they could not be satiated with that Divine Presence which excited their faith through the immediate contemplation of the Eucharistic species. During this last vigil there was reserved for the instigator of their zeal a favour which was to decide her future mission. But let us hear her own description of this divine communication, which no other motive than obedience would ever have prompted her to reveal:

'My time of adoration was from one to three in the morning. I sensibly felt the divine love, but I was not astonished; because for a long time I had daily felt a ray of light leave the Host and penetrate into my heart. But this time the impression was so strong that a violent rapture deprived me of my senses. The Eucharistic veils disappeared. I saw our Lord on the altar as upon a throne. He placed a gold tube to His Heart, placing the other extremity to mine; then He poured into my being a life which would have killed me had He not supported me. I felt lost in a superabundance of light and love. After this ineffable grace, which appeared entirely to have absorbed my own life, I regained consciousness a little, and I heard, though without words, the sense of what I now relate: "I desire adoration and reparation to appease the justice of My Father; but all these associations are insufficient: I wish for a religious consecration. I require souls who shall be continually in My presence to receive My life. I will place to their hearts a gold tube as I have just done to yours; but they must communicate this life that I give them to those souls who belong to Me in the world. I will also give them a tube to transmit the life which they will have received from Me." And then,' continues Theodelinda, ' I saw clearly the organisation of the work such as it now is ;* and never have I succeeded in banishing that sight. I may have doubted, because of my unworthiness, whether this vision came from God; but I never hesitated to think that if it were from Him, I should conform myself to it without modification.'

The vow of obedience which she had made to the Prioress obliged her to relate to that Mother all that she had seen and heard. She found the ground prepared for her communication; in fact, Mother Isabella had ardently desired to allow her Community to have perpetual Exposition of the Blessed Sacrament; but she did not know how to reconcile what appeared to her a command of God with the immobility of the rule of Carmel. More than once she had spoken on the subject to her confessor without obtaining a satisfactory answer. Theodelinda's disclosure to her would perhaps remove her perplexity. The latter, emboldened by her kind reception, went so far as to propose the establishment of *a third order of regulars with a secular branch*. This third order was to be united to Carmel, insomuch as it was not to be a new order, but it was to preserve as much independence as to be able to practise the devotion of reparation, and spread it without interfering in the mother order with the principle of the cloister and absolute separation. This proposition came as a ray of light to Mother Isabella. Nor was she the only one who applauded it: all the superiors and directors interested in the convent, all the virtuous and scientific men who were consulted, agreed in seeing in this idea an inspiration responding to the manifest wants of the day. From all sides, even from other countries, Theodelinda received

* This account was written in 1852, when the Congregation already existed, with its two branches, regular and secular.

encouragement. The one who hesitated most in giving his approbation was the Superior of the monastery, who raised several objections. She, however, successfully overcame them, without having recourse to any other means than the principles of faith and the plea of opportuneness. Her great motive, the command of Heaven, was a secret that she only revealed to her Mother and her confessor. But the enterprise was in itself a recommendation, and nothing could retard its execution. One month sufficed for the active Theodelinda to begin the foundation. Providence had, as it were, prepared the elements of this creation by placing in advance, under the spiritual direction of the future foundress, humble servants of God ready to follow her in the way she wished to mark out to them. On the feast of the Transfiguration, 6th August 1848 Mother Isabella assembled them to the number of eight behind the grille in the parlour, and placed them under the immediate authority of their new Mother. Thus God Himself hastened to fulfil His promise. But who would believe it? At the very time when Theodelinda found herself appointed, as if unexpectedly, foundress and superioress, she could not even then turn away her eyes from that perspective which revealed a Carmelite cell as the goal of all her undertakings. She really persuaded herself that this was a way of spending her life in the service of God, whilst duties to her father still remained to be fulfilled; but that later, breaking every tie with the world, she would leave to others the direction of the third order; and, free at last, she would enter the place of her rest. This she believed with perfect sincerity. But there is no repose for souls whom God has called to accomplish great things for His love.

CHAPTER VIII.
1848, 1849.

First year of religious life.—Novitiate.—The foundress's first coöperators separate from her.—Interior and exterior trials.—M. Dubouché generously agrees to his daughter's vocation.—Theodelinda's profession under the name of 'Mary Teresa.'

THEODELINDA'S was indeed a singular position—a superioress not yet professed, a foundress making her novitiate with her first subjects.

But the material condition of the infant order added still more to the singularity of this life. Whilst Theodelinda was receiving from the Prioress her maternal mission, her position had not altered in the eyes of the world; even her family was ignorant of what had occurred, and continued to see in her what she had been for so many years, viz. a pious person living a life more retired than ever, but admirably devoted to her family. About this time, her sister, her brother-in-law, and nephew visited M. Dubouché in his apartments, which were contiguous to the monastery; she shared their life, tending her father, ruling the house, and even receiving the friends who came to see the good old man; and no one ever guessed that at that very time, in the upper story, a community was being formed, whom she directed and installed in three or four rooms without furniture or money, and without any present or future resources. Thus commence God's works.

Nothing can give an idea of the confidence and energy of these holy souls. Inflamed by their Mother's zeal, they were ready to make every sacrifice. The Perpetual Adoration, both daily and nightly, had begun with the third order; the small numbers of the adorers obliged them to prolong their night-watches for two hours and a half; there were not sufficient beds for all, but they replaced each other there as in the chapel, and even found means to yield those they had to persons living outside, who took part in the adoration. In order to make room and set a good example, Theodelinda gave up her own bedchamber to these guests of prayer, and slept on a couch in her father's drawing-room; this was for six months her only bed.

So much abnegation, united to so much fervour, profoundly touched those who witnessed it. The venerated instigators of the Perpetual Adoration were never weary of admiring the poor members of the third order of Reparation. The most influential,* he who took the most active part in the institution of the Diocesan Confraternity of Adoration, often visited the little flock with words of encouragement, and merited, in this case as in many others, to be called the Apostle of the Eucharist. His attention was at that time directed to an organisation of the Perpetual Adoration, which would have comprised all the dioceses of France, and he thought of making the community which had sprung up under the shadow of Carmel the centre. He laid all his plans to this effect, and after obtaining the approbation of the Archbishop he communicated them to Theodelinda. This latter believed her foundation thus solidly established, and in her grateful joy repaired with her spiritual children to the monastery chapel to recite the *Te Deum*.

The future of the community was now regarded as certain, and it became necessary to have a rule. With the consent of the Carmelite Superior, Theodelinda drew up a rule which, in the month of October, obtained the provisional approbation of Mgr. Sibour. Some days later the Archbishop himself visited the new family, whose numbers were now doubled; he complimented them on their rapid increase, encouraged them in their vocation, and promised them abundant blessings.

About this time the diocesan authorities, renewing a point of discipline fallen into disuse, invited every community of

---

* Abbé de la Bouillerie, since Bishop of Carcassonne.

women to choose a Superior. Abbé Gaume already filled this office in the monastery of the Rue d'Enfer; he still retained it by the suffrages of the Carmelites, and the third order of the Reparation likewise chose him for their Superior. Thus the new congregation was becoming confirmed and regularly constituted.

Nevertheless trials were not far distant. The zeal of the foundress had led her to enter into correspondence with all those persons who, like herself, were animated with the ardent desire of glorifying the Blessed Sacrament; but, as it too frequently happens, unity of ideas did not respond to unity of hearts.

Theodelinda had no natural love for domination; nevertheless she firmly maintained the first idea of her foundation, and refused combinations which appeared to compromise in its regard the accomplishment of the designs of God. Having a different idea of the object of the foundation, and displeased at not being able to win her over to their way of thinking, several of her first coöperators left her, and there soon arose a kind of rivalry with regard to her institute. These persons having influence with the Archbishop, the plans for attaching the Perpetual Adoration to the third order were discontinued; in a new scheme, conceived on quite a different system, the third order was *forgotten;* later on even, it seems that it was only remembered to be opposed.* The infant institute, which appeared, but a few weeks previously, to answer serious and pressing wants, was now treated as useless; an Association would suffice; the new adorers had no need of a sanctuary; they were to seek to obtain Perpetual Adoration of the Blessed Sacrament in such parish-churches as kept up the Perpetual Adoration; likewise, they were to unite together only for the

---

* The correspondence of Mother Mary Teresa shows us that M. de la Bouillerie found out the falsehood of the insinuations of uncharitable persons. When these same persons sought to dispute with the Foundress the favours she had obtained from Rome, this latter found in the Bishop of Carcassonne a devoted defender, who has never since ceased to testify to her person and her society the truest esteem and the most cordial sympathy.

nightly adoration, *so as not to interfere with public devotion.* Such insinuations tended simply to destroy the barely-formed community, reducing its members to the rank of seculars, who were to perform many painful duties without being compensated by receiving any privilege. Then it was that the humble foundress felt to the full extent those trials which had begun for her with her functions of Mother. ' I was,' she said, ' at the first station of my Calvary.' And the better to mark this sad moment of departure, God permitted that the violence of her grief should bring on a serious illness, and for several days her life was even in danger. Whilst in this state she saw an abridgment of all that she would have to suffer. Like our Saviour at Gethsemane, she could meditate on and accept the chalice which was offered her; and like Him, comforted by love of the Divine Will, she became strengthened in constancy, and prepared herself for every trial.

It may not be amiss to consider here whence those dissensions arise which grieve us so much, appearing so often as they do, not amongst men enslaved to their selfish passions, but between souls equally animated by the love of God, and long united in the pursuit of the noblest aims. Those who are astonished at this show clearly that they do not understand what Divine things become after passing through human hands; the lives of the greatest servants of God give us examples sufficient to enlighten us on this subject, and to dispel the chimerical hope of ever finding heaven on earth, even in what would appear sacred ground. During all ages *saints have caused saints to suffer.* The principal and most obvious reason of this is doubtless the imperfection of the virtue of those even who are with greatest justice termed *perfect;* the dissension is generally caused by both sides, though in an unequal degree. One will, perhaps, be a little too stiff and unyielding in the application of a right idea; the other will display something of self-love in the defence of an opinion, of which a little more humility would have led him to acknowledge the falsity. Who shall determine as to which commits the greater fault? He alone who sounds hearts, who weighs in a just balance the merits and efforts of each individual soul, taking into consideration the faculties, lights, tendencies, and natural dispositions of each one and everything which modifies the moral act, and who alone can distinguish with infallible accuracy the elements of which it is composed. But to this first cause we must add another, viz. the diversity of opinion and ways of looking at things. Doubtless there exists a point of view superior to all others, one absolutely just and true; but it is placed at a height to which, by nature, God alone can attain, and to which He raises His servants only when He admits them in heaven to the participation of the Beatific Vision. Meanwhile, we must resign ourselves to know but one side of things, that one which has to do either with our interests or with our duty. The egotist stops at the first point, the virtuous soul clings to the second; the more disengaged he is from self-love, the more does he apply himself to the consideration of the task which God gives him, to the mission which He confides to him. Now works are of many kinds, and the various missions urge the envoys of God in different directions. Sometimes they journey on together and imagine that they are both tending towards the same goal; but the interior inspiration is not asleep, and when the hour of separation comes they regard it as a duty which does not, however, destroy their union of heart. They then separate, and, for want of seeing what the other sees, each one thinks that his neighbour has mistaken the command of God; whereas the truth is that each is obeying a different order. One can, then, conceive disunion without any cause, save a partial view of his own opinion on both sides; without there being any act of imperfection in either party. But the ordinary case is that the two causes combine, in an infinite variety of proportions, to produce those feelings of disunion and opposition, the sight of which so saddens disinterested lookers-on. Leaving to God the final judgment, we may say that he is right whose views are the largest, and whose abnegation is the most entire. If, in the impartial application of this *criterium* to contemporary persons and facts, the historian involuntarily pains some surviving actor of the scene he has undertaken to reproduce, he is the first to regret his misfortune; but he finds himself justified by the imperious exigencies of his task.

The history of the foundation of the third order has brought us to the end of the year 1848. But we must go back a little in order to resume that other more intimate history which describes to us the action of God in the soul of the Foundress. Loaded with a burden which threatened to become excessive, she sensibly experienced the assistance of Him who had laid it on her. Her communications with God became daily more intimate, and made her feel the necessity for a more enlightened guidance. It was a long time since she had seen F. Lefèvre. Yielding to a powerful impulse, and encouraged by Mother Isabella, she determined, towards the end of September, to travel to Tours, there to meet that guide who had so long kept the key of her soul. She met him at Marmoutier, where he was preaching a retreat; there during several days she revealed to him, though not without violent repugnance, the wonderful graces she had received; then she spoke to him openly of her designs concerning her community. The father approved not only of the spirit, but also of the organisation of the order as Theodelinda had conceived it. He even confirmed her against her own hesitation, telling her that her vow to do that which was most perfect did not permit her to draw back nor to choose for herself the sweets of a peaceful and retired life, when the will of her Divine Master so clearly called her to serve Him at the cost of her own repose. God seemed to wish to confirm interiorly the encouragements of her holy director. Before leaving Marmoutier, Theodelinda wished to visit the grotto of St. Martin and St. Brice; there, whilst her artistic soul imbibed those poetical emotions caused by the charm of the site and the majesty of its souvenirs, a powerful grace took possession of her, and during a lengthened meditation penetrated her with the thought that God was all in all to her. When overflowing with the consolations and lights which she had received from Father Lefèvre, she inwardly murmured at being deprived of this assistance when at Paris, a voice thus replied to her interiorly: *'You belong to Me alone; nothing that will be accomplished through you will come from man.*' 'Poor grotto,' she exclaimed later, when thinking of this favour, 'I would have wished to hide in your obscurity the delicious happiness I felt when I promised my Divine Master to seek assistance from *Him alone* in His enterprise !'

On her return from this journey, and in spite of the opposition which she encountered, her soul became dilated in the practice of her new duties. Great spiritual joys fortified her beforehand for the combats awaiting her; but above all, an immense and truly maternal charity for her children was bestowed upon her. One day, at the time of Communion, it seemed to her that our Lord gave her His heart, to communicate it to her children. 'O, sweet exchange of love,' she wrote on this subject to Father Lefèvre, 'by a change incomprehensible to the senses you become that mystery of unity announced by Jesus Christ! Anathema to *solitary hearts!* they will not enter the kingdom of heaven. He who journeys to that blessed country should desire to lead to Jesus crucified all those for whom that Saviour died.'

By these expressions, worthy of St. Teresa, it is impossible not to recognise an apostolic soul. How can we doubt that she belongs to the race of those to whom God has imparted the fecundity of His Church!

Another characteristic of souls destined to make new foundations is a clear sight of the aim in view, mingled with zeal and persistence in carrying it out. Almost always a founder meets with auxiliaries who pretend to aid the work without understanding it, and who, under the pretext of developing it, threaten to draw it from its object. The more sincere these coöperators are, so much the more difficult is it to get rid of their dangerous concurrence. In order to defend the primary idea against the friends who compromise it, as against the enemies who oppose it, great prudence and firmness are requisite; or rather, prudence and firmness do not suffice, there is likewise needed that strong faith which belongs only to the initiated. Occasions were not wanting for Theodelinda to give this fresh proof of her mission. Union with Carmel, nay dependence on it, was the soul of the new third order; and nevertheless, the special object, that of reparation, would have been wanting had this union led to fusion. Bound by a vow of obedience, and still more by the sentiment of filial gratitude, the *novice-foundress*, had she only listened to her feelings, would have placed herself and her children entirely at the service of the Mother Prioress. But she likewise understood that a religious family cannot exist without a spirit of its own; and each day, bringing with it fresh troubles, made a distinction between the two communities more necessary, and yet more difficult. This badly-defined position, which unceasingly threatened the very existence of the new community, seemed about to overcome the constancy of some of its members, and more than one *Réparatrice* began to envy the peaceful lot of the elder daughters of St. Teresa.

Whilst the Foundress was overwhelmed with these difficulties, her confessor involuntarily provided her with others. From the day when Theodelinda had seen in the future the existence of her congregation, she had conceived it in its fulness, with the distinction between the three orders of persons it was to include: the regulars, the seculars, and the associates. The devotion of reparation appeared to her as an ardent flame feeding at the Eucharistic centre. The regular sisters in the retirement of the cloister were to keep alive this sacred fire; the secular sisters were to carry it outside into some chosen families, to spread the rays of Eucharistic love beyond the monastery walls; in fine, the associates were to propagate in the world thoughts of faith, reparation, and love little familiar to ordinary Christians, and reawaken in a great many, by zeal for the honour of God, feelings of a disinterested religion. Of these three unequal branches, the most difficult to ingraft on the stem of Carmel was certainly the second. One can easily conceive cloistered religious, and one can likewise understand a number of pious persons forming an association and making the monastery the centre. But professed sisters living in the world; contemplatives without a cloister; obedience and, in some degree, religious poverty practised in the world—this was what formed, with regard to this new creation, the novelty of the conception and the difficulty of putting it into execution. Father Bertholon intended to assist the Foundress in the accomplishment of her cherished scheme; unfortunately he adopted quite a different one, and, unknown to her, laboured for its development. For a long time he had desired to introduce into Paris a work already begun in the provinces: its object was to offer a temporary asylum to young girls without work, and to find them places as servants; the house which had received them during their time of distress then became their place of meeting during their leisure hours. This excellent work was shortly after successfully established, and still continues to render inestimable services. But one can well understand that it was utterly at variance with the designs of Theodelinda. Whilst the latter was seeking for secular sisters, Father Bertholon sent her persons destined to be servants, and desired that she should in the mean time form them to virtue. He even did more than this: he invited to Paris two holy persons who had begun this refuge for servants in the provinces; he installed them in the house belonging to the third order, and placed them under Theodelinda's direction. The unhappy results of this proceeding were not long in becoming manifest. The novices of the Reparation were confounded by many with the poor girls without situation who were daily recommended to Father Bertholon. The discredit which thus fell upon the new community, whilst augmenting the material perplexity of the Foundress, caused her likewise a very lively grief which she could not hide from her confessor, who, in his turn, appeared hurt by her sorrow. Then, once more, his penitent experienced in his regard one of those temptations to reserve, mistrust, and coldness so painful to an obedient soul. Mother Isabella, whom Theodelinda consulted in this affair, shared her fears and regrets; and in order to deliver the Congregation of Reparation from a connection which compromised it, she let the apartment which had been given up for the use of the servants. This proceeding did away with every material difficulty, but it did not put an end to jealousy. Father Bertholon appeared less and less satisfied, and thus increased the interior trials of his penitent, who was no less anxious than incapable of opening to him her whole heart.

The winter of 1848-1849 passed amid these troubles. In the midst of so many obstacles, the third order continued to progress. A letter written at this period to F. Lefèvre shows us the increasing success of the scheme of reparation, in spite of the ever-increasing material obstacles. 'Humanly speaking,' she said, 'I see but embarrassments before me, both spiritually and temporally. Funds are wanting;* there is no work to be done. I am exhausting my resources: when they are gone, what will happen? I counted upon the association† providing for the wants of the third order, which would have lent all its aid to the confraternity; but if we remain separated, who will provide us with bread? Nevertheless, God seems to smile upon me. Everyday I receive new demands for admission from excellent persons; incessant retreats produce great fruit; several spiritual miracles have been effected more astonishing than the curing of illness; letters come from all parts—from Lyons, Bordeaux, Nantes, Bourges, Blois—asking me *what I am going to do*, and telling me *that they wish to do as I do*. O, what I am going to do, God alone knows!'

Amidst such rapid progress, it became impossible to prolong the provisionary and intermediate state, in which for several months a superioress without vows, and religious without the habit, had been living. Notwithstanding much opposition, the third order of Reparation began to reveal its separate existence: it was now necessary to give it an appearance corresponding to its actual state of being. The Superior informed Theodelinda that she could no longer openly fulfil her filial duty to her father and her maternal duty to her spiritual children; and that, if she intended to continue her foundation, the time had come for her to make her profession. Troubled as she was

---

* The reader will remember that to avoid a lawsuit she had given up her income for two years.

† She here speaks of the diocesan Association of Perpetual Adoration.

inwardly, and tormented exteriorly, Theodelinda did not hear this decision without feelings of anguish and terror. This time, circumstances forbade her to make her ordinary guides the confidants of her trouble. Fortunately her former confessor, Abbé B., was in Paris: he also was of opinion that she should take this step; but, with his usual kindness, he offered to make that communication to M. Dubouché which his daughter so much dreaded. 'It will be,' he added, 'a clear indication of the will of God. Naturally speaking, your poor old father will oppose this project. Well, if he testifies too great grief, capable of shortening or troubling his life, you will desist, at least for a time. If he should consent, you may conclude that God wishes you to act at once. Pray earnestly.' 'I prayed,' she said later, 'like a person whose whole fate is about to be decided.' Abbé B. soon reappeared, radiant with joy. 'It is truly wonderful,' he said to Theodelinda; 'do you know what your good old father answered? "Not only do I consent," he said, "but I am even happy to be able to give her to God during my lifetime. All that I ask is that I may be permitted to have a little corner in the house, that I may see her, and that she may assist me in my last moments."'

Thus were broken the last ties which bound the dove; she could now fly away to the place of her rest. But no; she was never more to enjoy rest. Instead of a quiet cell in the Carmelite Monastery, Theodelinda saw before her an uncertain and stormy future: the foundation irrevocably decided upon, when eight months of trial had revealed to her the full extent of the difficulties to be overcome; the burden of superiority henceforth firmly fixed upon her at a time when the weight of her own infirmities seemed more than ever insupportable, and when a trial (the renewal of that of former days) placed her in a dilemma between the desire to submit and the impossibility of confidence. Abbé B., to whom she confided her anguish of mind, regarded it as the pains of spiritual infancy, inseparable from the title of mother, which God was about to confer on His spouse. 'You have not,' he said, 'to ask yourself whether this is agreeable to you, but whether it is the will of God. You may have to suffer a martyrdom during your whole life, but of this you must make no account.' Theodelinda no longer hesitated. When called before the Superior to relate, as is usual, the history of her past life, she gave him an account of both her exterior and interior life; then the day was fixed for the clothing and profession. The feast of Pentecost was chosen for this double ceremony, which was to constitute definitively the community of Reparation.

It was necessary to prepare for it by a retreat. The Carmelites were about to have one, which was to be preached by a Jesuit whom Theodelinda greatly esteemed. She very much desired to confide to this father the direction of her retreat, and thus withdraw herself from the guidance of her confessor, her repugnance to whom seemed to increase. She had obtained permission to do so from Mother Isabella; but she was reckoning without the interior command of the Holy Spirit. The eve of the retreat she had an ecstasy, during which she was given to understand that she was to have recourse to Father Bertholon. She wept, she resisted, but in vain; the injunction was formal, and she must obey. How mysterious are the ways of Providence! who usually makes use of a certain sympathy to point out to souls the guides destined for them; but who, in this case, substituted violence for attraction when confidence seemed absolutely necessary. The truth is, that God wished to direct His spouse alone at this decisive period. Docile, but trembling, Theodelinda sought her confessor; revealed to him the reluctance she felt with regard to him, her intention to leave him, and the sorrow she felt at being urged to return to him. The holy man received these acknowledgments with perfect charity and humility. At that very moment Theodelinda felt herself changed; her heart opened, her anxiety ceased, and she began her retreat with a dilated heart. Again God was at hand to take from her all human support. She desired at least to follow the sermons of the Jesuit father; but from the first moment of solitude she fell into a passive state, in which she could hear only interior language: the plan of her retreat was revealed to her in this manner. But we must hear her describe it herself, in order to form an idea of the great heights to which prayer can raise a simple Christian woman, and one utterly ignorant of theology. 'The Divine Spirit gave me as a subject the three theological virtues as the foundation of the three religious virtues, of which I was about to take the vows: Faith in Obedience, Hope in Poverty, Charity in Chastity. I had never before conceived this idea; but I felt it with a superabundance of light which instructed me better than any book I could have read. This was not all. The three theological virtues and the three vows thus united were shown to me expressed and summed up in the three great divisions of the Mass; and I spent much of my time of prayer in meditating on the Holy Sacrifice, as a preparation for the sacrifice which I was about to make.'

The days of the retreat passed for Theodelinda in this lofty communication with God; and at the same time, to complete the entire oblation of herself, she settled all her temporal affairs like a person about to die. She disposed beforehand of her little fortune, and distributed among her relations and friends all her little treasures. Those who have never seen a beloved friend thus anticipate the business of death, and follow in its minutest details the consequences of a voluntary adieu to the world, can form no idea of the power of religious abnegation and the spiritual joy it produces—a joy far exceeding the bitterness of the sacrifice. Theodelinda experienced this joy. 'That was indeed a happy day,' she writes, 'when all my measures were taken for leaving the world. As I gradually deprived myself of those objects to me, so full of touching recollections, it seemed as if new feathers were being added to the wings which were to raise me to God.'

At last the days of Pentecost satisfied so many holy desires. On Sunday Theodelinda was clothed, and on Tuesday she made her profession. She passed but a day between those two great acts which influence a lifetime; but what else had her whole life been than a long novitiate, begun under the direction of God alone, amid a world a stranger to piety, and spent, notwithstanding a thousand troubles, in the laborious exercise of good works, in the daily practice of the contemplative life; finally crowned by ten months of a truly religious life in the midst of an infant community, in which the duties of mother and foundress, added to those of a religious, imposed on the novice all the burdens at the same time?

The reader will probably recollect Theodelinda's vision of the Blessed Virgin and St. Teresa covering her with their mantles. It was the living expression of the idea of reparation such as she had conceived it from the first: *the death of Carmel united to the simple and ordinary life of Nazareth.* She also desired to place her religious life under the patronage of these two Mothers. Henceforth, forgetting what she had been in the world, we shall call her by the name of *Mary Teresa.*

CHAPTER IX.

1849, 1850.

Spiritual joy caused by her profession.—She abandons herself to supernatural action. — Her extraordinary states alarm her directors.—Humiliating examination.—Frightful temptations which ensue.—The Blessed Virgin restores peace to her soul.—Incredible zeal for the sanctification of souls.—She commits her rules to writing.—Serious difficulties with Carmel.—Severe censure of the Archbishop.—The new congregation is on the point of perishing.—It is saved by the humility of the foundress and the devotedness of her daughters.

GOD alone knows what passed in the soul of the newly-professed at the moment of her consecration. Rapt in ecstasy, she remained for three hours immovable in a retired part of the chapel, without any one daring to approach her. On descending from this Thabor she was prepared for great struggles. Providence was indeed reserving her many, both internal and external: *Foris pugnæ, intus timores,*—struggles without, troubles within. This had been the complaint of St. Paul. It is the sad history of all great souls.

Nevertheless, the days immediately following her profession were to Mary Teresa days of great joy and interior consolation. A powerful thought animated her. 'I scarcely know,' she wrote to F. Lefèvre, 'whether I have any part in what takes place within me. I am afraid,' she added, 'that I am a little *exalted*, as people say. Happily, when my soul is about completely to go out of itself, God warns me of it, by sending a very great drowsiness. I then retire to my cell, and all takes place in accordance with the wishes of our Lord.' Continuing the account of her state, she added, with perfect simplicity: 'In my numberless exterior relations I can show gaiety and freedom of spirit; interiorly, I feel completely crushed, though calm. The *father* and *mother*' (her confessor and prioress) 'think that I am becoming more simple. Nevertheless, there are days when, *on returning from a journey*, I tremble like a leaf.' *Povera!* What will become of her? She always looks to see whether some hole will not open and hide her. That is putting herself on a level with the worms of the earth. Or, at other times, it appears to her that wings are at hand to raise her on high. From this passage we see that the mystical life had not crushed the imagination of the artist, nor robbed her language of the simple graces which it naturally possessed.

In this soul, so truly apostolic, all increase of virtue was developed into zeal. 'I have a great thirst for souls,' she writes at this time. 'Sometimes it causes me to suffer greatly: I see so many spiritual miseries unrelieved; and, what is still worse, so many pious persons thinking only of themselves! Jesus the Victim wishes to have a heaven upon earth; having established here His throne, He desires to have around Him angels and saints. In the absence of that purity which death alone can give, He is content with self-sacrifice; but He must have that.

'This century of egotism has destroyed every trace of that virtue. There are a great number of devotees, but there are scarcely any devout persons. O, how we should compassionate the Divine Bridegroom each time that, sounding the depth of a soul that we thought overflowing with love, we find in it nothing but self-love! Father, teach them, then, I beg of you, that the smallest sacrifice is of more value in the eyes of our crucified Lord than books of prayers recited from beginning to end.'

These zealous desires were soon to receive great satisfaction in the clothing of the first religious of the third order of Reparation. Even before the Foundress's profession, on the feast of the Compassion of the Blessed Virgin, eight of her children had made in her hands a consecration of themselves to Jesus the Victim. This seemed to be as an earnest of the gift they were aspiring to consummate. Mary Teresa had, then, in these columns a solid foundation for the new edifice. Later, she assured them with great emotion that, by their confidence and generosity, they had really founded the Congregation of Reparation, not fearing to engage themselves by a promise before their

Mother was bound by vows. Once professed, this latter bent her thoughts on giving her generous daughters the exterior signs of that holy state, the spirit of which they already possessed. Amongst the postulants, four were found worthy to be admitted to their clothing at the same time. They were as the twelve apostles of the foundation. The Superior examined them early in June, and they immediately began their retreat. At that time serious events seemed to be at hand: the Roman expedition, which was being brought to a successful conclusion, had reawakened the anger of the democratic party. It was everywhere feared that the month of June 1849 would practically recall that terrible anniversary. The government speedily took measures to prevent the projected movement; but the alarm had been great, the sinister echo of the cannon had troubled the pious silence of the solitaries. Mary Teresa admired in this circumstance an indication of Providence, who once more revealed the tie existing between the new foundation and the necessities of the times. Nothing was more fitted to cause her daughters to enter fully into the spirit of their vocation of reparation. Faithful to this grace, they calmly followed their retreat; and on the 13th June, the feast of the Sacred Heart, they joyfully put on the religious livery which outwardly dedicated them to the ministry of repairing adoration. One year previously, on that same feast of the Sacred Heart, Mary Teresa had received from our Saviour, in the vision *of the gold tubes*, the formal command to found her institute. One year had sufficed to make this inspiration a living reality capable of furnishing, by the clothing of twelve novices, a proof of its fecundity.

God alone could have been the Author of this unlooked-for success; but likewise His hand alone could preserve, in the absence of all human resources, the existence of the community and the courage and confidence of its members. During two years, some thirty persons were obliged to live in a few rooms, serving at the same time as dormitory, refectory, kitchen, &c. Sometimes even, in order to make room for persons who came for retreats, or for nightly adorers, it was necessary to restrict their space still more. Mary Teresa relates with her usual simplicity the kind of life she and her children led :

'A few palliasses constituted all the furniture of some among us. With regard to the necessary household utensils, we were often obliged to have recourse to the ingenuities of Robinson Crusoe, for we were in want of almost everything. Moreover, our mothers (the Carmelites) had arranged that we should be their tourière-sisters; so we were obliged, each in her turn, to traverse Paris in every direction,* and, in spite of every fatigue, to spend two hours in adoration every night; for, on account of the smallness of our numbers, we were obliged to double the hours, in order that there might always be two before the Blessed Sacrament.' So as to fatigue as little as possible both body and soul, Mary Teresa had arranged that each sister should have a change of employment every week; thus, the assistant, having for one week shared with her the anxiety of Superioress, passed the following week in the kitchen; and so on with the others. An admirable simplicity and perfect obedience rendered these singular changes easy and welcome to all.

No sooner did Mary Teresa find her community exteriorly constituted by the clothing of its *twelve apostles* than she endeavoured to assemble around this centre as many adorers as possible. To effect this, it was necessary to carry on the devotion of Reparation in a larger church than the small sanctuary in which it had arisen. This was likewise the opinion of the Carmelites, who planned, on their side, the augmentation of their choir. The work was quickly determined upon, and on the 26th June, the anniversary of the death of Mgr. Affré, the foundation-stone of the chapel was solemnly laid. M. Dubouché was present at this ceremony, happy to see founded before his death the congregation to which he had sacrificed his daughter. It was then believed that those walls would be the definitive centre of the institute: on a steel-plate, fastened to the foundation-stone, an inscription was engraved, stating the destina-

* This relates to the time when the Sisters of the Reparation had not yet their habit; after their clothing they only served the Carmelites as porteresses.

tion of the building. Future events showed, however, that before Mary Teresa could be really a foundress, she would have to seek elsewhere the necessary liberty. But nothing as yet revealed any change in the destinies of the third order of Reparation. More than ever, Mary Teresa became attached to Carmel, as the branch to the trunk; it required all the strength of her maternal vocation to enable her to make the sacrifice of that repose in a Carmelite cell which she had promised herself. Sometimes even now this dream of the past returned forcibly to her mind. The building of the chapel of the Reparation had necessarily suspended for a time the enclosure of the convent. Mary Teresa profited by this circumstance to go into it and converse with Mother Isabella more freely: she never entered without leaping for joy, nor left it without shedding abundant tears. One day even, when the time for leaving her came, she cast herself upon her knees before the Prioress, not being able to make up her mind to retire. The Mother was moved, encouraged and embraced her. On leaving the monastery, Mary Teresa went to pour forth her sorrow and her humiliation before the Sacred Face: she felt there was a weak point within her, which was a peril to her new institute. But it was not for her to break those ties which were, after all, but those of supernatural affection and religious obedience. Providence, by sending her fresh trials, was providing her with the means of freeing herself.

Before making her vows, Mary Teresa had undergone the canonical examination in presence of the Superior: she had replied with candour to the questions asked her; but the interrogators had been satisfied with asking general questions, and had not obliged the postulant to give an account of those intimate secrets known only to her director. Since her profession, the sensible graces which she received threw her more frequently than ever into extraordinary ecstasies: when meditating on the Passion, she experienced all the pains of the crucifixion; and then, seeking refuge in her cell, she found consolation in praying on her knees, with her arms in the form of a cross. Full of confidence in Mother Isabella, and fearing, if too reserved, to be wanting to the vow of obedience which she had made to her, she daily related to her, with perfect confidence, the supernatural effects produced in her soul and body by these celestial communications. The Prioress listened in silence; but these avowals caused her great secret uneasiness. The ardent temperament of Mary Teresa, her lively imagination, her artistic nature, her past life, which, although austere and pure, had known days of too human exultation— these appeared to her to be so many motives for receiving with a certain mistrust all in this soul that was out of the common way; and the vocation which, from the commencement of her religious life, had called her to the double position of Foundress and Mother, added new weight to these recommendations to prudence.

On the other hand, many motives tended to reassure the Prioress. She knew enough of her spiritual daughter to recognise in her a soul still more strong than sensible, a naturally reasoning spirit, more inclined to resist divine action than to anticipate and supplement it by dreams; and lastly and principally, a profound humility too often proved by great trials, easily to become the plaything of a foolish pride.

Thus wavering between fear and confidence, Mother Isabella thought that she should no longer remain sole depositary of a secret accompanied by so much responsibility. After remaining silent on the subject for some time, she at length spoke of it to her Superior. The latter was a man prudent even to excess; a declared enemy of all eccentricity, who viewed with suspicion everything removed from the ordinary. Having heard Mother Isabella's scruples, he immediately shared them, and resolved to question Mary Teresa himself. The Prioress was charged to acquaint her with this resolution: 'My child,' she said to her, 'I felt myself bound to mention your singular states to the Superior; he desires to have an interview with you to-morrow.' The humble girl was struck dumb with astonishment, which only increased upon reflection. She had always felt frightened of *examinations;* her candour with her confessor and the Prioress was the work of grace and the result

of a long confidence; but had not this confidence been abused ?*
The secrets of her soul had been revealed to one who, she
thought, was not authorised to know them. She would have
cared little had they published her sins and defects; but they
had divulged what it had cost her most to reveal, even to her
confessor—that supernatural action against which she had struggled so hard until the time that Father Lefèvre had taught her
not to distrust God. And what could be the motive for this
fresh examination? Had she not before her profession undergone the one commanded by the constitutions? If the Superior
wished to know her secrets, why had he not then questioned her
concerning them? But the examiners had declared themselves
satisfied; they had permitted her to bind herself by vows, take
the title of Mother, exercise its functions, and assemble her
new community; and now, after the lapse of a month, everything was again at sea. They doubted her capability to bear
the burden imposed on her; and all this because, delivered at
length from her fears, reassured as to her vocation by the success of her foundation, and joyful at the result of her sacrifice,
she had abandoned herself to the graces which actuated her.
But she must then be the plaything of some frightful illusion!
Mother Isabella would not have been alarmed without motive;
perhaps the devil was the author of what she considered
the action of God. In one instant frightful doubts filled her
mind; she remembered the days of her greatest trials, when an
insufficient and close direction led her to fight against God, to
flee from herself, and to live amid torments and suspicions.
Well, the end was now at hand If she were a monster of
pride, a miserable visionary, it was necessary that she should
know it: she now desired the dreaded examination; she would
hasten to it; she would hide nothing that might justify the

* We here give from Mary Teresa's own writings the thoughts which
crowded through her mind when the trial was most severe. Do we by
this mean that we also see a usurpation of the rights of conscience in this
communication made to a third person? We do not go so far. The
Prioress acted in the manner she thought most conformable to the interests of the soul she was directing; and God, who wished to try that
soul, made this conduct appear to her a trial.

fears of her guides. It was in this state of energetic resolution, but of profound humility, that she appeared before her Superior, like a criminal before his judge; in the fear of excusing herself, she interiorly condemned herself beforehand, and calumniated herself outwardly by her replies. Exaggerating in her answers all that might be suspected, she neglected to add the invariable testimony which her conscience rendered to the uprightness of her views. Later on, when relating this strange scene to her confessor, she added, 'One thing alone astonishes me, and that is that I was not there and then excluded from the community.'

In spite of the care she had taken to show herself in the worst possible light, the Superior was far from arriving at so rigorous a conclusion. He did not express his opinion respecting the extraordinary states just revealed to him; but, whether they were from God or not, he regarded them as dangerous in a Superioress. '*When one experiences these states, one should be a simple religious, otherwise injury might accrue to those under one's charge.*' Such was the very natural conclusion at which he arrived. But the measures which he thought proper to take in consequence seem to have surpassed what was necessary. Without telling Mary Teresa his opinion respecting her, he desired the Prioress to trace out for her a new plan of life: no more spiritual direction; brief confessions and to the Superior alone; and not to give way to any supernatural impression. This was condemning an anxious soul to the most complete isolation; this was playing with her repugnance, forbidding all her aspirations, delivering her to the fury of the tempest which they had raised in her bosom. A less firm character might hereby have suffered serious injury. Mary Teresa suffered frightful tortures. Grace, which does not take counsel from man, delayed not to visit her. On awakening at night, she found herself in a state of ecstatic prayer. Here was a fresh subject of uneasiness. Had she not yielded to some bad principle? Had she not been wanting to her vow of obedience? Thus, when God made Himself felt within her, she believed herself to be in a state of sin.

But what, then, is grace, if all that resembles it is perilous? Does God take pleasure in making fun of His creatures? Does the danger of incurring His hatred increase with the desire to love Him? One can imagine how perilous such thoughts must be to the faith. For the first time in her life Mary Teresa knew the torment of this temptation, the most cruel of all, since, whilst provoking the soul to struggle, it threatens to take from under her feet the very ground on which she stands. But when the soul has not drawn down this punishment upon herself by pride or infidelity, the greatness of the danger is far from corresponding to the bitterness of the trial. Plunged in a sort of despair, doubting herself, doubting men, and violently tempted to doubt even God Himself, Mary Teresa, when her tribulation was greatest, suddenly felt the friendly hand which saved her from shipwreck. Without giving her warning, or allowing her time to resist, grace seized upon her as the eagle upon his prey: she, who but a moment before had believed herself damned, suddenly found herself lost in ineffable sweetness, which renewed both her soul and body. On coming to herself her doubts returned; she sought to reassure herself, saying: 'This time, at least, I did not foresee it; I did not wish it; I have had no part in it.' This consolation lasted but a short time: pride might again have blinded her; another, in her place, would have recognised the enemy before falling into his power. But how was it possible to regard as an enemy that which for an instant had transported her from hell to heaven? And so, between consolations and anguish, she was torn in pieces: the *Miserere* and the *De Profundis* became her constant prayers, the spontaneous cry of her heart.

Let us consider the situation of the Foundress in the midst of her children, whilst labouring under such trials. She saw them but little; but she was obliged to see them at times, meet them all with a calm and smiling countenance, receive their spiritual confidences, and draw, from a soul bathed in sorrow and darkness, counsels of light and words of peace. 'What a martyrdom I suffered,' she exclaimed later, 'when these poor children approached me! It appeared to me that I was about to give them the plague.' She wrote thus to Father Lefêvre: 'The souls which confide in me have the grace of blindness. How I envy the priesthood and their sanctity! Jesus Christ only works His wonders in those who possess either one or the other of these prerogatives.' And whilst she was uttering this sigh God was working wonders by her, because her humiliations cloaked true sanctity, and that her maternal vocation gave her, for her children, part of the graces belonging to the priesthood.

The cruel trial we have described lasted during six weeks. On the feast of the Assumption, Mary Teresa was at the height of her anguish: the pains of the crucifixion, which she had felt for some time in her body, depressed her soul. But the Queen of Heaven had reserved to herself to put an end to her tortures. On the morning of the feast, Mary Teresa awoke full of the thought of the Blessed Virgin, and began a fervent prayer on her knees before that Mother. Suddenly her soul became inundated by an extraordinary sweetness: it seemed to her that Mary was seeking to console her, and that she showed her Father Bertholon, whilst she heard these words distinctly pronounced: '*Do all that he tells you.*' The reader will recollect the rigorous prohibition she had received to confess to any other than the Superior, and to enter into no spiritual communication with any one soever. Transported with joy at these words of Mary, she no longer thought of the prohibition: she went in search of Father Bertholon, and, saying to him, 'I must speak to you,' she entered the confessional. Then her soul, so long oppressed, entirely overflowed itself. Commiserating her state, the father promised to use his influence with the Superior to cause this cruel prohibition to be removed. He kept his word, and after a long conversation with M. Gaume he obtained the desired permission. It was a true deliverance. The same divine favour which had restored to Mary Teresa her friend and guide gave to this latter the lights necessary to direct her.

Who can fail to admire in this the power of grace? This confessor, who in a single conversation had restored her soul to life, whose every word now filled her with joy and strength, whose counsels banished all her doubts, was the very same whose simplicity had formerly weakened his authority in her eyes, the same for whom quite recently, at the time of her profession, she had felt a repugnance which she had only conquered in obedience to an imperious aspiration. So true it is that in supernatural cases the instrument is nothing, grace everything, and God dispenses at pleasure, to some light, to others confidence.

The sweet intervention of the Mother of God, who had restored calm to the soul of Mary Teresa, made itself felt within her during an entire month: not a day passed but she received from that Divine Mother some grace or particular lesson. Little initiated by her early training into devotion to Mary, she had been led to it by her familiarity with Jesus. It will be remembered how, when making the Stations of the Cross, she had met the Blessed Virgin, and what gratitude she had felt for her compassion for the sufferings of the Redeemer. But if, at the commencement of her mystical career, she had been led by love of the Son to that of the Mother, now, when there was question of arriving at a perfect union, it was the Mother who was to guide her to her Son. In the difficulties of a delicate position, Mary presented the Child Jesus to her as her model. Reversing human wisdom, which would have counselled calculation and artifice, celestial wisdom taught her that simplicity was the only art worthy of a spouse of Jesus Christ. Once even it seemed to her that Mary placed the Divine Infant in her heart, with all the virtues of the Holy Childhood. In another vision she again perceived Mary, to whom she presented her spiritual father; the Queen of Heaven blessed them both, and assured her daughter that this father would conduct her whither God pleased. The impression of happiness left in her by these communications lasted for many years, surviving new and bitter trials, and ever linking in her soul the name of Mary with the remembrance of the sweetest and most strengthening graces she had ever received from God.

The year 1849 was drawing to a close. Towards the commencement of October the building at the monastery was finished. The third order of the Reparation had at length its own chapel, which communicated with that of the Carmelites by means of the sanctuary, so that both might assist at will at the Exposition of the Blessed Sacrament, but a separate enclosure was reserved for the exercises of the Sisters of the Reparation and the devotions of their associates. The increase of the spiritual family corresponded to the enlargement of their sanctuary. About the feast of the Immaculate Conception, ten more postulants received the habit of regular sisters, and six others that of the seculars. Deprived of the preacher upon whom she had reckoned for the retreat, Mary Teresa was herself obliged to supply the want. 'It must have appeared very strange,' she said in one of her letters, 'but those truly filial hearts accepted all: the soil was so good that even pebbles would have taken root.' The devotedness and confidence of her children were, in fact, the worthy recompense of the zeal their mother had displayed in providing for their spiritual and temporal necessities. These latter were not small: poverty, that inseparable companion of every work blessed by God, continued to try the faith of the Foundress, whilst it multiplied her cares. 'I always desire to consume myself with the glory of Jesus Christ in the Blessed Sacrament. My delight is to remain in His presence; but it is my passion to serve Him as He pleases, even were it in begging by the roadside; and this supposition naturally arises in my mind, for the times and the uncertainty of our material resources render this extremely possible; but all this I would welcome, if Jesus and Mary will beg with me.'

In fact, nothing could equal the ardour of her zeal for the service of her Master. Worthy imitator of the sentiments of St. Ignatius, she desired no repose, not even the repose of heaven, so long as she was able to labour for the glory of God. One day when, overwhelmed with fatigue, anxiety, and physical sufferings, she was thinking of a holy friend who had just left this earth, she thought she heard our Lord proposing to deliver her from the mountain of difficulties which was weighing her down, by calling her to share the happiness of that liberated soul; and she replied from her inmost heart that 'she did not desire it.' When relating this to Father Lefèvre, she added, 'Our Divine Master has need of workmen; when the weather is bad, the head of the family hires beggars from the high-road to work for him; and when were the times worse than at present? O, no; I will not leave my Spouse in the time of trial! A thousand years of sufferings and crosses, if necessary, if I can but leave behind me a few hearts who will love Him!' Crosses were not indeed to be wanting to this generous soul in the accomplishment of her mission. The difficulties before mentioned became more apparent every day. The existence and increase of a community, a branch of Carmel, but distinct in its spirit and exercises, might appear a very simple thing to Mother Isabella, with whom the third order had originated; but it became a natural subject of uneasiness to the other monasteries of the order. They feared, and not without reason, the danger of relaxation to Carmel in two religious communities living under the safe roof, who neither observed the same cloister nor the same rules. They could understand a new and independent foundation; but they protested against the third order. On account of this almost general feeling, the Prioress was necessarily obliged to be more reserved in her dealings with Mary Teresa. She required of her a promise to determine the connection of her community with Carmel. This, it would seem, tended to the complete separation of the two houses; but this solution, which was one day to simplify everything, was then entirely unthought of by the two Superioresses. The Prioress seemed even to claim more than ever for her order the creation of the order of Reparation. 'My child,' she one day said to Mary Teresa, 'it is we alone who found the third order, since it is in our chapel and under our obedience that you carry on the adoration.' This reply, besides testifying the Prioress's devotion to the new foundation, gives evidence of the inherent contradiction of their position. From that time Mary Teresa, restricted between the double necessity of commanding and obeying, and responsible without independence, saw before her a future of inextricable difficulties. 'But,' she said later, when remembering these circumstances, 'supported by grace, visited constantly by the powerful and sweet love of my Saviour, if I felt my heart wounded with sorrow, my mind at least was not troubled by any doubt. The Divine Face which I had for some time continually seen in my soul, gave me the most earnest assurances that it would uphold its work of mercy.'

It required nothing less than this supernatural confidence to strengthen the humble Foundress in her undertaking. But the protection of God was manifest even amid trials the best calculated to make her lose heart. She knew how to keep to herself and her spiritual guides the sad secret of her difficulties, never ceasing to testify to the Carmelites her accustomed deference, and to her children and to strangers her pristine confidence in the future development of her institution. Whilst her letters to Father Lefèvre reveal the agitated state of her soul, her correspondence with her friends, which became gradually more rare, contains at this very time warm expressions of the joy and peace which she said she had found in her new vocation. And we must not regard this as duplicity or calculation. No; for there is room in great souls for the most diverse movements, and when God, as Master, takes possession of them, He multiplies their faculties in a wonderful manner. He gives them at the same time a peace of which the world knows nothing, and subjects of alarm which the world cannot understand; and the link between these opposite feelings is that strong and generous love which renders them insensible to their own interest, and delicately jealous of everything relating to the service of God.

Let us not, then, be astonished at finding Mary Teresa thus writing to her friend Clémence C—: 'Amid the complications of an overburdened position, I have never experienced a sweeter peace, a more sensible happiness in God, than now; it seems as if I were gliding along a torrent of mercy. I do not feel wounded nor repulsed by any obstacle; for when any arises I look to my Pilot, and abandon myself to His infinite wisdom. If I still occasionally weep, it is to see Him so little loved. My title of spouse, consecrated by the Church, has communicated to me a new life.'

If contradictions did not trouble the serenity of her soul, still less did they shackle the activity of her life. Never had she been more devoted to others, more overwhelmed with work. 'When I think,' she would laughingly exclaim, 'that formerly I considered myself busy! I have now very rarely any time to myself; but, all being done for HIM, that is of no consequence. To be *His* tool is my greatest ambition; I shall have eternity to adore Him.' The same letter gives us an account of her accumulated occupations. Her community already numbered thirty regular sisters; the extern sisters and persons recommended to her increased the number of those who received spiritual direction from her to fifty; add to these, persons continually making retreats in the house, and whose maintenance gave fresh anxiety to the charitable Superioress; for the wants of the soul are bound up, in more ways than one, with the exterior circumstances of life, and Mary Teresa could not interest herself spiritually in any person without at the same time rendering her all kinds of services. We see her, then, begging for shelter, succour, and protection for persons who had been to her to receive advice. She writes: 'I, who am so proud, have become a mendicant sister; I do nothing but beg.' But she was doing something else besides; she was working, and causing others to work. Whilst her children applied themselves, in obedience to her wish, to those employments which enable poor families to earn their living, she stole from her incessant occupations a few seconds of her time, so that, palette in hand, she likewise might earn her daily bread. The artist's cherished brush had become, in the hands of the humble 'Réparatrice,' the means of necessary labour. Her poor body, worn out with fatigue, sometimes gave way. Then she retired to her cell for just sufficient time to obtain, in silent and solitary suffering, the only kind of repose she loved. In the midst of so much anxiety she could not forget her aged father, who, in return for his generous consent to sacrifice his daughter, had only asked the happiness of seeing her every day for a little while, and of dying in her arms. She daily left her community for a few minutes, to carry a ray of joy to the old man. But there, again, fresh sorrows awaited her. The state of her sister's soul, her nephew's future, were permanent subjects of anxiety which she could not avoid, so great was the authority that her matured judgment and great virtue gave her over all the members of her family. Her letters to Clémence C— bear the trace of this anxiety. She learned how to apply herself to her domestic duties quickly and earnestly; then the next minute found her completely separated from the world, wholly preoccupied with her vocation of Réparatrice and of mother.

These multiplied occupations filled up the year 1850, but they were by no means the whole of her work. The inevitable consequences of a badly-defined and contradictory position became daily more evident, to the great detriment of the Congregation of Reparation. The rapid development of the new community increased the fears already expressed by the various Carmelite convents in France; but at Paris, instead of admitting the necessity for separation, the only idea was to arrest the increase of the third order. Mary Teresa was formally ordered to promise that she would not found any establishment elsewhere, unless dependent on a Carmelite monastery. To make this promise at a time when the difficulty of the union was greater than ever would have been equivalent to passing a sentence of death on the Congregation of Reparation. Although not then thinking of any foundation out of Paris, Mary Teresa felt and declared that it was her duty and her right to reserve a liberty, the abdication of which would have exposed her work to certain ruin. Her ordinary confessor and the extraordinary confessor of the community encouraged her in this line of action, assuring her that it was the only one consistent with her engagements; but the effort she was obliged to make to effect this resistance had destroyed her strength. Already ill, she fell into that state of languor in which she only lived to suffer. Supernatural action mingled itself with her physical weakness, and often left her for hours senseless, and to all appearance dying. Her children, who wished to attend her as they would have done any other invalid, unknowingly made her suffer agonies; for during these violent fits one thing alone could soothe her, viz. solitude. This illness lasted for a whole month, but was not less fruitful in graces than in suffering. Habitually united during that time to our Saviour in His Passion, she more than once saw Him 'rejected and despised of men.' She understood by the light of God the full extent of the trials and humiliations to which her mission destined her; and though trembling at the trial before her, she sincerely and resolutely accepted her chalice.

It was then with increased ardour that, on her recovery, she set to work to perfect her foundation. '*I cannot understand*,' she writes, '*but I can sacrifice myself;*' and this sacrifice, so frankly made, left in her heart no rancour against any one whosoever. 'When I think,' she said, ' of the purity of intention and the sanctity of those who are the cause of my sufferings, I cannot accuse myself of a thought or a judgment opposed to charity.' Admirable effect of self-forgetfulness! Without this heroic abnegation Mary Teresa would have been unjust to the Prioress, who, while yielding to well-grounded fears, still remained a holy Carmelite and an affectionate Mother : to hasten a conclusion which it was still necessary to defer for a time would have probably compromised for ever the existence of the institute. On the contrary, silently crushing her grief and anxiety, she waited for a clearer expression of the Divine Will, and left Him to give the signal for her deliverance.

Nevertheless, however great might be her trust in God, she felt that she could do nothing if her children's faith in their own vocation and in that of their Mother did not correspond to her own confidence. Already she thought that some were beginning to be discouraged. The difficulties which the Foundress wished to bear alone could not be so hidden that they did not sometimes become manifest. Mary Teresa determined frankly to communicate them to her spiritual daughters.[*] For this purpose she assembled them, and explained to them with much

---
[*] During the Lent of 1850.

animation the aim and objects of her foundation ; but at the side
of this picture, well calculated to inflame souls with faith (for
the means, as well as the aim, were all supernatural), she
placed before them the trials which were awaiting them, the
obstacles to be encountered in every new creation, and which
threatened this one in particular; then she explained to them
the inconvevience of what she called ' *her physical and moral
incapacity.*' ' Sound well your hearts,' she said to them ; ' try
and understand clearly what you wish : there is still time to
retreat. Those who simply seek the ordinary advantages of a
religious life will find them far more surely at Carmel or in any
other old-established community.' Finally, to put them still
more to the test, she appealed to their delicacy. ' Consider,' she
said, ' that I am now risking everything—my reputation, my
family position, my fortune, my spiritual life. If you are not
convinced that God will give you grace to continue with me to
the end, leave me. I need your fidelity ; if you even hesitate to
trust me, go. Leave me with my aged father and my nephew,
who are dependent on me.' Her children could only reply by a
burst of tears. They cast themselves on their knees before her,
and swore to be faithful. One alone remained unmoved, and, profiting by Mary Teresa's proposal, left the third order. She was one
who had been with her from the first : thus it happens in every
foundation. This defection greatly grieved Mary Teresa, but
it made her value the more the choice which her other children
had so generously made to remain with her in spite of all their
difficulties. Reassured as to their fidelity, she devoted herself
more assiduously than ever to their religious education. When
her increasing infirmities' rendered her incapable of instructing
them *vivâ voce*, she wrote conferences for them, which comprise
a whole treasure of spiritual doctrine. Thus it was that, unceasingly upheld by the words and inspiration of the Foundress
and supported by Carmel, the new institute had up to this time
done without a rule ; but its rapid growth rendered the composition of a written rule necessary. To this composition Mary
Teresa now directed her attention, and it formed not a small
portion of the difficulties we have before mentioned. From the

moment that it was determined to give to the third order of Reparation a definitive form, it was necessary to settle that most delicate point of all, its connection with Carmel. On the other hand, the special privilege of the third order—perpetual Exposition of the Blessed Sacrament—gave rise to fresh opposition even within the monastery. The reader will probably recollect the very active part taken in the first foundation of the institute by a venerable priest, very devout towards the Blessed Sacrament, and the circumstances which had suddenly changed his former kindness into coldness. Now this priest was Vicar-General, and it would be necessary to submit the new rules to the Archbishop. Mary Teresa feared in him an almost insurmountable obstacle; but full of confidence in God, and yielding to an inspiration which seemed to proceed from our Lady, she resolved herself to seek the Archbishop, and expose to him with simplicity her situation and her plans. Mgr. Sibour received her with paternal kindness. As she had foreseen, he was completely ignorant of all that concerned the new institute; but he heard with pleasure the extent of the work conceived and already set on foot for the greater glory of the Blessed Sacrament. Strengthened by the blessing of her chief pastor, Mary Teresa returned to her cell, and resolutely began the composition of her rules. She was alone to bear the weight and responsibility of this undertaking, but it was necessary that she should be mistress of her position. Left to herself, she would have had no difficulty in putting into shape what she had conceived; for this conception had been complete in the vision *of the tubes of gold* whence the institute had sprung; but, intimidated by the objections which were raised on every side, she hesitated to express an idea which was to her quite clear; and, wavering between the consciousness of her mission and the fear of displeasing her directors, she found herself again plunged into those interior troubles which had so often before distracted her soul. Later, she reproached herself with culpable weakness in not having upheld her views as to the foundation in a sufficiently courageous manner. However, she thanked God for having forced her, in spite of herself, to reconsider concessions which had been extorted from her, and to carry the most important points.

The question most anxiously debated was that concerning lay-sisters. Mary Teresa's views on this point, which at length triumphed, are sufficiently remarkable to deserve an explanation. Religious orders of men comprise two classes of subjects: the fathers, who are priests, and engaged in the functions of the Church and the apostolic ministry; the lay-brothers, who, bound by the three monastic vows, without receiving Holy Orders, devote their time to manual labour for the service of the community. A similar division was introduced in the great orders for women between the *choir-sisters*, who are cloistered, whose business it is to chant the office, and who alone can rule the monastery; and the lay-sisters or *tourière* sisters, whose duty it is to attend to all domestic work: the former inside, the latter outside, the convent. Simple peasant-girls without education, the absence of which would otherwise have prevented their entering the religious state, thus found the means of consecrating themselves to God; and charity, that powerful link between souls, formed of these two classes of persons one single religious family. This division, admitted in all the religious orders properly so called, has been adopted in the communities of men by all the various congregations of regulars who have successively arisen since the sixteenth century (the Jesuits, Theatines, Barnabites, Oratorians, &c.). In these, however, the distinction was quite natural, being between priests and those who were not in Holy Orders. But in the congregations of women the nature of the institute could alone decide the question. The new congregations who, following the example of the old orders, were cloistered, and whose members devoted their time to interior occupations, such as prayer, the divine office, and even the education of young girls within the monastery, were necessarily obliged to have lay-sisters and tourières for the service of their houses. On the contrary, the hospital-sisters, who were founded to tend the sick, to visit the poor, and instruct the children of the lower classes in the public schools, had no occasion to introduce amongst them any distinction of class, since, cloister not existing, the exterior and manual works were common to all the sisters.

But to return to our point. It was necessary to decide which course the third order for Reparation would adopt. According to the principles just laid down, it seemed that lay-sisters should be admitted; for, although the cloister was to be less strict than at Carmel, the life of the Réparatrices was quite interior, and the assistance of the active members appeared necessary to the existence of a contemplative community. The Superior was of this opinion, and his reasons were weighty ones. There was not only the question of providing for the material service of the community, but it was necessary to provide it with the means of living. They had not, as in the teaching orders, the resources of the pupils' pensions. To expect all from charity, when they had neither time nor liberty to solicit it from without, would be carrying confidence to a pitch of temerity beyond even that of the mendicant orders. They would then be obliged to fall back upon the dowries of the sisters. But was it not to be feared that, for want of a distinction between the two classes, those persons who did not fancy such perfect equality would become disgusted, and quit the institute ? The community would then gradually become composed entirely of persons of the class of lay-sisters, and every hope of obtaining sufficient resources for the institute would thus disappear. It being his duty to watch over, in a special manner, the material interests of the community, the Superior insisted on the introduction of a distinction which appeared to him necessary.

Mary Teresa had nothing to oppose to these prudential reasons; nothing, save that she was the Foundress, and that she viewed the foundation in another light. She followed the course of faith; she had accepted, with terror and under the constraint of an imperious vocation, the duties and responsibility of her undertaking. How, then, could she consent to denaturalise it ? Now it was nothing less than denaturalising it (according to her views) to hinder, through human motives, the inspiration which might call simple but generous souls to the honour of the mission of Reparation. At the very thought of this interdict, which would oblige the poor and the ignorant to desist from entering the sanctuary, her heart swelled within her and her eyes filled with tears. Nevertheless this leading point must be settled. The Superior continued to insist, so that Mary Teresa yielded, or at least thought that she had done so. But no sooner had she reëntered her cell, and was about to write the rule, than she felt herself stopped by an irresistible force. Then a violent struggle took place within her soul as to which command she should obey. Scarcely recovered from her illness, she was greatly shaken, and, after a painful crisis, she lay down on her bed trying to seek repose. But being unable to sleep, she stretched out her hand to her New Testament. The book opened at the parable of the invitations of the father of the family to his son's wedding. 'From the first lines,' she wrote later to her confessor, 'my heart beat violently, and a divine impression took possession of me. It seemed as if I no longer read, but received a lesson and a command from our Lord Himself. *By the refusal of those that were invited*, He gave me to understand that the great ones of the earth—the learned, even the devout—having abandoned the Holy Eucharist, He had determined to make use of the poor, the little, the ignorant, the imperfect, to accomplish that work of faith and love; and I saw, so sweetly and so clearly, that this was the divine reason why I and my children had been chosen, that I was rapt out of myself. I was struck with ineffable admiration. I saw in it a complete doctrine, a spirit removed from all prejudice, a strength similar to that which established Christianity. I kissed that sacred page with passionate ardour. It was to me as a letter brought by an angel from our Lord.'

After this signal favour, Mary Teresa would have considered that she was betraying her conscience had she abandoned a point which was to be the characteristic of her institute. So she returned to the Superior, and, by means of firmness, overcame his resistance; more fortunate than St. Francis of Sales, who had had similar views and desires when founding the visitation, and who lived to see his work transformed through the influence of strangers.

Thus was equality introduced amongst the Réparatrices: all were to take part in the watchings before the Blessed Sacrament and in the interior work of the house. There remained, however, out-of-door commissions and different services incompatible with cloister.

Instead of employing strangers, the Foundress determined to confide these duties to the uncloistered members, whom she called associated sisters. Notwithstanding this concession to the exigencies of the cloister, the principle of equality still existed, since, on the one hand, the enclosed sisters had to perform those household duties usually reserved to lay-sisters; and, on the other, such persons, who elsewhere would only have been received as tourières or lay-sisters, could here aspire to be admitted to the enclosure upon the simple condition of having a true vocation.

Thus was the new order constituted; it included three branches: the *regular sisters*, who would elsewhere have been called *choir-sisters*; the *secular sisters*, bound by the two vows of obedience and chastity, and living in the world to spread the spirit of the devotion of Reparation; the *associate sisters*, who rendered the community those services which the cloistered sisters were unable to perform. Finally, the association, which had been the foundation of the institute, remained connected with it to enrol pious persons in the holy League of the Perpetual Adoration.

The principal thought, then, in this creation was one of zeal: to draw hearts to Jesus Christ in the Eucharist, such was the aim which the Foundress proposed to her children; they were to attain it, first and principally, by sanctifying themselves interiorly by praying, and externally by giving the example of devotion; also by labouring in various ways for the sanctification of souls. The work of retreats, so actively undertaken by Mary Teresa, was to remain one of the duties of her community. She unceasingly explained to her children the beauty of self-renunciation and her horror of selfishness; she represented to them their vocation as a ministry which consecrated them to the service of souls. It was to comply with this ruling motive that she had thought it advisable to lessen the severity of the Carmelite rule as regarded the cloister. In the same way as the devotion of Reparation caused our Lord to leave the 'prison of the Tabernacle to expose Himself to the adoration of the faithful, so were His new spouses to remain in communication with the Christian world. Their choir was to have no wall separating it from the church; their parlour, no grilles to render them invisible. Whilst differing on this point from the rules of St. Teresa, she still hoped not to lose the right of calling her her mother. 'St. Teresa of Jesus,' she said, 'had the heart of an apostle; she envied the apostolic life; she would have desired to journey round the world to redeem souls. This admirable mother will then see the efforts which her children of the Reparation are about to make to unite the contemplative life to works of holy zeal. She will bless the aim of our vocation, which is no other than to place ourselves, as a piece of wood, in the furnace of the love of Jesus the Victim; and, instead of letting it burn for itself alone, to withdraw it when it is well lighted in order to carry heat and light to other hearts. My God, in these times of indifference and contempt, faith cannot be revived without Magdalens, Veronicas, Teresas traversing, with the Blessed Virgin, the crowd of executioners of Thy divine Son! It is not to seek repose that we have left the world, but to follow Jesus to Calvary, to preach His cross, to proclaim to all His never-dying charity!'

In fine, the ambition of this apostolic soul was carried to a still greater extent in her aspirations. As St. Teresa had reformed the order of the Carmelites, her faithful imitator heartily desired to see a community of men following the same divine aim of Reparation, with the double power of sanctity and the priesthood. She never thought of creating such an institute herself; but she earnestly implored Heaven to raise up a founder. One day she had a supernatural light on this subject, worthy of being related. Notwithstanding the many works which have since been set on foot by holy and venerable priests, there is still none existing exactly corresponding with what she saw in the future. But the principal points of this vision recall in too striking a manner what has been revealed to several great servants of God not to be worthy of serious attention. The following is her account of it to her confessor:

'During Mass my soul was rapt in God. I saw nothing save His brilliant immensity. My intellectual faculties as well as my senses were completely in abeyance. I was in an entirely passive state. In this space and in the midst of this light I saw a new people arise in the midst of the Christian world. These saints were of all sexes and conditions, characterised only by their great sanctity. They were religious; but they formed a society of persons practising the evangelical counsels in their perfect purity, rather than a regular community living in a monastery. The principal thing I saw was the glory they gave to God by spreading abroad the life of our Lord Jesus Christ in the Blessed Sacrament. I saw these people continually prostrated at the foot of the Eucharistic throne, and the priests of this order propagate Divine Love in all hearts. I saw these new apostles of the charity of Jesus living in the midst of the world in a state so angelic, so full of dignity and simplicity, in a word, so conformable to Jesus Christ Himself, and the entire society imitate so faithfully the Holy Family at Nazareth, that I could not endure the vision of so much happiness; I thought that I should die of joy, and I fell senseless in the chapel. Those present thought that I had fainted, and they carried me to the sacristy. This was the first time that anything so exterior had taken place within me.'*

* We cannot refrain from quoting here a remarkable passage from Father Grignon de Montfort's *Traité de la Vraie Dévotion à la Sainte Vierge*. The feeling which led Mary Teresa to seek for the accomplishment of her desires in the Marist Congregation establishes another link between the two documents. Finally, the last words of what we may call Father de Montfort's *prophecy* serve as a reply to those who, in the absence of immediate actual results, regard as illusions what Mary Teresa saw so plainly in the future: 'But who are these servants, the slaves and children of Mary? They will be the ministers of the Lord, who will spread the fire of Divine Love; children of Levi, who will introduce the

Thus did God reveal to the Foundress the full extent of His designs concerning her institute: the third order of Reparation with its three branches; the association which spread the spirit in the world; and finally, in the future, known to God alone, a society of men, assisting the mission of Reparation with all the power of the priesthood. Except this last point, which was left entirely to Providence, all the rest was a reality. After undergoing much opposition, Mary Teresa at length finished her rules, in which her firmness had triumphed in the long-run over all obstacles concerning the principles which she looked upon as essential to the accomplishment of her mission.

But whilst she was putting the finishing stroke to her work, the storm, which had been threatening for more than a year, broke over her. We have said that the fears and protests of different Carmelite convents had found an echo in the archbishopric. Mgr. Sibour's benevolent reception of Mary Teresa in the spring of 1850 had for some time counterbalanced this influence; it had even been determined to approve of the foundation of Reparation, giving it the form of a congregation. But unfavourable opinions had gradually arisen within the council. The constancy of the Foundress in her own views was treated as obstinacy; if she only intended to establish a third order, what had she to fear from the great Order? If she wished to preserve her independence for a future time, she had

---

gold of love into the heart, the incense of prayer into the spirit, and the myrrh of mortification into the body, and who will everywhere be the good odour of Jesus Christ to the poor and weak. They will be like clouds fleeting in the air at the least breath of the Holy Spirit, who, having no attachments and being astonished at nothing, will spread the rain of the Word of God and of eternal life throughout the whole world. They will be *true apostles of the latter times*, to whom the Lord of Hosts will give words and strength to work wonders. They will have in their mouths the two-edged sword of the Word of God; they will bear on their shoulders the bloody standard of the Cross, the crucifix in their right hand, the rosary in their left, the sacred names of Jesus and Mary in their hearts, the modesty and mortification of Jesus Christ in their whole conduct. *These are the great men who are to come!* But when and how will this happen? God alone knows. We must be silent, sigh, and wait.' (Grignon de Montfort, *Traité de la Vraie Dévotion à la Sainte Vierge*, 1ère partie.)

no right any longer to seek shelter under the shadow of Carmel. But in that case she would have to show herself in her true light, an ambitious novice; it would be necessary to found a new institution openly, at her own risk and peril; she would then immediately encounter the *veto* of the ecclesiastical authority, which was little disposed to sanction an institution which did not inspire confidence. Such were the suggestions continually made to the prelate's councillors. They were not informed that Mary Teresa's great desire was to remain united to the stem of Carmel, and that those who reproached her for her ideas of separation from it were the very ones who rendered the union impossible; that, in spite of every difficulty, the union still existed; and that, when refusing to promise to maintain it always and everywhere, the Foundress was only taking a necessary precaution, at the same time that, by her very silence and submission, she daily gave unequivocal proofs of her attachment to Carmel. Completely absorbed in her duties in the bosom of her community, she was ignorant of the measures being taken against her, or voluntarily neglected to send in her defence. Thus it came about that the council, in perfect good faith, formed a most unfavourable opinion of the Foundress's institution. Soon, labouring under this conviction, the same authority, which has since never failed to shower down on the work of Reparation the most precious testimonies of its approval, was then led to denounce it in severe terms which might be considered as a condemnation.

In fact, the rules of the new institute, definitively drawn up with the approbation of the Superior, were only waiting for the approval of the Ordinary to give the Congregation of the Réparatrices that regular existence which had been promised to it. Instead of this approbation, the council sent, towards the end of October, a peremptory note, which Mary Teresa was ordered to communicate to her community. It ran thus: 'Separated from Carmel, the third order of Reparation has lost its reason for existence, and cannot possibly inspire any confidence. The persistence of the Superioress in her views can only be considered as rash ambition.'

Without a moment's hesitation Mary Teresa assembled the chapter, not, as six months previously, to sound the intentions of her children and make sure of their fidelity, but to obey in all sincerity an ecclesiastical command, and divert her spiritual children from a path which was declared dangerous. There was yet time: no professions had yet been made, the community being composed of thirty novices or postulants. Mary Teresa, on her knees before them, read, not without many tears, the note which condemned her. Then, recovering her calmness, in the midst of the general consternation, she rose, and in a firm voice, with that energy with which she knew how to sacrifice herself, she unfolded to them the reasons which, she said, bound them to seek elsewhere, and in safer paths, the happiness of serving God in religion. They must make a sacrifice of the rest, since Providence seemed to refuse them His support.

Nothing could have been said better calculated to disperse them, except to have added what would not have been true, viz. that they were no longer permitted to persevere in their present state; for, on really examining the case, the prohibition was not real. The Diocesan Council, acting on the supposition that they desired to separate from Carmel, blamed the act, refused to sanction a distinct Congregation of Reparation, and declared that, *by the fact of its separation*, it ceased to exist. But this separation was neither accomplished nor wished for. Nothing, then, prevented the members from remaining in the same situation which had been so seriously misrepresented. In remaining united to Carmel, and accepting the subjection and annoyances which would result from this union, they no longer came under the sentence, which was soon to be effaced from the minds even of the members of the Council themselves by the sure information they received that their act had been premature.

The question was simply this: Would the Réparatrices have sufficient attachment to their vocation, sufficient faith in the future of their institute, to submit to the inconveniences of a situation more dependent and more contradictory than ever? This question Mary Teresa had just proposed to them, whilst she neglected nothing which might set their consciences at ease, should they consider the foundation hopeless. But, in spite of the novelty of the circumstances, their answer was still the same as on the previous occasion. Their devotedness, becoming stronger in the moment of trial, manifested itself in burning expressions of affection and confidence, and rendered it impossible to their Mother to abdicate a title which her children's fidelity insisted on bestowing on her.

They then resolved to continue their work as before, and leave to Providence the task of averting the perils which menaced their institute. An unexpected event was at hand which justified and recompensed their confidence.

CHAPTER X.

1850-1852.

The foundation at Lyons.—Fearful trial occasioned by the infidelity of the local superioress.—More favourable dispositions of the Diocesan Council at Paris.—Astonishing prosperity of the new institute.

WHILST the third order of Reparation was menaced in its very existence at Paris, it received from every part of France daily-increasing proofs of sympathy and admiration. Everywhere holy souls, inflamed with the thought of so pure and salutary a devotion, entered into correspondence with Mary Teresa, made inquiries as to her spirit, her means, her rules, often expressing their earnest desire to see her institute founded amongst them. But, without considering the difficulties of execution, the humble Foundress was too sincerely submissive to Carmel ever to think of voluntarily withdrawing herself from a dependence it had been thought necessary to impose upon her. So, without a thought of the future, she applied herself to her daily duties, trusting to Providence to break her chains.

Her ideas, especially those relating to an order of men, had particularly struck her confessor, Father Bertholon; for this thought was not by any means foreign to the Society of Mary, of which he was a member. The Rev. Father Collin, of holy memory, founder of this society, had formed the design of adding to the active branch already existing a contemplative branch, specially devoted to the adoration of the Blessed Sacrament. At the time of which we speak he was at Lyons, thinking over the best means of putting this idea into execution. Finally, about this time Cardinal de Bonald was likewise meditating and preparing to establish in his diocese a work of

Reparation, in honour of the divine Eucharist. In such a concert of holy desires there seemed to be something providential, and it wanted only an opportunity to blend into one common effort all these individual schemes.

A pious young lady, a tertiary of St. Dominic, had met Mary Teresa in her travels, and their casual meetings had sufficed to give her a knowledge of, and a relish for, the ideas of the Foundress. Becoming acquainted with the designs of the Cardinal, she spoke to him of what was being effected in Paris, and represented to him the possibility of transplanting to Lyons the young tree growing under the shadow of Carmel. Nothing could have better corresponded with the prelate's wishes than to find his work already established elsewhere, and to be able to lean for support on a religious community, as a common centre, in a devotion which he hoped to see spread throughout his diocese. Without delay he commissioned a Marist father to write to Mother Mary Teresa, and invite her to found at Lyons, under his patronage, a house of Réparatrices. The religious who served as interpreter to the zealous Cardinal was Father Eymard, who afterwards left the Society of Mary to found that of the *priests of the Blessed Sacrament*.

This unexpected invitation, which so strongly contrasted with the mistrust with which she was treated at Paris, greatly embarrassed Mary Teresa. Could she accept such an offer the day after her community, threatened with total destruction, had only been spared on condition of an entire dependence on Carmel and a complete union with it? Again, would it not be folly to seek at a distance the chances of a new creation when the existing community could scarcely support itself? But, on the other hand, how could one fail to see, in this invitation from so high an authority, and in the concatenation of circumstances which had paved the way for it, an indication of divine Providence? And if their position in Paris, which was already greatly compromised, were one day to become utterly impracticable, did not Lyons offer a refuge ready prepared by the goodness of God to save the foundation from shipwreck? Mary Teresa was not long in balancing these opposite reasons. Her community had a Superior, the direct representative of the Diocesan Council; she communicated to him what had taken place. At the same time the Cardinal renewed his entreaties, and asked for details respecting the spirit and form of the institute. Compelled by two more urgent letters from Father Eymard to come to a decision, Mary Teresa still waited for the resolve of her Superior. The Abbé Gaume's reply was positive: '*You must go.*' She no longer hesitated. Taking with her one of her novices, she set out for Lyons in the beginning of December 1850. It was in this unexpected, simple, and rapid manner that the act was accomplished which decided the future of the Congregation of Reparation.

On her arrival at Lyons, Mary Teresa immediately repaired to the Marist Monastery, thinking that he who had taken so lively an interest in the foundation would have secured a suitable house for the establishment of a community. Nothing was, however, prepared. Father Eymard recommended the travellers to some good people whom he knew, but the lodgings they offered were inconvenient; they again applied to Father Eymard, who this time installed them in a hospital, where a charitable person received servants out of place. Mary Teresa and her companion rested for several days in the dormitory of these poor girls. At length she found a small apartment without a fire, in which they could find shelter; charity supplied them with food. Thence it was that they issued daily to seek a house suitable to become that of the Reparation. Thus did evangelical poverty preside over their establishment.

The Cardinal welcomed Mary Teresa in a most fatherly manner. 'You are fulfilling my dearest wishes,' he said; 'for ten years I have been dreaming of what you have now accomplished.' He himself procured them a house in Bellecour-square, which might answer the wants of the foundation. Mary Teresa evinced some reluctance to establish herself in the most fashionable part of Lyons; she never felt at ease when not protected by poverty. The Cardinal calmed her scruples, and gave her to understand that it was his desire that the new foundation should be begun in that house; she obeyed, and immediately set to work to prepare things for the coming installation; nevertheless, the affair fell through, thus leaving the Foundress's humility victorious. At last, after many researches, her choice fell upon an old and poor house in the Rue de Tramassac, in front of the cathedral-church of St. John. This house had formerly served as a *pied à terre* to the fierce Baron des Ardrets, so celebrated for his cruelty to the Catholics during the religious wars of the sixteenth century; a singular coincidence, in which we may remark a particular design of Providence, drawing from oblivion, after three hundred years, the old dwelling, and changing the abode of crime into a sanctuary of reparation.

There was much to be done before the house could be fit for its religious destination. Nevertheless, without even waiting for the repairs to be commenced, Mary Teresa resolved to establish her community provisionally by summoning eight of her children from Paris. On the 3d of January 1851, the little flock was assembled and inaugurated the exercises of community life amidst the confusion of an installation and the cares of poverty. The future chapel not being ready, these pious women were obliged to dispense with the presence of the Blessed Sacrament, and this was to them a great privation; but their Mother taught them to supply it by faith, by glancing actually or inwardly through the large windows of the old cathedral to the sanctuary where their Lord lay.

Mary Teresa's life was now more active than ever. The inhabitants of Lyons welcomed the new institute in the most favourable manner; the protection of the Cardinal and of the Marist fathers was a pledge that inspired confidence; and the Foundress had to receive daily crowds of persons who came either to ask for explanations or to introduce new candidates. The institute had appeared from the first in its full development, with its three branches; and this very variety pleased many, by satisfying varied desires and employing persons of unequal capacities; but an imperfect knowledge of the real design of her institute occasioned great confusion. Mary

Teresa was advised to do impossibilities; postulants were recommended whom she could not accept, but whom it was difficult to refuse, being patronised by powerful protectors. Thus, even the good-will of persons of rank was sometimes a source of great annoyance. But still greater trials were at hand. The Carmelites of Lyons were those who best understood the utility of an independent congregation of Réparatrices, but they were likewise those who most feared the vicinity of the third order of Reparation; so that if, on going to Lyons, Mary Teresa had hoped to escape from the difficulties which surrounded her at Paris, the event would doubtless have given her reason to repent her resolution by raising similar difficulties in the new asylum where she was seeking a refuge. But such had not been the determining motive of her undertaking; and her soul, ever firm and obedient to the requirements of duty, did not recoil before the Cross.

In fact, never had her generous firmness of character been more necessary. To the external difficulties which we have named was now to be added a domestic trial, the greatest and most acute that could afflict her maternal heart. As before all the great trials of her life, she was supernaturally warned of the sufferings God had in store for her. Amidst all the fatigues of this new undertaking, she had until now felt herself upheld by a sensible grace which rendered all things easy and agreeable to her. But shortly before her return to Paris, as she was meditating upon the Passion, she suddenly saw herself in the place of our Saviour, like Him, loaded with opprobrium, betrayed, calumniated, abandoned: she was given to understand that a heavy cross awaited her; and from that moment a mortal sadness took possession of her soul. She did not cease, however, to apply herself diligently to every duty, and to conclude as quickly as possible the business which detained her at Lyons, though all the while trembling at what might be in store for her.

The building was actively carried on, so that towards the end of January the little chapel was ready to receive the Divine Guest. The Cardinal honoured the house with a visit, and conceded without further delay *perpetual Exposition*. The following day, the 29th January, Father Eymard blessed the humble sanctuary, and a few days later the holy Archbishop celebrated Mass in it, and gave to the community fresh proofs of his kindness and of the joy with which he welcomed the new foundation. Pious souls were attracted to this centre of prayer. 'Would you believe,' wrote Mary Teresa to her children in Paris, 'that every evening we have more than a hundred persons adoring, and certainly from two o'clock to nine in the evening, not less than twenty? During the day priests come to say their office, and soldiers likewise repair to our chapel *for their hour of guard*.' Thus from the outset was the privilege of perpetual adoration justified by the fruits which it produced, and the members of the third order for Reparation had already begun to fulfil their mission, which was to draw souls to the adoration and love of the Blessed Eucharist.

The community of Lyons was now fully constituted, and the Foundress was anxious to return to the cradle of her institute. But before leaving her new family it was necessary to name a Superioress; she whom Mary Teresa had at first destined to fill this office was not in a fit state to do so; it was not an easy task to find in a community of novices a Superioress capable of carrying on a new foundation. Father Bertholon wrote from Paris recommending a certain Sister Anne, in whom the Foundress had not much confidence. However, she thought herself bound to follow the advice of her spiritual father and overcome her repugnance; a dangerous submission, for on such occasions instinct is often the best guide. Sister Anne was sent to Lyons and installed as Superioress. Mary Teresa returned to Paris in the middle of February, after an absence of two months and a half, but leaving behind her the instrument of her suffering ready prepared.

From the date of this journey commences a long and admirable correspondence, continued until her death, with the houses at which she was not residing. Later, the community of Chalons shared in this colloquy, in which sentiments of the most affectionate tenderness are mingled with prudent counsels, sometimes with mild reproaches, and always with lessons of the purest and most sublime mystical doctrines.

On her return to Paris, Mary Teresa was scarcely allowed time to experience the joy of reunion with her cherished children. During her absence the state of things had not improved. A new Prioress had succeeded Mother Isabella. God, who watched over His little flock, did not permit this change to be detrimental to the new institute; but at first it added to other causes which gave Mary Teresa great uneasiness. The extreme poverty of her community did not afflict her, for her great faith led her to see in it a sign of the protection of her Saviour. But others were not of her opinion, and those who had mostly contributed to deprive her of all human aid brought forward her precarious pecuniary position as an objection to her foundation. This reproach made a lively impression on her, and she one day addressed Father Lefêvre thus: ' What can I answer to those persons who say, " *You are useless* " ? What proof can I give of my mission when no other is sought than money ? To speak the language of Jesus Christ is an extravagance which only meets with ridicule. They say to me in other words, " *If you are the Son of God, come down from the Cross.*" I doubtless deserve every punishment for my past life; but must my poor children, so generous and confiding, suffer for my incapacity ?'

But it was only rarely and with her two spiritual confidants, Father Lefêvre and Father Bertholon, that she allowed herself the consolation of complaint in her sufferings. Never did she outwardly reveal the sufferings inflicted by men, nor did the opposition she encountered cause her ardour to relax for a moment in the performance of her daily duties. In spite of every obstacle the institute continued to increase in regularity and fervour. Mary Teresa wholly devoted herself to the formation of her two families of Paris and of Lyons, to the religious virtues, and to the special spirit of the order of Reparation. By conferences and letters she gradually initiated them into the sublime thoughts by which she had been supported in the development of her undertaking. She wished that the Sisters of

L

the Reparation should not be content to honour Jesus Christ in His Sacrament and draw souls to Him, but that they should endeavour to reproduce in themselves the traits of His Eucharistic life. In that seemingly inimitable mystery she never ceased to propose to them a model; and what they did not find in the severity of the rules and the cloister, she taught them to seek in conformity to the Eucharist. This doctrine seemed to her to conciliate the requirements of humility with the interests of zeal. 'To live hidden in God is not,' she would say, 'to become sterile and incapable of doing good. O my dearest children, a mother may speak of herself to her children. I speak from daily experience. The more one gives, the more does God give in return. God is charity. To hide oneself in Him means to love, to devote, and forget oneself. Daughters, spouses of the Sacrament of love, you should, like Jesus Christ, live hidden in God; through humility alone is He veiled, and this veil none can take from Him; He remains hidden in the midst of splendour.'

The spring of that year was entirely devoted to the exercise of this spiritual formation. Whilst the Congregation of Reparation was thus internally gaining strength, it developed externally. In the little town of Crouy-sur-Ourcq, in the diocese of Meaux, there arose at the instigation of several pious ladies, friends of the Foundress, an association affiliated to the institute. The Bishop of Meaux approved of the rules, and granted Exposition of the Blessed Sacrament once a month, for the exercises of Reparation. Similar aggregations took place in a great number of parishes with the approbation of the Bishops. Providence permitted this favour to be bestowed on ungrateful towns, withering under the scourge of religious indifference, and everywhere it powerfully contributed to rekindle faith in souls. The associates bound themselves to practise all Christian duties, to set an especial example of keeping Sunday as a day of rest, and of respect for the holy name of God. On the monthly day of Reparation, they succeeded each other without interruption before the Blessed Sacrament, exposed in the church, and the day ended with a sermon on the Eucharistic mystery. Simple peasants have displayed an extraordinary zeal for this sublime devotion, and their fidelity in following its exercises and contributing to enhance its splendour has won for them wonderful graces for the sanctification of their interior life.

About this time Mary Teresa began to reap the fruit of her self-denying conduct during the tempest which had threatened her foundation with destruction. The unfavourable impressions produced on the council at Paris through certain misrepresentations were promptly effaced. The alarm of the Carmelites soon diminished; so that, notwithstanding the foundation at Lyons and the change of Prioress at Paris, the relation between the two communities became even more affectionate and sisterly. The idea of forming the third order into an independent establishment was now favourably received; measures were taken for the accomplishment of the project, and the Carmelites, who six months previously would have regarded such a step as injurious to their order, now lent all their efforts to insure its success. Mary Teresa sent word to her children at Lyons of this happy change. But, as if she had already had too much prosperity, she whom she had appointed their Mother was at that very time preparing for her fresh trials.

Every society, even a religious one, is in danger of possessing among its members one of those restless spirits who, incapable themselves of creating anything, do not know how to respect the work of others, and whose genius is devoted to destroying under the pretence of reforming. It rarely happens that a founder or foundress of any good work does not find a troublesome subject, whose pretended submission conceals real jealousy, but whose actual capability has fitted him or her for some important post. But when this miserable ambition puts on the garb of devotion, when intrigue clothes itself with the religious habit and a virtuous exterior, the evil is not only more odious, but it is far more hurtful, and it requires the powerful protection of Divine Providence for a foundation to resist this dangerous trial.

When admitting Sister Anne into her community, Mary

Teresa had introduced the scourge of which we speak; and when, in spite of her own reluctance, she had appointed her Superioress at Lyons, she had confided to infidel hands the weakest and most exposed part of her flock.

The new Superioress took to Lyons her own ready-formed ideas, which were entirely different from those of the Foundress. She had assisted at the birth of the Institute of Reparation, and even then, ever ready to criticise, she had laid down, in a writing intended for her confessor, her own views on the foundation. Speaking of Mother Mary Teresa, and of those who shared with her the sufferings of that laborious undertaking, she said: 'They require to be taught how to set about a work of reparation.' A little later, after entering the Community of Reparation, and whilst still a novice, she carried her presumption so far as to prepare a rule according to her own ideas. She was thus occupied when the Foundress's order called her, even before her profession, to the government of the new house. Before leaving she had completed her plans, and determined on the form in which she would mould her community. Unable to enter into the great and deep views of Mary Teresa, respecting the apostleship of the Eucharist and the alliance of zeal for souls with a contemplative life, she strongly objected to the branch of secular sisters, the charge of those who were making retreats, the connection with the associates, in a word, to all that constituted the apostolic part of the foundation. If she had been less engrossed in her own views, she would have been better able to understand those of the Foundress, who certainly no more desired her children to lead an *exterior* life than she did herself. She would have been struck by the admirable lessons that Mary Teresa addressed to them on the hidden life; and finally, if, after a serious and impartial attention to the teachings of her Mother, there had been anything which she could not understand, it was her religious duty to lay her doubts before her who could solve them, and not to make use of them to contradict her teaching and bring it into discredit. But not having sufficient light to discern the truth, nor sufficient discretion and modesty to keep quiet, she misrepresented the thoughts of her Superioress in such a way as to render them objects of suspicion even to the best-informed persons. She then promised herself an easy success, her criticisms were agreed to by every one, and there was nothing to prevent her making in the new institute such modifications as she pleased. But was it not to be feared that the consequences of such conduct would go beyond her wishes? After depriving Mother Mary Teresa of the confidence of those who had summoned her to Lyons, was she sure that that confidence would be granted to herself, and would not the discredit cast on the Foundress rather fall back on the whole institute, and involve in ruin a foundation still in its infancy? This was a serious question; but to imagine it, it was necessary to have less pride; for a proud soul never sees anything wrong in what she herself undertakes.

Circumstances seemed likewise greatly to favour the designs of Sister Anne. The first period of a foundation in which everything was new—place, rule, and members—and where everything was wanting—furniture, money, and resources of every kind—rendered many proceedings unavoidable which momentarily disturbed the repose of the little monastery. Add to this the crowd of pious persons who, edified by the new community, wished to know more about it, and the reader will be able to form an idea of the entirely accidental causes which obliged the Superioress to spend a great part of her time in the parlour. At Paris, Mary Teresa had reserved for herself this transient annoyance, and had besides, even when most pressed by exterior occupations, found means to devote much of her time to prayer and the interior formation of her novices. Sister Anne preferred to take advantage of this circumstance to exclaim against constitutions which imposed on *contemplatives* the distractions of an active life. Cleverly represented, this objection had its force; it greatly impressed the mind of the Cardinal, who watched with kindly interest the progress of the foundation. At the same time, like all who wish to withdraw themselves from obedience, the new Superioress obtained much advice, all of which she appeared to receive, but which she really dictated. To be more sure of directing herself, she took a multitude of directors; it was discovered later that she confessed to six different ecclesiastics or religious, each of whom believed that he possessed the secret of her heart, whereas she only revealed to each so much of her designs as would obtain his approbation and support. At the same time, with a prudence which a holy religious afterwards qualified with the term *diabolical*, she prepared for herself a retreat in case the authority of Mother Mary Teresa should finally triumph over her intrigues. Through the interposition of one of her confessors, she had asked for, and obtained admission into, the Order of Poor Clares, at the same time being firmly resolved not to profit by it unless she were forced to abandon her position. Deceived by this unhappy creature into becoming her accomplice, this confessor encouraged her to persist as far as she was allowed, and to leave the institute the very day she was deprived of her functions of Superioress.

Such was the state of things when Mary Teresa, suspecting part of the danger to which her new foundation was exposed, resolved to set out for Lyons towards the middle of June 1854. Her arrival was a heavy and unexpected blow to Sister Anne. She at first thought of retiring immediately; but, seeing that her Superioress did not reproach her, she took courage and resolved to face it all. Mary Teresa had indeed resolved to observe in silence before adopting any serious measures. The evil was certainly much greater than she had anticipated. Interiorly she no longer recognised her good and affectionate children, towards whom her feelings were still the same, but who had not been able to resist the unfavourable impressions produced by the insinuations of Sister Anne. Externally she found the Cardinal prejudiced against her and her institute, and all the priests who loved the house had been won over to the ideas of the local Superioress. Mary Teresa thus found herself completely alone, compelled to struggle against every one if she wished to maintain her work. But God gave her the grace not to doubt for an instant either her right or her duty. 'They treat me in a manner as cold as ice,' she wrote to the Carmelite

Prioress in Paris; 'but I do not appear as if I observed it. I have very briefly explained the state of things to our confessor, without showing the least fear; I have spoken still less—simply, but briefly and seriously. I cannot help feeling my isolated position, but, as it appears best to me, I quietly follow the direction of our Divine Master. O, how profitable it is to give oneself up to prayer; but how much more consoling it is practically to abandon oneself! Who would have thought that this hour of humiliation, of desertion, I might almost say of treason, would have been so sweet?' Actuated by this interior grace she feared nothing. She sought the Cardinal, who received her coldly, and appeared displeased at the exterior development she wished to give to her work. Mary Teresa respectfully begged him not to regard her intentions as they had been reported to him by a person whose interest it was to deceive him, but to seek information from her superiors at Paris. She then briefly explained the institute such as she understood it, adding her willingness to obey the prelate in all things, and to give to the establishment at Lyons only such development as he should deem fit. She, however, declared that she felt herself in duty bound not to abandon any of the characteristics of her foundation or sensibly modify the pristine rules, but that the application of them she would either modify or leave to the will of his Eminence. Satisfied with this reply, the Cardinal turned the conversation to the conduct of the local Superioress. He agreed that she had acted contrary to a true religious spirit; that Mary Teresa should resume and exercise her rights as Superior, even so far as to send Sister Anne back to the novitiate if she should think it necessary. Finally, he commissioned her to regulate, as she should see fit, the temporal and spiritual affairs of her community. Relying on this approbation, she no longer hesitated to declare to her unfaithful child that she was to return to Paris and go through a fresh apprenticeship in the novitiate. This latter replied that her directors had made her promise to leave the institute if she ceased to be Superioress. Confounded at so much pride, Mary Teresa sent her to the Cardinal, who treated her severely, and the separation, which was now unavoidable, did not take place without many tears, both on the side of the Foundress, who still loved her wandering child, and on that of her who at the last moment bitterly repented of her fault, and suddenly lost that confidence in the future of which, by means of such unworthy proceedings, she had tried to assure herself.

Thus ended in a few days that painful conflict which might have caused the destruction of the institute at Lyons and have greatly compromised it in Paris. In the latter place objections were only lulled; and what then would not have been said against the third order, if the first attempt to establish it independently had proved an utter failure, not exempt from scandal? Mary Teresa's firmness, her loyal conduct, so full of faith and straightforwardness, had restored the confidence of her former protectors. The Cardinal, who, at the request of Father Collin, had several times heard her confession, had conceived a great esteem for her spirit and virtue; her children recompensed her for a moment of coldness by redoubling their affection and confidence; those persons in the world who loved to regard the Community of Reparation as a centre of edification, rejoiced to see it confirmed by the authority of her who had founded it. All these testimonies were a sweet recompense to Mary Teresa; but here and there, especially among the clergy, there remained an unfavourable impression which was destined later to serve the designs of her enemies; and whatever might have been the dispositions of men, God, who had supported her, alone knew what her heart had suffered inwardly on account of this trial, and outwardly from the betrayal of her trust and the terror of seeing her beloved foundation exposed to perish ere it had scarcely begun.

The remainder of her stay at Lyons was occupied in completing the preparations for the installation of the community in the old house in the Rue Tramassac. Some of the old tenants had up to this period continued to inhabit it, and their departure left the community more room. They were able to enlarge their chapel, form a separate choir for the sisters, and give to each a cell. A cell—what a joy for the poor religious, who, until now, both at Lyons and at Paris, had been forced to have simple dormitories! Mary Teresa wrote an account of the good news to her dear absent children; and in her letters, which teemed with charm, quiet fun, and tenderness, yet were full of firmness, discretion, and prudence, we are surprised to find a thorough knowledge of all the conveniences and delicacies necessary to the religious life, when we consider that in her, this knowledge was not the fruit of experience, which she had been unable to acquire, but the consequence of a sure instinct and a kind of divination. Such are the signs by which we recognise an extraordinary mission in a soul.

The improvements which gave the community so much spiritual joy produced consequences both unfortunate and amusing. The departure of the tenants had been followed by three successive invasions of different insects, whose immense numbers brought to mind the plagues of Egypt. The consequent episodes occasioned frequent merry remarks, which served to enliven the recreations, whilst furnishing the lovers of mortification with more than one occasion for practising it. 'Imagine,' wrote the Superioress to her children at Paris, ' a dark cloud descending on us, and on myself in particular, who, being the most guilty, merit most this purgatory. Like true children, this calamity was a source of amusement to us; but any other than a Réparatrice would have considered it a misfortune.' Scarcely had these insects disappeared when they were succeeded by *cafards*.* 'Which of you knows what a *cafard* is?' she writes at another time; and then she set to work to describe those large black insects, their agile feet, their invading propensities, and, the better to make herself understood, she sketched the outline of the animal life-size. Another time, there came a swarm of winged ants, which persecuted the poor inhabitants of the old house with their bites; and in the Superioress's letter we find mingled with the lively description of these trials, warnings of a vigilant zeal and lessons of sublime spirituality.

Amid these little annoyances, and urged on by an energetic

* Blackbeetles.

will, the building was at length completed. The rules for the community of Lyons, written entirely by Mother Mary Teresa, had been presented by her to the Cardinal, who approved of them.* The new local Superioress, an angel of piety, but, unfortunately for the community, already ripe for heaven, had begun the exercise of her functions under her Mother's own eyes. There was now nothing to keep the Foundress away from the cradle of her institute. Towards the commencement of August we find her again at Paris with her children, whom she had taken by surprise.

She found all things in perfect order; the dealings with the monastery more affectionate than ever; the Archbishop favourably inclined; and the Superior wholly devoted to the institute. Postulants were not wanting; but the Superioress was severe in her choice, applying with constancy the principles she had succeeded in laying down in her rules, and which, setting aside all human advantages, made a true vocation not only a sufficient, but the necessary condition for admission. Happy are those religious societies which, at their origin, are governed with that firmness which faith alone inspires. Their progress may be slower, but their spirit is more vigorous; their mission better fulfilled; their existence more sure and respected: even the world is not deceived, and admires those who do not carry into the sanctuary those interested views which suit earthly purposes alone.

Poor Mary Teresa's soul—that soul so many times bowed down by sorrow, that she thought it incapable of experiencing a single joyful feeling—now, however, tasted the happiness of that prosperity which, after so many trials, appeared to her as the sweet approbation of her Master. She stole a few moments from her multiplied occupations to break the long silence she had maintained with regard to her oldest friend, and to confide to her her joy. 'My poor Clémence,' she wrote, 'you know

---

* It was necessary to constitute the new foundation distinctly, under the diocesan authority, for as yet the institute bore only the title of the Third Order of Reparation; and where it had no longer the support of Carmel it required another.

what my life has become, or rather you cannot know. Even I myself cannot understand it, and I rub my eyes asking myself how I shall continue to the end with this daily increasing burden. But strange to say, now, when it is impossible for me to move this mountain alone, I feel a profound peace. I devote to it all my time and strength; and leave to God what I do not do, without feeling any uneasiness. As I have no leisure to examine myself, my conscience has never before been so free of scruple. I quickly ask pardon for those faults which I know, and for the rest, mercy. It is sufficiently great to cover me. There is now no repetition of the tears of the Abbaye-au-Bois! I no longer shed any, save of gratitude.'

The project of a foundation in Paris separate from Carmel, which in the spring had seemed likely to succeed, had just failed. Another had been attempted, but with no better success. 'Providence,' she said, 'wills our condition to be a provisional one. *Fiat!* It will keep us in the path of humility.' Meanwhile the institute continued to progress; one of Mary Teresa's best-loved children had, it is true, died in her arms; she was death's first victim in the bosom of the community. But what is death to a soul whose whole life has been an immolation? 'Mother,' she exclaimed at her last hour, 'give me wings, that I may flee away.' And the faith of those around her was so great, that none thought that they would lose that companion because she was about to become invisible to their eyes. No; she was going to heaven as others had gone to Lyons; she was there going to begin what Mary Teresa called *Sister Victorine's foundation.* A few days later, three postulants took the place of the departed angel by taking the habit of novices. At the same time the association at Crouy was prospering so far as to oblige the Foundress to repair hither and confirm the good already begun. A small religious family had there been formed, who, no longer content with the ordinary practices of the associates, aspired to live in community. Mary Teresa had first sent them a secular sister, but she was now obliged to obtain permission from the Superior to visit in person these pious zealots of the Reparation. She set out on this excursion of a few days towards the end of October, and found in it repose both of soul and body. The sight of the beautiful autumnal tints roused her artistic soul; and, still full of the sweet emotion she had experienced beside the bed of her beloved sufferer, she gave vent to her thoughts in a mystic song, in which inexperience in versification is doubtless visible, for the number and rhyme are often incorrect, but in which the poetical inspiration and sentiment* are not at fault. But the

> * Ma Mère, il ne vient pas,
>   Mon doux époux, ma vie;
> Je l'appelle trop bas,
>   Je suis anéantie.
>
> Ma Mère, parlez-lui
>   De sa fille fidèle :
> Pour sortir de la nuit
>   Oh, donnez-moi des ailes!
>
> Oui, je veux m'envoler
>   Au séjour de lumière :
> Je voudrais respirer
>   Dans le ciel la première.
>
> Tout disparaît, tout fuit,
>   La terre n'est pas belle :
> Pour sortir de la nuit,
>   Oh, donnez-moi des ailes!
>
> Des vengeances de Dieu,
>   Non, je n'ai pas la crainte :
> Ce doux Maître des cieux
>   N'est pas sourd à ma plainte.
>
> Du Sauveur j'ai l'appui,
>   Sa charité m'appelle :
> Pour sortir de la nuit,
>   Oh, donnez-moi des ailes!
>
> De ton Christ vois la face,
>   Mon Dieu, vois sa douleur!
> Que ta puissance efface
>   De mon front la rougeur!
>
> Console mon ennui,
>   Vois mon cœur qui chancelle :
> Pour sortir de la nuit,
>   Oh, donnez-moi des ailes!

happiness of meeting pure souls, devoted to Jesus Christ, was the principal joy derived from this journey. She returned enchanted, and wrote to her community at Lyons *that she had become better.* 'I there found,' she wrote, ' a little *brother of the Reparation:* he is a child twelve years of age. I persuaded him to relate to me his manner of praying, which is admirable : he has his day of Reparation, and when I said to him, " My child, what do you like doing best ?" he replied instantly, " Mother, my hour of Reparation." " What do you do, then ?" " I speak to the good God." " And does He answer you ?" " O yes, Mother." ' And she added with tears, ' What a Mission of holiness could be undertaken in those poor countries where there is no direction for interior souls !'

Nevertheless, notwithstanding the consolations she met with, obedience and charity alone could keep her away, even for an instant, from her real family, whose sanctification was her task as well as her joy. She returned before the feast of All Saints. Providence, who, at this time seemed to remove all those difficulties which had threatened the institute at Paris, again procured for Mary Teresa an unexpected happiness, viz. that of being able to offer her chapel for the exercises of the Perpetual Adoration. Another community having been unable to comply with the request tendered to it, it was the same vicar-general, who, after showing himself at first a zealous friend of the new institute, and afterwards seemed to share the unfavourable opinion respecting it, now asked of the Réparatrices the hospitality of their little chapel for the *triduum* of adoration. He himself celebrated Mass and preached ; the crowd was great. All rivalry had then disappeared, and one only wish triumphed, that of doing honour to the Blessed

---

Divine Eucharistie,
  Ombre du Sacrement,
Je t'ai toujours chérie
  Jusqu'au dernier moment.

Mais l'espérance à lui
  Des clartés éternelles :
Pour sortir de la nuit,
  Oh, donnez-moi des ailes !

Eucharist. Thus, notwithstanding the opinion of weak souls, too prompt at being scandalised, true devotion is still the best guarantee for fraternal charity; and if it should not succeed in preventing all disagreement, it sooner or later reconciles those whom diversity of views may separate, but whom unity of aim cannot fail to draw together again.

A mark of confidence of still greater importance was now to efface the last traces of past difficulties. Only one year previously there had been a question of almost suppressing the institute; finally, its existence in Paris was tolerated, on condition of its remaining dependent on Carmel, and not being extended elsewhere; since then, the authorities had become more tolerant; the foundation at Lyons, though contrary to the imposed condition, had raised no opposition; and now the state of things was such that the Superior no longer feared to ask Mary Teresa for the definitve digest of her rules, so as to obtain the canonical approbation of the diocesan authority to their right of establishment as an independent congregation.

Whilst she was occupied with these religious cares, political events once more brought on Paris the horrors of civil war. The 2d December and its consequences, however, did not trouble the existence of the Community of Reparation. 'Now is the time to test our vocation,' said Mary Teresa to her children, on hearing the report of the cannon. And they understood her so well that, though still free, as none of them had yet made their profession, they would not yield to the entreaties of their terrified friends who came to withdraw them from supposed danger. 'Now,' they said to their Mother, 'we feel how entirely we belong to you.' However, the troubles of those evil days did not approach the house of Carmel. Henceforth, strangers to the world, entirely devoted to their Réparatrice vocation, Mary Teresa's first companions were to receive the recompense of a long novitiate of three years, amid the trials of opposition and poverty. The approbation of the rules was not delayed. Before the end of December the congregation of the Adoration Réparatrice was regularly constituted; henceforth, submissive to its own Superioress, under the authority of the Archbishop, the new institute could establish itself where it willed, and had now no connection with Carmel save of deference and charity. Great was the joy of the community at this good news; profiting by it, twenty-one novices immediately prepared to make their profession. As if to set the seal to his work, Mgr. Sibour determined himself to receive their vows and give the habit to five postulants. It was on this occasion that the professed sisters received the cross and red ribbon which complete the religious costume of the congregation.

It seemed that every one should have been satisfied with the turn events had taken; for the high approbation of the ecclesiastical authorities reassured secular persons with regard to the undertaking, whilst the independent existence granted to the new institute completely separated its destiny from that of Carmel, and freed that venerable order from every subject of uneasiness. The danger of lukewarmness, which the monasteries had to fear from the vicinity of a third order, was no longer to be apprehended from an alien congregation; and the present arrangement was what the Carmelite Mothers had proposed when objecting to a third order. Yet there still remained dissatisfied persons among those who had formerly united their efforts to those of Mary Teresa for the establishment of the nocturnal adoration, but who had then separated from her, and now accused her *of robbing them of their plan.* Mary Teresa might have replied that she had begun to act before becoming acquainted with those persons; that consequently she had taken nothing from them; and that to have persisted in her views with the approbation of her spiritual directors at a time when these momentary coöperators wished to give the institute a form of which she disapproved was assuredly not a step of which she was likely to repent. But she reserved this apology for the outpourings of spiritual direction: to her detractors she displayed only a silent and patient firmness.

These latter, seeing the foundation firmly established at Paris, did not give up the hope of disturbing it at Lyons.

They had succeeded in filling the Cardinal's mind with fresh fears, so that he hesitated to confirm the privileges previously granted, especially that of perpetual adoration. This suspense did not tend to inspire confidence in the future of the foundation; their protectors withdrew; the society of nocturnal adoration ceased to give the aid which appeared necessary; resources failed; and Mary Teresa, who felt the danger of a contemplative community entering into imprudent engagements, had firmly resolved not to incur any debts. The Cardinal, still kindly disposed notwithstanding his fears, encouraged her to induce her children to make their religious profession, assuring her that confidence would then gradually return. But, on the other hand, the Superior in Paris warned her that, if they were one day obliged to leave Lyons, the mother-house could easily take back novices, but not those who had made their vows in another diocese. The congregation, in fact, had not as yet any general government, and each house was to depend directly on diocesan authority. Those who made their profession would thus run the risk of being excluded from the institute by that very act which should consecrate them to it.

Such was the situation of the poor community of Lyons at the time when all was prospering at Paris. A visit of a few days to Lyons in the month of December had added to Mary Teresa's anxiety; and on her return, she had almost decided on recalling her subjects. She wrote disconsolately to F. Lefèvre: 'Henceforth, without assistance, without money or credit, I am on the point of abandoning this foundation, the fruit of so many tears and so much fatigue. This little community, a model of piety, charity, and zeal, will be expelled from Lyons. They do not remember that ten young girls have for a whole year kept up the perpetual adoration day and night, in spite of privations of every kind; they do not see that Jesus attracts a crowd of adorers to that little sanctuary.' But with her accustomed faith, she regretted none of the successes that had been accomplished. A year of homage and adoration procured to our Lord seemed to her a more than sufficient recompense and consolation. 'I have great trouble,' she said, 'in reconciling myself to the thought of destroying that pretty little Throne of our Beloved; but I cannot expose it to be seized by the bailiffs. And notwithstanding all, I am consoled; and I cannot repent of having made an act of Reparation at Lyons: on leaving it, I shall ask that our prayers and sufferings may have been of use to that city, where, as in Paris, vice and virtue strive for the mastery.'

Once more, however, God was satisfied with the accepted sacrifice without requiring it to be consummated. An unexpected benefactor supplied the most urgent necessities, and it was decided that the novices at Lyons should be admitted to profession at the beginning of February 1852. There, as at Paris, the Pastor of the Diocese in person received the vows of the 'Réparatrices;' and Mary Teresa, seeing in less than three years, her humble family increase to the number of sixty members, set up in the two capital towns of France the Altar of Reparation, and receive from two archbishops the title and privileges of a regular congregation, when, on the outset, she appeared to meet with nothing but obstacles, and now, as on the first day, she knew not whence would come the morrow's bread,—Mary Teresa, seeing, as we have said, these results, could not grow proud, for the hand of the All-Powerful was too visibly at work in the matter: but she might well rejoice in the happy thought that God had made use of her as His instrument for an undertaking of which He was the real author.

Her visit to Lyons on this occasion was but a brief one. This time she departed with the more confidence, as she left her dear children to the paternal care of Father Bertholon, who had been summoned to Lyons by his superiors. The affectionate vigilance of this guide was to stand in place of their absent mother, whom a mournful presentiment urged to return to Paris. The mortal career of her aged father was, in fact, drawing to a close; and, in reward for the generous gift he had made of his daughter to God, he was about to receive the grace of a holy and blessed death. His daughter, become the mother of a numerous posterity, could offer to the old man the prayers and pious intercessions of a whole spiritual family, the hundredfold promised in this world to those who sacrifice the object of their most cherished affections. Nothing extraordinary marked that end, except what astonishes those who see nothing beyond the present life: I mean the serenity of a soul who abandons the world without an effort. The Sacraments ardently desired, hailed with faith, received with love; the calm with which the preparations for death and the last tender adieux were made; the firm and tranquil hope of a future reunion; one last look, mingled with confidence, at that past which God had purified, then for ever turned away from visible things to fix itself on the bright dawn of eternal realities; the hands twined round the crucifix; the lips murmuring a last prayer; and the entire man, peacefully recollected, waiting for his last sigh,—such is the sight which ever makes a Christian death the astonishment of the impious, the consolation of the just, and one of the most eloquent witnesses which God gives of Himself here below.

CHAPTER XI.
1852, 1854.

Mary Teresa devotes herself to the government of her institute.—Characteristics of her direction.—Solidity of her mystical doctrine.—The institute obtains from Rome a *Laudative Brief*.—Project of a foundation apart from Carmel.—Reasons which determine the choice of the old Ursuline Convent.—Laborious life of the community at the time of their installation.

No important event to the institute signalised the remainder of the year 1852. Troubles, which are the lot of all Superiors, were not, of course, wanting. Sickness cruelly visited her convent. Death was about to snatch from her at the same time as many as four of her children; and, notwithstanding her tender care, she could not save two of them. One was a young postulant, eighteen years of age, whom she had brought from Lyons, and who gently faded away, as a true child of the Reparation, without even having time to adopt its livery; but she possessed the spirit to such a degree as to serve as a model to the professed sisters. 'Let us take care,' said Mary Teresa to them, 'or this child of benediction will one day be our judge.'

The other loss was still more keenly felt. The angelic Sister Veronica of the Passion had very soon felt her strength belie her courage; or, rather, as we learn from a confession of her mother, she had offered her life to God for the foundation of the Reparation. Decline having declared itself, it became necessary to deprive the community of Lyons of this treasure. There is a particular charm in hearing saints speak of saints; the following is what Mary Teresa wrote to her children at Lyons respecting their late Superioress: 'I am preparing our dear Sister Veronica for the last journey; or, rather, it is she who, by examples of heroic virtue, teaches me to continue mine on earth. She has raised herself so far above ordinary perfection, that I do not think the holiest of Saints could have been more edifying. Since my return from Lyons I have not succeeded in discovering in her a single imperfection. As she takes no food, her weakness is extreme; nevertheless she receives Communion daily, and remains whole hours in the presence of the Blessed Sacrament. O, if you knew how we love to see her motionless, with her large eyes fixed on the Monstrance! It seems as if all her life were there. The Divine Sun takes pleasure in consuming with His rays this young plant; then when He has done so, He will revive her, so that she may blossom in the immensity of His heavenly love.'*

---

* Mary Teresa's letters to her children of Lyons contain many precious details relative to this death. We will give a few extracts: 'No, no; do not complain. I feel the love of our Jesus glorified by the death of this elect one; my joy is greater than my sorrow. Love is stronger than death. The doctor having warned me that each day might be her last, I told her of her position; and every morning in Communion she makes an act of resignation. Nevertheless she thinks but little of herself; her life, her death belong to the institute, especially to the community at Lyons, to her beloved sisters; it is her only anxiety. When she sees me she says, "Mother, have you any letters from our sisters?" Her dear novices, who love and venerate her as a saint, rejoice that God still leaves her to witness their happiness and bring down graces on their consecration. I hope that she may be able to assist at it. She glides about like a shadow; it is wonderful how she lives, continually a prey to fever, without food. It is supernatural.'

Again: 'Pray for our dear departing one; for although her soul is at peace, her body is in continual suffering. Last night she called me and said, "Mother, I am in Gethsemane: God is punishing me." The subjects of her meditations are the words of Jesus which express the deepest sorrow. This was necessary in order to render her conformable to the holy victim, and to give us an admirable example of what pure faith can effect, even to the last breath, in a soul united to God.'

In another letter: 'My very dear children, you weep, but your tears shall be turned into joy! Our Lord alone can change a day of mourning into a time of joy, and this wonder He is operating in us. We felt happy in surrendering to God that beautiful soul, worn out by suffering. To the last moment she maintained the combat with love and courage. A few minutes before her death I was at her side, when I received a letter from you. I said to her, "My child, here is a letter from your loved children at Lyons; you offer yourself for them, do you not?" "O yes, Mother,"

It required nothing less than the beauty of this scene to console Mary Teresa; for in this saint who was leaving her she not only lost a cherished daughter, but a support, a confidante, a friend. The strongest souls sometimes stand in need of such

---

she answered, with a sweet smile. I gave her the letter to kiss, and placed it on her heart. For thirty-six hours she had tasted nothing; nevertheless, on Friday night, she said to me, "Mother, I say nothing, but I constantly think of my Beloved. If I could communicate I should be so happy; but as you wish, Mother; I do not ask you to allow it. I like better to obey than to communicate." I acquainted the father with her desire, and he determined to give her this last consolation. We made a pretty reposoir, and she received her Divine Spouse for the last time on earth. Since then she tasted no other food. In the evening, finding her worse, I assembled the sisters for the prayers for the dying. We ended by the *Stabat*, which she wished to be sung. This heavenly song was very beautifully sung by our sisters, who seemed at the last verse to be opening heaven to their dear sister. The whole night seemed to be the last minute. She wished me to place my hand on her head, and it consoled her to hear me pray. Once she gave a low groan, but immediately asked pardon of God; having spoken to me in a manner which she did not deem sufficiently respectful, she likewise begged my pardon. I then blessed her, and told her to be at peace: she replied, "O yes, I am at peace, for you are my Jesus Christ; I will place my soul in your heart, and you will give it to God." However, she said to me next morning, "You are tired, Mother. Go to the first Mass; *I will wait.*" Relying on her promise, I went; and on receiving our Lord I felt assured of her eternal happiness. I returned quickly to her to impart to her the divine virtue I had received. I was very happy, and she understood it, smiling sweetly; but, always forgetful of herself, she begged me to go and breakfast, and she would prepare herself. She had always wished Mary to offer her to Jesus, and God granted her request. On Saturday, during the nine o'clock Mass, which was being offered for her, she expired. On Sunday she was borne to her last resting-place; the altar, instead of being in mourning, was covered with flowers, it being the feast of the Dedication.

' I felt greatly consoled when confiding her remains to the empty vault in my family chapel. I am sure that she will prepare a place for me in heaven. Everything terrestrial is now at an end for this angel; but her true life is beginning. I cannot tell you how consoled I am when I think (and I do so constantly) that her dear soul is living with you, for you have a right to her. When she arrived in your midst the institute needed reparation, because it had been betrayed. God was pleased to accept her sacrifice, because He wished to bless this foundation. Joy, courage, my beloved children, in the midst of your sufferings. Other trials are awaiting you; but they are only childish sorrows. When you have spread in the world the fruit of Mary's womb, you will be joyous! Pray that I may soon be able to sing with you the *Magnificat* for our dear saint.

assistance; but, unlike weak souls, when God deprives them of it, they know how to profit by the privation—by attaching themselves more firmly to Him. Besides, supernatural friendship participates in the immortality of the souls it has united;

Yesterday, during the Holy Sacrifice, I felt as if assisting at her espousals, and, being her Mother, I felt glorified in her greatness. Father Julliard experienced the same impression. He saw her every day for three weeks, and he told me that he had never found solid religious virtues carried to so high a degree in any other soul. Latterly she had constantly thought of St. Gertrude, and invoked her unceasingly.'

Again, to Mme. de L.: 'She was my *second soul*, supplying, encouraging, and upholding me in all things. God has sealed her with the seal of a victim; for a year she has been constantly on the point of departing, and yet she still continues to suffer. Pray for her: she will certainly reward you in heaven. I wish I could give you an account of the heroic virtues of this holy and privileged soul. At twenty-five God had gifted her with that maturity which caused her to be chosen for mistress of novices. Notwithstanding her sufferings, she is still the life and soul of our numerous novitiate. She is called Sister Veronica of the Passion, and is the true image of her crucified Spouse.

'My heavy burden will be still heavier; nevertheless there is in my soul a hidden joy which sustains all; she is on the point of being so happy, and the communion of saints unites heaven and earth! You said to me, "I have angels in heaven;" I shall have saints; and we shall see them again on that day when, in our turn, we shall all plunge ourselves in the immensity of the love of God.'

Let us give one more extract, from a letter written the following year:

'She became so quickly the true image of the Divine Spouse, who called her to Himself about four months since: my sacrifice had been made long before, and the union between us had become so intimate, that I felt that we were not separating, but that a part of myself was going to heaven. On the day of her burial, during the Holy Sacrifice, it seemed as if I were assisting at the great festival of her espousals; and from that time this sweet impression has never left me. Her happiness and glory lighten the weight of my exile: when I suffer most I cast my eyes on her, and peace returns to me. She had promised me that it should be so, and God permitted her to keep her word. She died the death of a saint; our whole community became embalmed with her admirable virtues, which made her an angel on earth! Humility and obedience were the guardians of her deep love. The energy of this ardent soul was hidden beneath a candid childlike simplicity: I alone knew the extent of her intellect and her strength of character. But it would require a pamphlet to relate her life, which was interesting even in a worldly point of view: and if I could tell the beautiful prayers which she uttered aloud during the last fifteen nights that I spent beside her, it would prove that God does not forget the world, and that the deposit of the holy love of the Saints is still preit establishes between those whom death appears to have separated, a link which is not merely that of remembrance: there is a spiritual presence of the liberated soul, which makes itself felt by those who survive, and sometimes even reveals itself outwardly by visible tokens of answered prayer. Five months after Sister Veronica's death, Mary Teresa, when speaking of her to her children, testified to the truth of this presence; she then added: 'And now, this is a secret between us. The day before her death she felt a buzzing in her ear, which gave her pain. She said to me, "Allow me to offer this suffering that Sister —— may be delivered from this misfortune." (This sister was threatened with deafness.) On the day of the funeral, Sister ——, *who knew nothing of what had passed*, came to me, saying, "*Mother, Sister Veronica has cured me.*" There was also a soul who for two years had been possessed by the devil, and was suffering cruel pains. I persuaded her to make a novena to our sister, and on the fourth day she was cured.'

---

served in a few elect souls. God was very good to inspire her to ask permission, when alone with me, to speak freely and out loud, for constraint augmented her fever. I sat behind a curtain, so as not to disturb her, and listened religiously. She always made use of the Gospels or the Psalms which she had committed to memory, and made from them admirable applications to her soul and the institute.

'Mgr. de Bonald, who had seen and appreciated her whilst she had been Superioress at Lyons, was then in Paris, and came to give her his blessing on the eve of her death. He afterwards praised her virtues to the sisters of Lyons in words very consoling to us. She had a singular love for the Blessed Virgin. After the prayers for the agonising, she expressed a wish that our sisters should sing the *Stabat* at her bedside. Although not beautiful, her face, which was extremely expressive and angelic, seemed at that moment celestial with joy and love.

'A holy religious having asked her, "What do you regret on earth?" she replied, "My Mother (that is, in her spirit, obedience) and Jesus crucified." This answer is in itself a meditation, and may be of great service to such as still live in exile.

'Have I told you that, on her first arrival at Lyons, she said to me, "Mother, permit me to offer myself as a victim for the establishment of the institute." Her confessor having permitted it, he placed her act of oblation under the chalice on the feast of St. Magdalen. *Eight days later she brought me her handkerchief saturated with blood, smiling the while. Her sacrifice had been accepted.*'

Thus, amid the sweet emotions produced by this holy death, a year was closed, the opening of which had brought such unexpected prosperity to the institute, but which the Foundress had not passed without much anxiety and suffering. Notwithstanding these trials, she ceased not to devote herself to the interior formation of her two families. In the month of December 1852 we again find her doing violence to her infirm body in order to spend a few days with her community at Lyons. At Christmas she was again in Paris; and the New Year, which brought with it a change of government, found the 'Réparatrices' in that state of profound peace known only to those souls who live for God alone. Six weeks after the proclamation of the Empire the community was still ignorant of the event which had just agitated the world. Thus were justified the views of Mary Teresa, who, whilst introducing into the mission of her institute the care of souls and the solicitude of apostolic zeal, had promised to insure to her children the recollection and absence of worldly disquietude necessary to the contemplative life.

Her letters at this period to her community at Lyons are particularly deserving of attention. Whilst perusing them one cannot help recalling the burning exhortations of St. Paul, the tenderness with which he tempered the flame of zeal, those ardent feelings which rendered him sensible of the least wants of his children, but a thousand times more sensible to the interests of Jesus Christ. Whilst glancing over the correspondence of this mother with the apostolic heart we can imagine her exclaiming, '*My little children, you whom I bring forth in anguish until Jesus shall be formed within your hearts!*' 'My beloved children,' she writes to them, 'a cloud of sadness often passes over my heart when I remember that you are absent from this sheepfold. Do you know that here they are almost jealous of my yearning for you? To be happy in Paris I must have Lyons in my cell.' This is certainly affection; but it has nothing in common with those mixed earthly affections engendered by weakness and self-love. Another time she writes, 'The hearts of Jesus and Mary are in our hearts, and our solicitude is for all. I have remarked that since I have been a

Réparatrice, setting aside the souls of whom I have charge, *and those to whom God has bound me by a providential affection*, I find it difficult to feel more interest in one soul than in another. I never pray more especially for my friends, or the members of my family, not even for my nephew. God knows them; if He wills, He can bestow upon them what I give to Him. My family and friends are everywhere. There is but one kind of people from whom I shrink, viz. the Pharisaical race; those for whom our Divine Master did not pray, because they draw the children of God into the snares of the devil by clothing themselves with deceitful appearances. From such persons, with Jesus, meek and humble of heart, with David, with all the Saints and prophets, I turn away, saying, "My God, deliver my soul and the souls of my children from the jaws of the lion and the sting of the asp."'

Her zeal was not less than her affection. She wrote thus on the subject of a splendid ceremony which had attracted many people to the chapel at Lyons: 'If you but knew how I hunger and thirst for Jesus to have adorers in spirit and in truth, you would well understand that I do not always rejoice in what is brilliant and showy. I know that our Lord will remain sad and in the shade in the midst of the light which the world gives Him, and that He will be resplendent when a single loving soul consumes itself before Him. When you write to me, *We have found a victim of reparation*, then I shall rejoice more than in all exterior splendour.' Then, as if some one had answered her by bringing forward the desire she had so often expressed for the exterior adornment and glory of the B. Eucharist, she suddenly exclaimed, 'Do I no longer wish to attract souls? Do I renounce the task of procuring the glory of the Victim King? O no; but I wish to show you how ephemeral is the world's enthusiasm. Jesus was conducted in triumph to Jerusalem, and a few days later He was crucified in that very city! Besides, many persons will, I know, speak to you as St. Peter did when he did not wish to hear the divine secrets of the Passion of our Saviour. Many will say to you, "Well, sisters, Divine Providence has come to your aid; profit by this show, this splendour; leave your obscurity, and procure for yourselves powerful protectors; you will not be labouring for yourselves, but for the greater glory of God." But I say to you, Remain humble and little as Mary your mother; love the Eucharistic and hidden life. I do not deceive myself; now is the happy time of the infant family, now when it is struggling in poverty and evangelical simplicity. I hope to die before the dawn of another day.'

I think we cannot be wrong in asserting that such sentiments are very rare, and that such a detachment in the midst of practical poverty and daily privations is one of the most striking marks of the spirit of God in a soul.

But to exhort is not everything; it is necessary sometimes to reprimand. The Christian virtues, especially the religious ones, cannot be acquired without effort. However great may be the fervour of a novice, it is rather ardour than perfection. The meek and affectionate Mary Teresa had neither mercy nor affection for her children's faults. A letter that she wrote on the feast of the Compassion of the Blessed Virgin contains, in the form of an allegory,* such subtle and keen reproaches, such vigorous lessons of perfection, that, in spite of its length, we cannot help giving our readers an extract. From it will be seen in what the work of sanctification consists, what are the requirements of true religious abnegation, and what a rigorous employment of their time is demanded of those souls whom the unjust and frivolous world so lightly accuses of idleness. The letter begins thus:

'My dear children, I have just made a long visit to Mary at the foot of the cross; and, kneeling before her, close to her heart, I said, "Mother, tell me what are the swords with which my children pierce your maternal heart—you, who on this very day adopted them at the feet of Jesus the Victim." The Blessed Virgin looked at me sadly but affectionately, and re-

---

* We do not pretend to consider as her own invention what Mary Teresa relates as having been shown to her during prayer; but the allegory is found in the form under which the teachings of Mary were presented to her—a form which she reproduces in the letter to her children.

plied, "I will tell you." And you will see, my dear children, that these swords often pierce my heart also. The first sword which Mary receives is when one of you looks back. She said to me, "But see how ungrateful that soul is. My Son went in search of her; He worked miracles to bring her here; and now, when her sacrifices might glorify God, she brings forward cowardly excuses. Fed not only with the manna of grace, but with the bread of angels, she regrets the flesh-pots of Egypt. O, each time that I see that sister spend her hour of meditation in frivolous, earthly, illusory thoughts—thoughts opposed to the spirit of faith—my soul is pierced with a sword.

"Pride is the second sword. Do they not know that I have said, by the inspiration of the Holy Spirit, that God humbles those who make themselves the centre of everything? How the sword enters into the depth of my heart when I hear them wanting in charity, exalting themselves at the expense of their sisters.

"The third sword is tepidity—listlessness in every duty and exercise—no fervour or zeal for their own spiritual advancement. It is a serious matter, for God rejects the lukewarm.

"The fourth sword is, that my Jesus, who has given Himself unreservedly to them, who, in the ardour of His love, has espoused them, has not entire possession of their hearts. What, then, do they love? Who can they find more amiable or more loving than my Divine Son?"

'At this pressing question of Mary I knew not what to answer, and, my children, I was much ashamed. Nevertheless I was obliged to obey. "Mother," I said, "some are so engrossed with themselves and their own thoughts that, continually contemplating themselves, they forget your Son. It is true that they sometimes long to leave themselves a little for Jesus; but it then happens that He becomes angry, and hides Himself. Thus, though living under the same roof, they end by visiting Him so rarely that their love grows cold. Others are like Martha; under pretext of serving Jesus, they busy themselves about everything except that which is necessary. They consider their little talents as very important, and they live in anticipation of this or that office. . . . . If they do not succeed, all is lost; they spend their time in thinking that it was more or less through their own fault or that of others. O, the love of such souls is without wings; it crawls on the earth, and often clings to it; and, believing that they have left all things for Love, they really leave Love to attach themselves to everything. Finally, there are some who do not love because their hearts are too sensitive: these suffer much, for they have the instinct of love; but they confound it with enjoyment. They forget that they have espoused a crucified Love; they do not find any charms in His cross or His crown of thorns. . . . . As soon as they see Him they are terrified. . . . . They imitate the Apostles—they flee away." O my children, I wept when thus speaking to the Blessed Virgin. She appeared so sad on seeing that the victims of Love do not yet know the charms of Love.

'The fifth sword had entered so deeply that Mary seemed to suffer much from it. She said to me, "My child, you do not, then, instruct them in their vocation? What indifference to the very object of their mission! Do they think that a mere formula of the vows is its accomplishment? The Church has placed in their hands a source of boundless grace for sinners. And what do I see every day? This one in Communion, instead of thinking of my perishing children, is entirely occupied by some petty annoyance she has received on the previous day. Here is another who weeps during the time of prayer. Is it through compassion for those souls who are falling into hell? Alas, no; it is because her self-love has received a prick of a needle; it gives her so much pain that if she dared she would cry out in presence of Him who for her sake was spit upon and scourged."

'Mary showed me the sixth sword: it proceeded from the dispositions which had driven in all the others. "*Self-love*," she said, "holds them captive, and prevents the development of the work of salvation. The good angels of other countries come and ask me for the Institute of Reparation. I dare not present their prayer to our Lord: you can scarcely maintain your two houses. I say to the good angels, 'Wait a while.

Perhaps later.' But it pains me to be obliged to keep back the spring of living water which seeks to overflow on every side."

'The seventh sword is my secret! . . . .

'Prostrating myself at the feet of our tender Mother, I asked her the means of healing these wounds. She appeared touched, and answered, "Tell them that if they wish to do so, they can, instead of swords, offer me a crown; let them have it ready for the feast of the Assumption."'

Such is the outspoken and vigorous mysticism with which Mary Teresa fed her children. What God gave to her in prayer she transmitted to them with a truly maternal liberty. There are two snares to be avoided in spiritual direction: exaltation, which substitutes illusion and chimera for the sure gifts of faith; and a strict and scrupulous prudence, which compresses the motions of grace, and disputes with the Holy Spirit the right of acting as He pleases in souls. In this, as in everything else, the medium is difficult to find, and he alone succeeds in doing so who, forgetful of himself, does not seek under the name of holy liberty for a dispensation from the great law of interior mortification. Mary Teresa never ceased recalling to her children the essential truths of revealed doctrine; it was on this solid foundation of faith that she wished to establish the edifice of perfection. A short time after writing the above letter to her children at Lyons, she was again in their midst preparing them for the renewal of their vows (April 1853). The following is what she wrote to her community at Paris, revealing to them the graces of that retreat. 'The truths of the faith, well established and grounded, can alone produce and maintain piety. Everything decays, fades away, deceives us, save God. His sovereign dominion over His creatures, happiness in Him alone, sin, the cause of every evil, inevitable death, perhaps near at hand, judgment, hell, the sufferings of Jesus Christ which we renew by our ingratitude, His sacrifice which repairs all—O, how speedily do these deep and severe meditations solve all difficulties! How easily do they destroy all illusions! Of what value are our little thoughts in presence of these sublime revelations which rule the entire Church, which make saints in every country, and which are *the great constitutions* to which every particular rule should be attached.' This is certainly a direction which the austere seventeenth century would not have disowned. Nevertheless the rigid and unloving character which French mysticism has preserved since that great epoch, or which it has only lost at intervals by losing at the same time its solidity, did not please Mary Teresa. At that time she had friends at Rome, one of whom expressed a wish for her institute to be established there. 'I do not know,' she answered, 'whether my Italian origin has preserved me from the *Jansenism*[*] of which you complain in our country, but I fear that I have not sufficient of *that method which makes saints in France*. I will tell you what I only say in the secret of direction. The congregation of the Reparation will only be exceptionally understood in this country, where the strangest liberty in matters of faith is disguised under the mantle of cold argument.' And again, 'I have felt that, like our Jesus, I must hide myself well beneath my veil in order to be *tolerated*, and that, in this country, the existence of every bold thought will only be pardoned if it adopts the usual form and the commonplace language which reassures them.' And finally, replying to entreaties from Rome, she continued, 'And I also ardently desire the happiness of seeing the Eucharistic work develop under that beautiful sky which I have all my life longed to contemplate. " Veder Roma, poi morire," has ever been the cry of my poor heart, which from my very youth has been imprisoned and restrained within the narrow circle which in France represses equally the feelings of a poor artist and those of a poor nun. Certainly, what formerly occupied the artist, she now rejects as childish. Uncreated beauty throws created

---

[*] Without accepting this qualification, of which the Italians are so prodigal, it cannot be denied that Jansenistical rigour has contributed to dry up French devotion. Relaxation, proceeding from weakness of faith, has done away with rigour, whilst tepidity still continues to exist: hence the infirmity of contemporary mysticism, which is now neither vigorous nor tender.

beauty into the shade; but the same want of largeness of spirit still urges the religious to seek a freer air, where she can breathe more at her ease.'

This spirit of liberty and submission is really no other than the spirit of the Gospel. Whilst Mary Teresa was trying to instil it into her children, she ceased not to direct their hopes to what seemed to her to be the perfection of her foundation—a congregation of priests consecrated to reparation. This foundation, which she never thought of attempting herself, occupied nevertheless, for several years, a large place in her thoughts, desires, and prayers; she spoke of it to many persons whose aspirations resembled her own: to Father Hermann, who had recently entered the Carmelite order after a most striking conversion; to the Founder of the Marists, who, until it existed, thought that he had done but half of his work; to Father Eymard, who, four years later, left his first coöperators in order to undertake it; finally, to that friend who had written to her from Rome, making overtures which proved fruitless. If we were only to seek in the life of Mary Teresa for actions accomplished and visible results, it would be superfluous to speak at length about what proved, as far as she was concerned, unreal dreams. But what we desire, above all other things, to study in the Saints is their spirit; and their spirit is discovered in their desires as much as in their works. It rarely happens that a Saint chosen to endow the Church with a new institution does not look beyond the field that he sows; God thereby maintains in him a zealous ardour, which he uses in working out what God has given him to accomplish; whilst others are sent later, with a fresh mission, to bring about the realisation of the hopes he had been obliged to hide in the secret of his own heart.

The close tie which connects the priesthood with the Eucharist was the deep theological reason which persuaded Mary Teresa that the congregation of the Reparation would never be completed by her; she used to say that the holy women had preceded the Apostles to our Saviour's sepulchre, but that Peter and John followed in their steps. If then a few poor girls had contributed to bring Jesus in the Eucharist from the obscurity of the Tabernacle, if they had been the first to form a guard of honour before the throne of His perpetual Exposition, should not the successors of the Apostles, those to whom the interests of the Eucharist are intrusted, should they not also take part in the joy of this Resurrection? 'The Divine Eucharist,' she wrote, 'has given me the grace of prayer for the *priests of the Blessed Sacrament;** for two years I have ardently longed for them. I have offered my sufferings, my sacrifices, all, that this great privilege which has been bestowed upon us may be placed in the hands of those who alone are worthy of this sublime vocation. I await the day of the manifestation of the Eucharistic glory; this glory poor women are not called upon to produce, but only to protect. Such an institution requires the sublimity of the sacerdotal ministry. True saints are needed in order to keep the Sacred Victim raised above the earth.'

When writing these words, Mary Teresa had reason to believe 'that the time of the Lord was come.' The following year she saw the foundation on which she had rested her hopes disappear, and she was obliged once more to confide to Providence the task of accomplishing this great work at the appointed time. But, notwithstanding difficulties and deceptions, she never lost the conviction that sooner or later the institute would be established. 'I suffer much,' she said, 'on account of the branch for men: I desire it; in all my prayers, I feel that God wishes it, that our congregation cannot be solidly established and developed without the apostles of the life of Jesus in the Blessed Sacrament. I am convinced that the apostles of the work will, by some divine sign, receive the necessary call to this sublime mission. As for me, I must humble myself and remain silent, not being worthy to kiss the dust from their feet.'

Whilst abandoning herself to these holy desires, Mary

---

* The congregation which bears this name was not founded at that time; but Mary Teresa gave the title beforehand to the institute she so ardently desired to see founded.

Teresa received a powerful encouragement. The existence of her foundation had been reported at Rome, and, in spite of the contrary efforts of persons whose interest it was to oppose it, the zeal of some pious persons, seconded by the recommendation of diocesan authority, had just obtained from the Holy See, in favour of the new institute, the first degree of approbation, styled a *Laudative Brief*. It is well known with what prudent slowness the Court of Rome proceeds in all cases submitted to her consideration. Long experience has shown that where it is a question of praise or blame, the encouragement or suppression of an enterprise, time is a necessary element in the consideration of the subject. It is only time, in fact, which can add the control of experience to the enthusiasm of some, the criticism and mistrust of others, in any new work. If there be question of a new form of religious life, for instance, the Congregation of Bishops and Regulars set on foot an inquiry into the aim, origin, spirit, and practices of the society. If the result of this inquiry prove favourable, the congregation obtains from the Sovereign Pontiff a brief, congratulating the authors of the enterprise, declaring their praiseworthy intentions conformable to the interests of the Church and the good of souls. This brief is not as yet an approbation, properly so called: the institute which has received it is not yet canonically instituted in the universal Church;* it still continues to depend in each diocese on the will of the ordinary. Usually a period of ten years must elapse before fresh steps can be taken to procure the *approbation*: even then that which is granted only regards the institute itself; and another delay of ten years must occur before one can obtain the approbation of the Constitutions.

The Institute of the Reparation had only reached the first step of this wisely-ordained gradation. The Foundress was destined to conduct her institute almost to the second degree; but, after dearly purchasing the joy of this hope, she was not permitted to live to see it. Her death preceded the desired approbation by three years.

* The approbation of a religious order is one of the cases reserved to the Holy See by the Fourth Lateran Council (1215).

Nevertheless this first benediction of St. Peter, this first tie which attached her infant family to the unity of which Rome is the centre, caused the profoundly Catholic soul of Mary Teresa to bound with happiness. A venerable prelate, who then exercised the functions of auditor of the Rota, and whose whole life was devoted to the glory of the Holy Eucharist,* brought her the *Laudative Brief* from Rome in the July of 1853. She immediately ordered prayers of thanksgiving in her two houses; and her gratitude found vent in touching letters, which show us what lively faith can do, the price it sets on every word issuing from the lips of the Vicar of Christ, and how, in regard to that supreme paternity, it excites the feelings of a truly filial heart.

In this life there is no rest, and this the souls devoted to God know well; when their designs receive from God that blessing which renders them fruitful, although their hearts may be consoled, their burden is increased. The time had come when the development of the congregation of Reparation rendered a separate establishment indispensable; the poor house which the hospitality of Carmel had for five years granted them was no longer able to contain the number of novices; the health of the sisters suffered from such close confinement, they not having even a garden in which to take the air. But the thought of incurring the chances of a removal, of assuming financial responsibilities, of being obliged to leave the quiet sanctuary to order and oversee the works, this thought alone made Mary Teresa shudder; and it was only her desire to raise a better throne for Jesus, to form for Him a larger court, and draw a greater number of adorers to Him, that enabled her to overcome the repugnance she felt to again taking part in exterior work. Moreover her health, which was gradually failing, rendered all active exertion exceedingly painful. Her voice often failed, obliging her to correspond in writing with those immediately around her. Great weakness often deprived her of the power of moving, whilst she at the same time suf-

---

* Mgr. de Ségur.

fered intense pain in every member. But these she would call her good moments; for she had no longer then to ask herself whether she were not bound to struggle and to act, since, at such times, exertion was impossible, and she had only to shut herself up in her cell and enjoy, in suffering, the happiness of being united to God. Notwithstanding her state of continual illness, she fulfilled with ardour the multiplied duties of her office, seizing every minute of respite which illness allowed her, exhausting her remaining strength, receiving visitors in her cell when no longer able to walk, writing when unable to speak, and, as soon as she could rise, spending her time in a manner that would have fatigued even the strongest person. The journey to Lyons, which, during the early days of her institute, she was obliged to undertake several times a year, added to her weariness. But the sufferings that preyed upon her body did not succeed in conquering her soul. She was of opinion that what gives pain does not injure, and that a Christian should not consider such trifles as subjects for sorrow. 'Poor children,' she wrote gaily to her community, 'I am grateful for your goodwill to cure me; but I warn you that you will not succeed; on the contrary, God wishes to destroy me gradually.' And again, 'Infirmity and weakness have fallen to my lot. God be praised! It is well that the poor tool should be sharpened and polished for the trial; it may then be good for something. At present it is impossible to form a good opinion of myself: I am nothing, absolutely nothing. No more a superior, no more a religious; a poor thing, scarcely able to say a *Pater*.' It was in these words that she spoke of herself in the beginning of the year 1854, after a crisis more than usually severe. We shall see by the use she made of this year the manner in which she struggled against her weakness.

For some time past she had received from several French towns petitions for fresh foundations. Urgent entreaties had come from Marseilles and Poitiers; but the prudent Superior thought with reason that, when the members of a community have not had time by a long fidelity to become penetrated with the spirit of their institute, a multiplicity of foundations, far from being advantageous, does but threaten the congregation itself with dissolution and ruin. Two houses founded within five years from the commencement seemed to her a sufficiently rapid progress. Besides, in a new congregation where could she find Superiors to direct new communities, or old professed sisters to teach them the traditions without which there can be no religious spirit? Nevertheless the offers were tempting ones; and more than once the idea presented itself to Mary Teresa's mind of simplifying matters by abandoning Paris in favour of one of these towns. As they were obliged to leave Carmel, to remove thither would not be more difficult than to go elsewhere, and the temporal prospect seemed more promising. It was difficult to decide. Whilst at Lyons an association had been spontaneously established to defray the expenses of the perpetual Exposition of the Blessed Sacrament, thus freeing the poor community of its heaviest responsibility. At Paris no such succour was granted. Parisian charity is generous; it is ardent and takes the initiative; but it prefers an accidental call to a perpetual one; that which makes a show to what is hidden; in a general way it shares the prejudice of the world against the contemplative orders: finally, it is hasty in judgment; and when it does not from the first seize the object of an institution or its distinguishing characteristic, it does not hesitate to decide that it is useless or unnecessary. Perhaps these are, after all, but pretexts to hide the embarrassment they feel when attempting to reconcile the ever-increasing demands of charity with the requirements of luxury and life in the great world—requirements which there less than elsewhere can be dispensed with, even in Christian families. Thus few places are less propitious to works of pure faith, which cannot be justified by any apparent result, which cannot bring into play the human merit of benevolence, and which, to be appreciated, must be viewed from a supernatural point of view alone. Thus a praiseworthy prudence seemed to urge Mary Teresa to seize the occasion which presented itself, and transport the Institute of Reparation far from its cradle, to a place where poverty would still continue to be the safeguard of fervour, but where they would not have continually to strive against material impossibilities, not less hurtful to the religious life than an excess of prosperity.

These considerations would have been decisive had the Foundress been able to lose sight of what she considered the aim of her institute. She ceased not to repeat to her children that if they simply wished to be religious they would do better to seek in more ancient and better-established orders the advantages of venerated rules, illustrated by the practice of saints, and consecrated by centuries; that, in order to remain her children, it was necessary to feel a special call to the life of Reparation. This conviction, which she endeavoured to instil into others, was with her the fruit of long and ripe reflection, which left no room for doubt; in it she had drawn strength to sacrifice to God the spiritual repose she had promised herself at Carmel, courage to encounter fatigue, dangers, deception, and all the innumerable trials awaiting her in the creation of a new institute. Now if her aim were reparation, where could it be better worked out than in a great city where sin abounded?

What city could stand more in need of protection from the arrows of divine justice than Paris? Where then could the audacity and gravity of crime call more loudly for expiation than in that immense town where the vices of all nations find a rendezvous? 'I should find no consolation,' wrote Mary Teresa, 'did I renounce the task of making atonement for Babylon.' This argument, based on her vocation, carried the day. She resolved to remain in Paris, accepting at the same time all the anguish of a situation in which even the necessaries of life were wanting. We might here apply to faith the words of a philosopher concerning the heart: *it has reasons which reason cannot understand.*

Towards the commencement of the year 1854 we find the Foundress resolute in her determination and actively employed in reducing it to action. After much search, she had fixed on the house destined to be the seat of the Institute for Reparation; this was the old Ursuline Convent in the street which still bears the name of those religious. Having for sixty years been used for private dwelling-houses, the old monastery preserved but few vestiges of its original destination; but this very circumstance appeared favourable; for, situated as they were, a purchase was impossible, and the total rental, which would amount to 380*l.*, was only practicable on condition of letting a great part of the rooms. Besides, by choosing their tenants, they might manage so as to attain one of the chief aims of the foundation, by grouping round the sanctuary of Reparation pious adorers, who, as secular sisters, as associates, or merely as persons making retreats, would insure to the community a peaceful and religious vicinity.

These considerations, highly approved of by the Superior, decided Mary Teresa's choice. At the last moment unforeseen difficulties arose, and, as if to try her fidelity, Providence at the same time directed their attention to another house, humanly speaking, far more advantageously situated; but if the interests of the community would be more benefited, those of the congregation, on the contrary, appeared sacrificed; it was to be feared that they would not possess the necessary independence, and that the situation of the house in a quarter removed from the centre of Paris threatened to discourage the zeal of the adorers. Encouraged by the counsels, full of faith, of the Abbé Gaume, Mary Teresa did not hesitate any longer to consider supernatural reasons before the counsels of prudence, and the lease, making over to her the Ursuline Convent, was signed on the 22d March 1854. This event was signalised by a remarkable coincidence. For obtaining the sum to be paid down on signing the contract, they had counted upon the generous offer of a secular sister; but at the very last moment she found herself unable to provide the full amount, and Mary Teresa would have been obliged to face the lawyers without being able to keep her word had not a private loan made by a person far from wealthy, and who did not know the house, solved the difficulty in a providential manner. Mary Teresa related to her community at Lyons the way in which she put her signature in the following terms: 'When in presence of the lawyer, I made the sign of the cross, saying interiorly to God and Mary, "It is for your Son that I am about to pledge myself." I then returned to the chapel to place this act at the feet of my Divine Spouse; my heart beat violently; then I suddenly felt a profound peace, and it appeared to me that the will of God had been accomplished. I am as happy and calm as if I were rich. The poor widow of Sarepta has filled her cruise to the full without having any oil!'

Great was the joy of the poor community of the Rue d'Enfer on learning that the Institute of the Reparation had now its own house; the Mother, as if to moderate the transports of her children, hastened to tell them that the promised happiness, which was still four months distant, would have to be purchased by much fatigue. This did but inflame their zeal, and she at once proved it by setting them to work to prepare the decorations for the future chapel. But before herself joining in the work she determined to prelude by a retreat and by prayer the exterior life she would soon be obliged to lead. Lent was at hand; she set out for her house at Lyons, where she could, in peaceful solitude, meditate on the Passion. Recollection, difficult to ordinary to souls, is the repose of the saints; the violence which others have to use to snatch themselves from external cares, souls united to God have to impose on themselves in order to interrupt their conversation with heaven; and when duty no longer keeps them back, they joyfully return to it of their own accord, attracted by that force which St. Augustine so justly styled *the weight of love: Amor meus pondus meum.*

On returning to Paris after Easter she urged on the labours of the new installation. Part of the house was to be transformed into a chapel and cloister; the rooms destined to receive lodgers had to be fitted up; and furniture and all the objects necessary for religious worship were to be found, for the furniture which the community had used until now belonged to the Carmelites. Whilst the workmen were busy in the new house, the one they were leaving had likewise become a workshop, where the sisters exercised their talents in painting, tapestry, and gilding, so that the decoration of the new sanctuary might cost as little as possible. 'Do not fear,' wrote Mary Teresa to her community at Lyons, 'that our prayers turn into quietism. We love God *in action*, with all our strength, and with more than our strength.' None had more right to say this than herself, for, after the painful infirmities which had for several months reduced her to a state of powerlessness, such activity seemed perfectly wonderful; it is true that she was one of those persons who work even when unable to do so. 'Though tottering,' she wrote, 'I still go about; as soon as I rise I lean against a wall, and whether well or ill, I give the orders of the *Master of the house*, at the same time praying hard that I may only do what He pleases. I cannot help thinking that Blessed Mary of the Incarnation, who built this monastery, is now superintending the workmen.'

But here again want of money placed her in a difficult and painful position. She had to write letters, beg unceasingly, ask of one a chalice, of another a monstrance, a clock—in fact, ornaments of every kind. To beg thus is a hard penance, bringing with it often more humiliations than alms, and fatiguing both soul and body more than the bodily effort. Mary Teresa, more than most people, was of a nature to feel it acutely; but the service of her Master was in question, and that rendered all things easy. 'I have resolved,' she wrote, 'to make every effort to prepare fittingly the poor Nazareth of the Reparation. I have put self on one side for good; of what consequence are trifling humiliations if they do but render greater glory to Jesus the Victim? Like a soldier who has served in a campaign, I begin to be braver.' Then, still seeking to sanctify even her smallest actions, she continued, 'These temporal affairs are well known to our Saviour. When staying with His poor creatures in His Sacrament, Jesus knew well that, as at Nazareth, He would hear petitions respecting houses and human necessities. He takes an interest in them as He formerly did in the duties of Mary and Joseph, who likewise lodged and fed Him.' Always attentive to preserve the interior spirit amid the inevitable confusion of the time, she did not content herself with elevating by these sublime thoughts the souls of her children, who were busy at work: she took care that prayer should not be neglected; the regular devotions continued calmly in the Rue d'Enfer; and the month of Mary was celebrated with particular devotion; every evening, when the work of the day was over, the sisters meditated together on the Litany of the Blessed Virgin, in which Mary Teresa found an inexhaustible fund of holy thoughts.

The building was actively carried on during the whole of the following month, and on the 2d July the community was at length installed in its new dwelling. It was the Feast of the Visitation, the day of the Magnificat; never had Mary's canticle been so heartily repeated. It was in the chapel in the Rue des Ursulines that the sisters of the Reparation began to sing Office in common, adding to each of the canonical hours praises and blessings addressed to the adorable Name of God. This touching custom has been preserved in the various houses of the institute, and consoles in a singular manner those Christian souls who witness this daily and nightly protest made by the spouses of Jesus Christ against the blasphemies by which His name is being continually outraged.

When taking possession of their new abode, Mary Teresa's greatest joy consisted in being able to reduce to practice every point of the rule and establish the traditions of her religious family. Although for several months they were obliged to put up with the inconvenience caused by the presence of the workmen and to devote themselves to the fatigues incumbent on a change of residence, yet she took care that the exercises of the community should not be neglected; and her children's fidelity corresponded so well with the pious requirements of their Mother that, when beholding the chapel filled with the perfume of prayer, it seemed, she said, as if the old Ursulines had never left the place. Sometimes, in the midst of a fervent prayer, raising her eyes and seeing that little sanctuary resplendent with lights—that throne where our Saviour was seated in his Eucharistic glory, that choir where consecrated souls perpetuated their adoration—she became dizzy, and thought that all before her must be a dream; she could not understand how it had been accomplished; and, notwithstanding the surprising reality, the part she had taken in it seemed to her the least real. Thus does God glorify the humble by working great things through their means; and whilst encouraging their belief in their own weakness by the difficulties and insufficiency of the means, He astonishes, by the importance of the results, those whom He has made use of to bring them about.

CHAPTER XII.

Vicissitudes of her interior life.—Journey to Rome.—Poetical and religious impressions.—Return to France.—The order for men appears on the point of being founded.—Spiritual relations of Mary Teresa with Mgr. Luquet and Brother Francis.

THE temporal and spiritual cares consequent on the recent removal to the house which was to serve as a model for others kept Mary Teresa fully occupied during the second half of the year. She had great difficulty in setting apart a few days in September to refresh herself by a retreat, and, again, a few days towards the end of November, to visit her sisters at Lyons, and determine for them, as she had done at Paris, all the little points of usage which the rule had left undecided. But she was of the number of those in whom exterior activity never suspends or dims the interior life. Amid the labours and temporal cares which we find described in her letters at that period, we can follow the continual progress of that soul whom nothing could turn from her mystical destiny. 'Next to the loss of God,' she said one day, 'the greatest misfortune is not to attain to that degree of love to which God has destined us.' This thought is a compendium of her whole life, which to the very last was but one long and indefatigable effort to attain that desired end.

Her confessor, F. Julliard, who directed her since Father Bertholon's departure, obliged her to give, in writing, an account of her impressions and her spiritual state. He was a pious and prudent man, and had not failed to recognise in his penitent an elect soul, whose ways of spiritual progress should be respected. He directed her for five years with great advantage, and became himself deeply penetrated with the spirit of the order of Reparation. It was in accordance with his command and insistance that the autobiographical sketch was written which has furnished us with materials for this work; we are likewise indebted to him for being able to read, as if in an open book, the history of Mary Teresa's interior life, thanks to the many written communications addressed to him. We are surprised, when we compare these writings with what was going on at the time, to read of such trials, such interior struggles, and ecstatic communications with God, hidden under the appearance of common everyday life, and united in the same person to the multiplied cares of what one would imagine to be absorbing occupations. Illness, it is true, came to her aid, giving her the right to retire to her cell when duty no longer called her elsewhere. But her love of simplicity, joined to her great energy, prevented her profiting by this relief as often as would have been advisable to spare herself those violent struggles which so greatly weakened her physical strength. No sooner was she able to rise than she disregarded her state of exhaustion and compelled herself to exertion; but often, even whilst occupied on business in the parlour, or applying herself for the good of the community to the direction of souls, she felt herself overwhelmed by the action of Divine Love, and, fearing to attract attention, she resisted it with all her might. But scarcely was she again alone when cruel sufferings and the sensible reproaches of her Divine Spouse caused her to expiate her resistance. One day, when gently complaining to Jesus Christ for having left her in a prolonged state of dejection and dryness, she heard this reply: 'For a long time you have withdrawn yourself from the action of My Grace, wishing to do that which I do not will; this is the source of your troubles and faults. You belong to Me: I wish to do with you what pleases Me, and you constantly baffle My designs. You belong to Me: when you feel My presence, know that I require you to return to your solitude. Your perfection is not what you deem it to be; it consists in passive submission to My dictates. You are deceived by a remnant of self-love; you desire to escape the humiliation of acting in an eccentric manner; but you will not be able to conquer Me. It is false humility which leads you to seek the ordinary path: your path is to be my plaything—without reasoning, without foresight, without human respect, without fear.'

The exact and severe direction which Mary Teresa had for a long time undergone had greatly strengthened within her the natural disposition which led her to misdoubt all outward appearances; a right disposition, but one which she carried to excess. One state demands one line of conduct; another, another. What was yesterday prudence, may to-day be a fault. Having reached a certain degree of union with God, the soul should rise above all things human, even no longer to fear to please Him; she should be as indifferent to the admiration of creatures as to their contempt. God alone has then the power to speak and act; but it must be really He who makes Himself heard, and not the perfidious echo of self-love. It is not for the soul of herself to bear witness that she no longer walks in the common path: until God draws her from it by the powerful action of His Grace, she does well to remain in it and to hide herself; and a direction which inspires her with a great repugnance to all that can attract the eyes of others, even when it sins through excess of rigour and mistrust, is still useful to a soul, and demands its gratitude. Mary Teresa was well aware of this when she declared that for many graces she was indebted to her former director, who had nevertheless so little understood her, and caused her so much suffering.

At the epoch we have reached, amidst the alternate sorrow and joy which chequer the course of the spiritual life, her soul was in an unceasing state of interior suffering, which sometimes admitted of, and sometimes excluded all, consolation. In every page of the narrative now before us we find the expression of this varied state of feeling; at one time her accents are sad, at another a joyous note may be distinguished; but in both phases we find ever two things: suffering and love. When God reveals to her her weakness, she is annihilated. 'Nothing is pure within me,' she exclaims; 'I am odious to myself; a stinking corpse, whence issue the exhalations of original sin.

I seem to have a horror of it, and yet not remorse: I have no hope, save in the mercy of purgatory. Formerly love seemed to me a purifying fire; but now I feel myself burning with a love as hard and dry as hell. I cannot flee from God; yet, in order to approach Him, fear and desire struggle so hard that no suffering can be compared to it.' But when God hides from her the sight of her own miseries, in order to reveal Himself to her, she again assumes tones of joyous happiness: 'I saw the God of love taking possession of a human heart and incorporating this atom into Himself. In an ecstasy of love I repeated these words of the Communion: " *Corpus Domini*"—the body of God. I feed on the body of God; and he who eats it shall live eternally with God; and God is Love. And I have long thought that it is a more impenetrable mystery to be able to love anything else than God, than to believe His presence in the Divine Sacrament.' Between the leapings of joy and the tremblings of anguish there is an intermediate stage in which love speaks alone, without feelings of either pain or pleasure: 'I am neither upon the earth nor in heaven just now; and I have reason to consider myself the most miserable of creatures, and yet the happiest: why happy? Can I be happy without the sentiment of love, since happiness consists in love? This is what makes one think that there is a love which does not realise what it feels, which is the action of God Himself: a happiness as mysterious and incomprehensible to the senses as the divine essence. This action strengthens and consoles, *but without visible means*. They who pass through this state of absolute annihilation can recognise it only by feeling that the First Cause could alone produce such effects.' Finally, there are times when Divine Union seems to have supplied natural life: 'God impresses on me I know not what feeling which gives me to understand, in one moment, what I am, not of myself, but in Him. In that moment I feel that I exist, but I feel none of the functions of natural life. I understand how the Omnipotent dispenses with all created means to communicate, when He pleases, to His creatures strength, love, and light. In these sublime moments the soul is invested with a power proportioned to the gifts which she receives; she is neither astonished nor alarmed, she is happy and great as on the day of her eternity. She also regards every event, whether good or evil, as of small importance; the will of God predominates; what He wills is easy, what He does not will is nothing. This prayer annihilates self (*le moi*) far more than suffering; it separates me from creatures more effectually than hatred could do, and it gives a charity that nothing can diminish. My God, to be united to Thee in this manner for the space of one hour, from time to time, I accept every possible suffering, if Thy Grace will but sustain my weakness.'

The Holy Spirit breathes where He wills. His operations are mysterious. He would indeed be rash who would wish to limit or regulate His action. In order to describe the states of which He is the author, we are obliged to make use of human language and the operations of the human mind, imagine divisions, ascribe, as far as one can, the supernatural impressions to the different faculties of the soul, to the various sentiments existing in the human heart; but this artificial arrangement is far from corresponding exactly to a reality which defies all description, and those who think they can discover in it either contradiction or confusion must lay the fault on the unavoidable imperfection of the formula. The essential point is, that the translation of these superhuman words should contain nothing which is not conformable to revealed truths; dogmatic theology cannot supply the place of mystical theology, but it has the right to control it. We have not to fear this control in the writings of Mary Teresa. Although little familiar with the science of dogma, she never departs from doctrinal exactitude; and in the same way, although a complete stranger, by education, to the study of mystical authors, she notwithstanding coincides with the best masters in a striking conformity of views and expression.

The fear of fatiguing our readers by repetition leads us to confine ourselves to the few extracts we have given to make known what was passing, at the time of which we speak, in a life so often marked by the sign of the cross. Like all who have received the grace of fecundity, she brought forth in pain, and that state of crucifixion was to last during the whole of her life. The more her institute increased and prospered under the hand of God, so much the more painful did her path become. She attributed this severity of the Divine Love to the bad dispositions of her own heart, crying out, 'It is not Thou, O my God, who causest me to suffer, but the opposition of my corrupt nature; if I were pure when Thou approachest me, I should enjoy the happiness of heaven; but, my flesh being guilty, Thy sanctity consumes it. I dread Thy visit as a wound dreads the caustic.'

And in the state of abjection into which the sight of her 'baseness,' as she termed it, cast her, she trembled when receiving the respect and submission of others. 'They must be blind,' she would say. 'Considering what takes place within me, the greatest act of self-abandonment is to remain Superioress.' But, whilst allowing that human infirmity might have had a share in bringing upon her the rigour of Divine Sanctity, we must seek another explanation of her sufferings, and we shall find it without difficulty in her vocation of Reparation. Called to point out to many souls that thorny path, she was destined to follow it first herself, and her progress in perfection was to mark a similar progress in her state of victim. We shall soon see a striking proof of this in the event which transformed the remainder of her existence into a true martyrdom.

Meanwhile, in spite of the state of debility in which she appeared to languish, she had not ceased, since the removal to their new convent, to bestow on her community all that anxious care which the spiritual and temporal welfare of the institute demanded. The year 1854 had drawn to a close, and nothing remarkable in the exterior history of her life occurred until the month of March in the following year. She then set out for Lyons; but this was but the first stage of a longer journey, the object of which was kept secret, but which was to conduct her to Rome.

Two years had not elapsed since the Holy Father had honoured the new congregation with a *Laudative Brief*, and eight more must pass before it could obtain the favour of the *Approbation*. This was not then the motive which determined Mary Teresa to brave the difficulties of a journey, at once expensive to her extreme poverty and painful to her body, which was worn out by infirmity. Her principal object, and one which she was obliged to keep secret, was the hope of obtaining from a person then resident at Rome an important temporal assistance. But many circumstances combined to render this journey necessary. The opposition which she had met with in Paris on the part of some of her former coöperators followed her even to Rome. It is not our intention to enter into the detail of the motives which actuated those persons, who were certainly pious and devoted to the Eucharist, but who jealously laboured to propagate views differing widely from those of the Foundress. There was already a question of founding another institute for Reparation, identical in aim, but differing in spirit and means.* This project, which was accomplished two years later, greatly troubled Mary Teresa; not, assuredly, because she was grieved to see a rival foundation, but because it appeared to her that, the aim being the same, a second creation following so closely upon the first had not a *raison d'être*, unless there were in the existing institute vices or deficiencies capable of depriving her of the confidence of her protectors. Now the interest of the authors of this new project, at the Court of Rome and elsewhere, might give to this unfounded supposition an appearance of truth. In such circumstances it was not useless to go to Rome and receive, in the blessing of the Holy Father, a fresh pledge of his benevolence.

The two communities of Paris and of Lyons knew nothing of this journey; but the letters which Mary Teresa wrote, when *en route*, to the Sisters Counsellors enable us to follow her step by step, and to read that soul so open to every noble impression. For the first time for many years she again found herself amid the beauties of nature; and the artist, who still lived beneath the saint, bounded at the sight with religious emotion. We

---

* The congregation of Marie Réparatrice was founded in 1857.

find her on the Rhone, on her way to Marseilles: 'I have meditated on and admired this grand river, which was carrying me away with such rapidity and energetic majesty. I thought that strong souls who know how to restrain their passions, as this bank restrains its strong current, must be pleasing to the Creator. who always assists those who struggle.' She thus salutes the sun of the south: 'How beautiful is the sun of my country! Yours at Paris is pale. When we shall arrive in our true country, the Eucharist Sun also will be eclipsed.' She is then afraid of scandalising her children by showing them that she has not lost the *sense of earthly admiration.* 'But no, my children, be not afraid: it is doubtless a sacrifice on this miserable earth no longer to see nature, the reflex of the Divine beauties; but my sacrifice was long since made. I can assure you of the truth of those Divine words, which promise a hundredfold to those who give up all for Him. Yesterday I was moved to tears by this thought of gratitude: God is admirable in His works; but His most wonderful work is to give to the soul, by means of contemplation and love, a joy a thousand times greater than could be caused by the entire creation.' At the period of which we write, the route from Marseilles to the East was intersected by numerous convoys carrying to our army under the walls of Sebastopol reinforcements and assistance of every kind. 'I have recovered my sensibility,' she writes, 'to compassionate our poor wounded men in the Crimea. Yesterday I said to myself, "If such were the will of God, I would willingly embark with the Sisters of Charity to assist them." Immediately recollecting myself, the Holy Spirit gave me to understand that a Sister of the Reparation should assist both camps; that the grace of Jesus the Victim was given to us for all the souls redeemed by His Blood.'

If the sight of the Rhone had enchanted her, how much more so the sea !—'the sublime spectacle of which,' she wrote, 'is well worthy of contemplation. Can one fail to discover God in this immense and majestic beauty?' Even the passage brought to her mind thoughts of her vocation. 'This voyage will be of great service to me by teaching me to conduct my vessel better.

How well on board ship one sees the necessity of perfect union between those whose duty it is to conduct it!' After the fine weather, however, a storm set in, and the poor traveller experienced all the miseries of sea-sickness. 'I cannot boast,' she said, ' of having entirely escaped human misery, but I often feel worse in my cell in the Rue des Ursulines, and every one congratulates me on my appearance. My poor fellow-voyagers are not all, like me, accustomed to guide a barque amid storms, and to conceal them from the passengers; moreover, they do not all possess that sublime consolation, the effect of the presence of God.' At length she reaches the shores of Italy, and, forgetting for a moment the inconveniences of the passage, she exclaims: ' This makes me think how soon we shall forget in heaven the miseries of earth' (' *le mal de terre*'). From Civita Vecchia to Rome the beauty of the scenery and of the climate gave her fresh strength. 'I ask myself,' she said, ' whether Italy is not resuscitating the old woman whom I have taken such pains to kill.' Her natural cheerfulness had not deserted her any more than her appreciation of the beautiful. ' At the gates of the Eternal City the passports are examined almost as carefully as at the entrance to eternal life. You know your old mother; in spite of herself she sees everything; I shall have many little anecdotes to relate to you, to enliven our recreations.' Scarcely had she arrived in Rome when a fortunate chance, taken advantage of by a devoted friend, procured her a close view of the Pope, who was making the stations at St. Peter's. Whilst the sublime grandeur of the edifice enchanted and bewildered her, the sight of the Vicar of Christ moved her inmost soul. 'Here,' she exclaims, ' we do not think of asking the reason why; we feel we touch the divinity of the Catholic Church. When the Pope, on his return, gave me his blessing, a thrill, such as would be caused by Jesus rendered visible, ran through my whole frame. My dear children, I cannot explain to you this grace; it is too great. But how also can I explain to you what St. Peter's is?' Then follows a description in which the artist gives way to enthusiasm; but the remembrance of the little sanctuary, in which her children pray and make reparation, is still the one on which her heart most dwells : ' Do not fear, my dear children ; I love Nazareth still better than St. Peter's.'

We cannot accompany Mary Teresa and her pious friend in all their pilgrimages, and the happiness caused by them. She had seized upon the good points in the Italian character; she was able to appreciate the charms of Rome, and to notice few or none of the real or apparent faults which diminish in the eyes of many the prestige of this incomparable city. If any one is of opinion that she showed bad taste in loving that simplicity of manners, that joyous eagerness in piety, that expansive good nature which, we must own, contrasts with our habits of reserve and discretion, we shall not attempt to prove the contrary. Tastes cannot be disputed; but at least all will acknowledge that it is a proof of greatness of mind to take into consideration, in the moral comparison of nations and individuals, the differences arising from temperament and customs, and to recognise the essential good qualities of each, even when the form in which they are invested is foreign to us.

Fifteen days sufficed for Mary Teresa to conclude in Rome the important business which was to insure to her community in Paris the possession of their new abode. After receiving the blessing and encouragement of the Holy Father, she at once set out for France. Staying but a short time at Lyons, she arrived in Paris about the beginning of May. Here an unexpected favour showed that God had blessed her journey. It will be remembered that in the commencement it had been resolved to make her institute the centre of the Diocesan Confraternity of the Perpetual Adoration, and the common focus of all great Eucharistic devotions. The defection of her first coöperators had ruined these fine prospects. In order to save something from the shipwreck, Mary Teresa had wished at least to obtain for the Superior of her house in Paris the same privileges and rights that had been granted to the Director of the Diocesan Confraternity. The Holy Father, prejudiced against granting this favour by persons whose interest it was to prevent it, had refused it somewhat energetically. The Superior, who had not counted upon a refusal, had promised the Associates of the Reparation that, at their reunion in the month of May, he would give them the Blessing of the Scapular, and bestow upon them other spiritual favours. Great was his disappointment, therefore, when Mary Teresa returned from Rome empty handed. The day for the reunion arrived: the associates had brought their scapulars, Mass commenced, and Mary Teresa was thinking with sorrow on the disappointment awaiting those good souls, and the discouragement which might ensue; for was not the refusal of such common favours equivalent to an expression of distrust and disapproval of the institute itself? Mass was nearly over when the Superioress was called away to receive a large stamped packet from Rome, which she found contained a grant in perpetuity of all the powers, graces, and indulgences demanded, accompanied with warm praises of the institute and the Apostolical Benediction. At the same time a letter from her pious friend informed her how the change had been brought about. No fresh steps had been taken; but the Holy Father, who does not usually attend to such business in person, had seen reason to change his views, and had consequently written to this lady, sending her back the petition, to which he had caused to be affixed the desired rescript. Invested at the last moment with the necessary powers, the Superior at once profited by them, whilst Mary Teresa blessed in the secret of her heart that paternal Providence which, by an interior inspiration in the heart of the Holy Father, had brought about the accomplishment of her pious desires.

Immediately on her return to the cradle of her institute, Mary Teresa applied herself more ardently than ever to the interior formation of her children. God, who intended soon to visit her by a terrible trial, and to accomplish, by material fire, the purification of her soul, allowed her six months more of an activity which, although far from being exempt from suffering and weakness, nevertheless did not deprive her of the power of following the inspirations of her maternal heart. Whilst her letters describe the humiliating state of weakness to which the

Lord, she said, had reduced her in punishment of her sins; whilst she wonders how they could bear with a worn-out Superioress, utterly incapable of doing anything when her body was not at rest; whilst she was making every effort to accept gently this condemnation to inertia, uselessness, and perpetual somnolence,—we find her displaying a wonderful activity, of which her correspondence affords ample proof. She was not satisfied with keeping up with that one of her two communities from which she was absent a regular succession of letters, conferences, and instructions; with giving special directions to the sisters counsellors and those in office; with writing down, in accordance with the command of her confessor, the thoughts produced by her meditations and retreats; with providing, by means of a few devoted friends of her institute, for continual and pressing necessities. No; this invalid, 'who was good for nothing,' as she said, still found time to follow and direct, from day to day, the progress and aspirations of two souls in whom she thought she perceived the requirements for the foundation of the order of men. These two persons attracted her attention in very different ways, and each required a different treatment. One was a Bishop,[*] who, already advanced in age, wished to renounce his exterior dignity and brilliant career, in order to devote his life to contemplation in a humble and hidden ministry. He had met Mary Teresa in Rome, and shortly after followed her to France; he acknowledged the ascendancy of her mind and exalted piety; and it was at the foot of the altar, prepared by her hands, that he resolved to seek the satisfaction of his holy desires. The Foundress was filled with gratitude, and deeply touched by the humility of the holy prelate; her lively faith took pleasure in giving to the episcopal character the veneration and deference due to it. At the same time she too well knew that the Holy Spirit breathes where He wills, to refuse to the soul of this priest the succour

---

[*] Mgr. Luquet, Bishop *in partibus* of Hesebon, who, after fulfilling a diplomatic mission in the name of the Holy See, had retired to Rome, where he met Mary Teresa at the house of a pious French family with whom he resided.

that he demanded of her. Her letters to him, true models of Christian simplicity, breathed both confidence and respect: the authority of a firm and sure doctrine, joined to the holy embarrassment of humility. The other person was a young man,[*] who had not yet left the world, but who already despised and fled from it. His soul was ardent, impetuous, extreme in its impulses; as austere as it was loving; and, even from his youth, he was captivated by whatever was most penitential and most tender in devotion: in fact, one of those souls who were formerly admired, but are now feared; and who would seem to be voluntarily misplaced in a century and country like our own, did we not know that God, who cares not to please men, reserves to Himself messengers to display, in their own persons, in all places and in all ages, the marvellous folly of the Cross.

Providence caused this young man to be introduced to Mary Teresa shortly before her journey to Rome; one meeting decided the union of these two souls. From the first moment the disciple penetrated into the furthest corner of the Mother's heart; and the Mother, without knowing it, became the sovereign arbiter of the destiny of the disciple. No sooner had Mary Teresa's words enlightened his path than he saw his life clearly traced out before him. He would be a priest, a religious, nay, even a saint; he would live and die in the service of the Eucharistic work. He was now no longer the son of a noble family, on whom all the affections and seductions of the world smiled, but simply poor *Brother Francis*, seeking, under that humble name, shelter from the eyes of all men. Although still wearing the secular dress, he was already seeking humiliations and contempt, taking pleasure in appearing at a family reunion in worn-out shoes, or hiding beneath an awkward and heavy exterior the natural vivacity of his character and the brilliancy of his mind. But it may be objected that this is not virtue. Perhaps not; but virtue and the germs of sanctity are hidden beneath; it is the wild, generous, over-exuberant vegetation

---

[*] Abbé Octave de Villequier, afterwards chaplain of the convent in Paris. He died in 1865.

which denotes the richness of the sap, and, whilst requiring the pruning-knife, promises an abundance of fruit.

Brother Francis followed Mary Teresa to Rome, and it was there, at the house of his sister, Mme. de L—, that Mary Teresa met Mgr. Luquet. Thus this fortunate journey loaded the Foundress with blessings; the union of two holy souls to hers would alone have sufficed to render it for ever precious in her eyes. The world judges severely of the friendship of saints. Accustomed to waste in frivolity or to profane in vice the purest treasures of the heart, it willingly suspects the holy liberty which unites so closely the souls whom God fills with a like zeal for His service. The best Christians but too often share in this narrow and jealous disposition, which leads them to judge the servants of God harshly and with unjust and uncharitable severity, and which, on the pretext of acting as a safeguard to the honour of piety and the purity of the priesthood, would go so far as to deny the existence of supernatural affections, did not the teaching of our Saviour and the example of the Saints give the lie to this disparaging and narrow-minded theory.

Observing scrupulously that sense of propriety which is the jealous guard of virtue and the extreme delicacy which preserves it, Mary Teresa had nevertheless a horror of that Jansenistical stiffness which dries up the sources of the heart; and, like all truly mortified souls, she found in the hatred of self the secret of loving with simplicity and devoting herself generously.

Whilst Mgr. Luquet held at Paris the rank of humble chaplain to the community in the Rue des Ursulines, Brother Francis commenced his ecclesiastical novitiate at the country house of the Marists at Lyons. At the same time Father Julliard, whom the Father-General had given over to the Institute of Reparation, devoted himself to it in concert with the Foundress; he was her confessor during three years, and greatly benefited her in her personal direction. But in all that concerned the institute, their parts seemed to be reversed; the direction appeared rather to come from the penitent, and docility was not wanting on the part of the priest: a touching exchange of submission and confidence which can only be explained by the deep feeling on both sides of the rights of God. The Holy Spirit chooses what organs He pleases, but it is always He who makes Himself heard.

A few extracts will, far better than any words of ours, give an idea of the manner in which Mary Teresa understood her direction of such different persons. But first let us ask why, instead of confining herself to the interior government of her two houses, does she so earnestly desire the formation of a community of priests of Reparation? The reason is that the priests may in their turn form the daughters of the order. The supernatural life can neither continue nor increase if not rendered fruitful by sacerdotal grace; and if there be a question of a separate vocation directing towards a determined goal the efforts of sanctification, priests are required who are imbued with the very same spirit that they are to communicate to the souls intrusted to their care. Although both Foundress and Mother, Mary Teresa yet felt that she was not everything to her children, and that what was wanting could not be completely supplied by priests ignorant of their *Réparatrice* consecration. 'O my dear son,' she wrote to Brother Francis, 'my heart tells me that your vocation is necessary, for my children have no fathers to conduct them to the mountain of sacrifice! We have sheep in the flock languishing in the midst of pastures for want of a shepherd. And let it not be said, " They have their Superioress." Superioress though I may be, I shall yet never touch the sacred Host. My children's souls have received a sacred character which requires a priest to develop its life. Again, who will understand my sorrow when I see these dear souls in pure hands, doubtless, but under the care of those who, misunderstanding the treasure God has confided to them, seek to utilise it by natural* means or in too human a manner? These souls feel that there is something wanting. In their trouble they eagerly turn to the maternal bosom; but as the time for weaning has come, milk fails them, and a more strengthening food is required—a food which receives life from

---

* Allusion is here made to several priests and religious who wished the Foundress to take charge of the education of young girls, in order to obtain for her institute sympathy and resources.

the sacramental words alone. Brother, join me in saying to our Lord, *They have no wine.*'

Thus enlightened from his first steps in the sanctuary respecting the course he was to follow, the future priest of the Reparation did not hesitate as to the means. He was destined one day to be, according to the energetic expression of Mary Teresa, *the sacrificer for the souls of the Réparatrice;* he was to do with them as the priest does with the *Host—offer* them, *break* them, and *bless* them. But it was first of all necessary that he should sacrifice himself. Of this Mary Teresa reminded him with much earnestness. On a note relating to some material matter we find these few words written hastily: 'None can serve two masters. Be the grain of wheat; remain alone, rot in the earth, for so it must be; from you will arise the Eucharistic institute.' But if this doctrine of interior mortification seemed severe on the mother's lips, she knew likewise how to be mild, and to moderate by gentle lessons the rude energy of the disciple. Nazareth was the model that she unceasingly placed before his eyes; Nazareth, the abridgment of the simplest, most sublime, and communicable perfection. 'In my stupid dejection,' she exclaims, 'I still cannot help admiring and adoring that divine life of Nazareth, pure without contention, without stiffness of heart; calm and recollected, without however depriving poor humanity of the support that its weakness requires; separated from creatures by the dignity of a real union with God, without allowing the barrier to be an obstacle to the approach of one's poor neighbour.' On this point she was inflexible. Nazareth was the mirror into which she continually looked, and showed to her children as the ideal of the Institute of Reparation. 'When I meditate upon Nazareth, my feelings are similar to those I experience when in presence of the Blessed Sacrament: in it there is silence, solitude, purity, light. It resembles a new terrestrial paradise containing two creatures, and the living God intimately united to them both. Such was Nazareth, and such also should be our communities. Nothing austere outwardly; the divine Son, exposed in the sanctuary, should reflect His light and beatitude on the temporal and spiritual poverty of the *Marys* and *Josephs* who adore Him. The Gospel does not desire the friend of the Bridegroom to become sad on the approach of the Bride. I see peace and joy reigning at Nazareth. They who approach are penetrated with celestial sweetness; yet what is it they see? Poverty, silence, separation from the world, the subjugation of the passions. After having been persuaded to draw near, many will retreat; for the language of Nazareth is as hard to the senses as that of the Eucharist; the life of Nazareth is an apprenticeship to the life of a victim.' It was love and imitation of Nazareth that had led her from the beginning to dispense with lay-sisters, and to render all her children equal according to the holy law of labour. On seeing the time for the Foundation for men drawing near, she did not wish them to be an exception to this law; the Priests of the Blessed Sacrament were to serve themselves and labour with their own hands; and if they had amongst them lay-brothers, the dignity of the priesthood would be their only preëminence, without that dignity insuring either exemption from labour or other privilege. This idea, which had never undergone the control of experience, may be regarded in various lights; but in Mary Teresa's mind it formed part of the substance of her mission; and as her disciple shared on this point the firmness of her conviction, she congratulated him as if on a celestial inspiration: 'O, Brother Francis, it is neither flesh nor blood that has taught you the excellence of evangelical equality in communities, but the goodness of your Father who is in heaven.'

But the life of faith is what is especially learnt at the school of Nazareth. In like manner Mary Teresa regarded pure faith as greater than any other grace; she attributed to her great imperfection the sensible and wonderful favours with which her first steps in the spiritual life had been strewn. 'Brother,' she wrote, 'how necessary it is that this institute should be based only on motives and means of faith! I was thinking to-day how miserable I must be to require that our Lord should give me the wounds of His Members and of His Heart to touch. Blessed are they who believe, and yet have not seen. I should be grieved were this, or anything of the kind, to serve as a support to our dear institute, whose existence is justified both by the Gospel and in the Commandments. The wonders which we need to prove the divinity of the foundation are those foretold by St. John the Baptist: "The blind shall see, the deaf hear, the mountains shall be brought low," &c. "It is by becoming upright and humble, seeing all things by faith, and listening to the Divine voice in prayer, that we shall establish the Eucharistic work with the practical form of Nazareth."'

The soul that Mary Teresa fed with this strong doctrine was one of those that require moderating: she did this with a wisdom full of firmness, though with great respect for his supernatural yearnings. Worldly prudence is quick in condemning, making no distinction between the really blamable excesses of an indiscreet zeal and the holy and legitimate rigour of penance. Christian prudence fears above all things to act in opposition to God and contrary to His inspirations: 'God forbid, my dear son, that I should draw you from the narrow path. A cloud of sadness overspread my soul on thinking that I might diminish within you, ever so little, the action of divine grace.' After this preamble, full of delicacy, she reminded him of the obligation of not depriving his body of what was *necessary.* 'I do not know,' she added, 'why I repeat this, since I have already said it, and you have answered, "Yes." The reason is that I know that the Holy Spirit tends to *destroy,* and in this He often appears as if opposed to Himself; for He wishes also to *produce;* and our poor judgment cannot always preserve the medium between these two tendencies. Hence proceed the two excesses which prevent God from carrying out His undertakings. The Holy Family of Nazareth found means to keep mortification and zeal in perfect harmony.' She ended this remarkable letter by relating a dream. 'God showed me two palm-trees; from one there came a dove, which, perching itself on my hand, roused my courage, and then flew away to heaven: "*Sister Veronica, pray for me.*" A second dove, similar to the first, descended from the second palm-tree. She nestled with me in her turn, but she did not fly away, at least not before I awoke in the land of the living. "*Brother Francis, labour and help me!*"[*]

Whilst she thus directed the young ecclesiastic, she was careful not to encourage him to withdraw from the obedience of his confessor; she even taught him how to draw profit for his vocation from what seemed to oppose it. 'I will not ask whether your director has a regular or secular vocation; that is of little consequence. God gives him to you for the time being: be therefore subject to him. Jesus was obedient even unto death; and it was the Pharisees who, taking advantage of His obedience, made Him accomplish His mission. *Saint Joseph would not have crucified Him.* . . . We should always mistrust the lights we receive concerning our own conduct. I would rather be directed by a seminarist than direct myself in my own path. And you also will know that the devil is laying a snare for you if you think that, even before the accomplishment of the great act, you will be able to dispense with a priest.' The wisdom of these counsels will be appreciated by those who know what a great temptation it is for generous souls, engrossed by a special call or vocation, to do without direction, when those who give it appear confined within common bounds, either from want of light or from system. Mary Teresa knew from experience the sadness caused in the soul by this obedience, being as it were reduced to choose between God and His representative; but she likewise knew that Providence hides in the mystery of this contradiction precious seeds of sanctification, which do not fail to spring up at the right time, when all has been sacrificed to obedience. She feared not to give herself as an example of this to her disciple. Respecting the new future, which seemed about to open for her institute in the foundation of the order of men, she also foresaw the opposition of those who directed her. 'They will be astonished,' she writes; 'they will prove this spirit; but I do not feel anxious; I shall be submissive. I have learnt that the will of God must be humbled by the will of man before it can

[*] Sister Veronica was, in fact, already dead, and Abbé Villequier outlived Mary Teresa by two years.

reign all-powerful in my poor soul; otherwise I should not be able to distinguish it from my own thoughts, which are naturally ardent.' Remarkable words, which, in our opinion, solve more than one of the difficulties in the lives of the Saints.

Whilst carefully guarding her dear son against the illusions of piety, she also knew how to encourage him in the right path and applaud his generous impulses. 'I have entered with joy,' she writes to him, 'into that abyss of graces which urge you on to your end; I have felt as grateful for these mercies as if they had been bestowed upon my own self. Sacrificed as I am to the work of love, what is given to the elect of the Blessed Sacrament is in my eyes more precious than what comes directly to myself. Be faithful, my very dear brother; penetrate thoroughly that rare and sublime light which has revealed to your soul the beauties of the annihilated and hidden life.'

It was with such prudence and firmness, such tenderness of heart and ardent zeal, that Mary Teresa applied herself to the formation of her chosen disciple. 'I bless you with joy,' she said to him, 'in the expectation that you will one day bless me.' Soon other young men presented themselves to Mgr. Luquet, to begin with him what Mary Teresa called the little *Nazareth of the men.* This was in the month of August 1855. The Foundress had just gone on a visit to Lyons; and Brother Francis, who certainly did not find what he wanted in the congregation of the Marists, had repaired to Paris and joined himself to the infant community, which comprised Mgr. Luquet, Father Julliard, and two young laymen. The venerable prelate joyfully set to work to perform the humble functions of master of novices, and for the smallest details had recourse to the inspiration of the Mother. This latter corresponded with simplicity to this confidence by revealing to him from day to day her views respecting the formation of her new family. God, who alone plants and plucks up, builds and overthrows, did not intend that her loving care should bring about the result which Mary Teresa so ardently desired. Her community of women had arisen, increased, and prospered at a time when all human means seemed wanting, and when she herself felt inclined to relinquish all idea of a foundation; and now that a powerful inspiration urged her to complete her work, when everything seemed prepared for its accomplishment, Providence did not allow her to make a durable foundation. The disciples on whom she relied were united but for a short time and they then separated, leaving to others, at a time which God only knows, but which has not yet arrived, the accomplishment of the most cherished designs of the Foundress.

The great fire which occurred towards the end of the year, and reduced Mary Teresa to long months of the most complete helplessness, was the exterior signal for this dispersion. In the commencement of the following year Mgr. Luquet returned to Rome, to the house of Mme. de L—, where Mary Teresa had first met him. Father Julliard, after great interior trials and an absence of a few months, returned to Paris, where, as a simple member of the Society of Mary, he continued his ministry as confessor and chaplain to the order of Reparation. The two young laymen followed another course. Brother Francis alone remained faithful to the Foundress' idea, and, in hopes of one day accomplishing it, he continued his ecclesiastical studies. He completed them at the French seminary at Rome, where the remembrance of his heroic virtues is still preserved. No sooner was he ordained priest than he returned without delay to place himself at the disposal of Mary Teresa. After serving in turn the two communities of Paris and Chalons, he was appointed chaplain to the house in Paris, where he remained until his death. He gathered together many of the town children, whose laborious and poor life he shared, and whom he endeavoured to form early to a vigorous piety, hoping to begin with them the nucleus of the work which was to give brothers and fathers to the Institute of the Reparation. Death overtook him in his task, showing once more that God's time had not yet come for this foundation.

Mary Teresa had promptly understood and willingly accepted the bitter disappointment of her dearest wishes. As early as 1856 she wrote to Mgr. Luquet: 'St. Ignatius has taught us that we must not spend more than a quarter of an hour in making the sacrifice even of an accomplished work.' At that time Father Eymard was on the point of leaving the Marists, in order to found the Society of Priests of the Blessed Sacrament. Whilst admiring the sanctity of this great servant of God, Mary Teresa might herself have had reason to regret, '*during a quarter of an hour*,' the so-much-desired union of the two congregations. But when the quarter of an hour had passed she acknowledged that all was well as it was, and that she must learn to wait. Brother Francis, it is true, remained to bear witness to her primitive idea; but she said of him, with great truth, 'The courageous Brother Francis appears to me to be more a *precursor* than a *founder*.' He had, in fact, something in common with St. John the Baptist: his virtue, though subdued and softened by grace, was severe, and he seemed destined by God rather to bear the standard than to sow the seed. His life was a model, his death a martyrdom. One day, we are convinced, his memory will be revived with his spirit in the midst of those whom God will raise up to accomplish that which he conceived, and was not allowed to carry out.

Meanwhile, and before bidding adieu to these names, so closely allied to that of Mary Teresa, it will be interesting to glance at the destinies of these three persons whom God had united in the love of the Eucharist. All three bore, during life and in death, the seal of the Reparation. Mgr. Luquet retired to Rome, to the house of Brother Francis's sister, and he lived there until the death of that virtuous lady; then, alone in the world and without resources (for he had given away all that he possessed), he obtained a cell in the French seminary, and there, clothed in an old black cassock, beneath which he hid his pectoral cross, he lived in poverty, sweeping his room, serving himself and giving himself up, in an absolute retreat, to the exercises of the contemplative life. In a short time he was seized with cancer on the lip, which led him to the grave, after an interval of eighteen months of the most acute and humiliating suffering. When death was near at hand the Pope sent to ask concerning his health, and to announce his visit. The humble prelate wrote to the Holy

Father, begging him to send him his blessing by another, not wishing for an honour which would have called attention to the last days of a life devoted to obscurity.

Mother Mary Teresa, half consumed by the flames, only survived the fire which had devoured her for eight years, that her martyrdom might be prolonged.

Brother Francis, who followed her to the grave two years later, died, in the flower of his age, of a strange malady which had suddenly overthrown his strong constitution, and left his body one whole wound. The disease began by a softening of the vertebral column in consequence of the loosening of the vertebræ whilst playing with his pupils. One of his friends, who had not seen him for a long time, one day entering his room, found him sitting in a straw chair, his body almost bent in two, whilst he was singing gaily the Italian hymn, *Evviva Maria*. 'What is the matter with you?' he asked. 'My dear friend,' replied Brother Francis, smiling, 'I have a spinal complaint.' 'But you should be in bed.' 'But I cannot rise; I have remained in this chair several days.' It was with difficulty that he could be persuaded to go to bed. The disease continued to increase: after the bones, it attacked the muscles; the skin of the back fell off in pieces; the legs were as if dead; the upper part of the body alone lived, and lived to suffer indescribable agony. Calm and smiling, the intrepid penitent never complained, save of the relief he was compelled to take. He had been removed to a spring bed. 'Formerly,' he said, 'it was customary to die on ashes; now one is made to die on a luxurious couch.' His friends had sent him some beautiful fruit; he distributed it himself to his little children, refusing to make any change in his eremetical diet, which he had observed for so many years. For a long time he had lived on cauliflowers, boiled with water without salt. 'Do you wish,' he would say, 'that, after labouring to mortify myself during ten years, I should give over at the last?' But when the doctor ordered him to take other nourishment, he did so, preferring obedience to sacrifice. At length Holy Week brought release. He had hoped to die at three o'clock on Good Friday; but at night he was still alive. 'Ah,' he said, on seeing the doctor, 'it is my confessor of whom I stand in need.' 'And why? are you not ready to die?' 'Because, when three o'clock struck, finding that I was still alive, I felt a movement of impatience.' He died on Holy Saturday, and we do not think that we presume too much on the goodness of God when we express our belief that he went straight to sing the *Alleluia* in heaven.

Who can fail to recognise in these three souls a common destiny, and a kind of relationship in immolation?

CHAPTER XIII.
1855-1859.

Fire in the chapel at Paris.—Mary Teresa is saved from the flames, half-burnt.—Her faith and energy amid sufferings.—She gradually withdraws from the government of her houses.—Her dealings with Cardinal Morlot.—Her abdication.—She causes another Superior-general to be elected.

WE left Mary Teresa at Lyons, whither she had gone to provide for the wants of her community. It required all her energy to undertake this journey, in the state of physical and moral weakness to which she was now reduced. We have seen how, not content with fulfilling the object of her journey, she provided from a distance, by an almost-daily correspondence, for the spiritual necessities of her daughters at Paris and of the brothers whom she hoped to give them. To infirmities of body and the fatigue caused by excessive labour were added trials of the soul. In this state of universal crucifixion she felt what all the great servants of God have experienced, that thirst for suffering which is excited by suffering; and before a crucifix* she made the offering of all her senses to God, accepting every suffering in reparation for sin. The offerings of the saints are not mere words; therefore God accepts them.

On her return to Paris, in September 1855, Mary Teresa had recommenced her ordinary occupations, though often interrupted by illness. During the Octave of the feast of All Saints she was obliged to keep her bed, and felt more than ever urged to ask for the cross. 'I ask our Lord,' she said, 'to send me some great suffering. I shall feel rebellious, but no matter;

---

* This ivory crucifix, the gift of Father Colin, the founder of the Marists, is preserved at the house in Paris, in the convent sacristy.

do not listen to my murmurs, and be assured that at heart I am resigned to Thee.'

In the evening of the 8th November she was not present either at supper or at recreation. One of the sisters went to find her in her cell. She found her sitting down and in tears. On being pressed to explain the cause of her suffering, she answered, 'My child, God is about to visit us: let us accept the trial; it will be great, but it will purify us.' Then, after a moment's pause, she resumed, 'Poor children! God knows very well that I would suffer still more for your souls.' And she added a few words concerning those who were the least faithful to their vocation. She then consented to join the recreation: on her entrance the sisters remarked on her face an expression of great sadness. Instead of enlivening them, as she was accustomed to do, by her cheerful conversation, she spoke to them seriously, telling them that she had begged God to lead them to perfection, at the price of many sufferings. 'Yes,' she added, 'were I to be burnt like straw, still I would accept any sufferings for my children.' Then, as if she wished by their own testimony to point out the two victims He had chosen, one of the sisters, the very one who was most seriously injured by the fire, knelt down beside Mary Teresa, saying to her, 'Mother, I do not want to have any purgatory; I wish to suffer here, to suffer a great deal, but no purgatory.'

After Benediction, Mary Teresa retired to her cell, and lay down on her bed without undressing. She was calm, although still sad and thoughtful. Meanwhile the sacristan was in the chapel, arranging the lights for the night adoration, when, unknown to her, the drapery caught fire, and in an instant the *reposoir* was in flames. The poor sister endeavoured to rescue the Monstrance, but failed, and fell down; although much burnt, she succeeded in leaving the chapel and calling for assistance. There were two sisters in adoration at the *prie-Dieu*: one remained, whilst the other ran to call Mary Teresa. 'Do not be troubled,' replied the Mother; 'be calm, firm, and courageous; the hour of sacrifice has come.' This sister then hastened to call Mgr. Luquet and Father Julliard. Whilst the community assembled in the court, and preparations were being made to give assistance at the entrance, Mary Teresa rose and entered the burning chapel, unperceived, through the sanctuary. She saw plainly that to approach the altar would be to endanger her life, but she could not consent to see the Sacred Species consumed without attempting to save it, no matter at what risk. Whilst trying to reach the altar her face and hands were dreadfully burnt. All her efforts were useless. Then only did she desist, and sought to escape; but she was already enveloped in flames and smoke, so that there was no opening left. 'I thought,' she said later, 'that all was over with me: I made my way to the confessional, and knelt down there, so that I might at least have the consolation of dying in the tribunal of mercy.' Suffocation obtained the mastery, and she lost consciousness.

In the mean time the sister who had remained in adoration at the *prie-Dieu* found herself, in her turn, surrounded by flames. She afterwards related that she had quietly knelt down, saying, '*Well, if I am to be roasted, let it be so.*' But suddenly, seeing a means of escape, she added, '*Here is a door: since I can get out, I will do so.*' Thus no one was absent when the names were called, no one except the poor Mother. No one knew what had become of her. The anguish of her children was frightful: one of them recollected having seen her pass as if on the way to the sanctuary. But, until the pumps had quenched the heat of the fire, it was useless to think of attempting to enter the chapel. They had good reason to fear that their beloved Mother would be found dead; a fireman, who had succeeded in exploring the sanctuary, had seen nothing of her. At length they were able to enter the lower end of the chapel, where they found Mary Teresa, terribly burnt and motionless. Whilst they were bearing her away she sighed; this was a ray of hope she was not then dead. A physician, who was passing, was called in; after the lapse of three-quarters of an hour he succeeded in restoring the suspended animation, and life returned with feeling; but the swelling increased, and the wounds were dreadful. The sufferer only uttered a few unconnected words; they were words of confidence and abandonment to the will of God, mingled with grief at the thought of the Blessed Sacrament having become the prey of the flames.

The Monstrance was, in fact, melted; and the Holy Host, reduced to cinders, still preserved its form within the crystal. A few days later Mgr. Luquet deposited it in a sealed reliquary, which is still kept in the chapter-room of the Mother House. This good prelate likewise took from the tabernacle the ciborium, which remained intact, and placed it in a room between two lighted tapers; in this manner the adoration was continued during the night. The following morning an oratory was prepared, and the community assisted at the holy sacrifice before the ciborium which had been saved from the flames.

The little sister who had so cheerfully accepted her part of roasting had also received serious burns, which threatened to endanger her life; she was delighted at the thought of dying of burns occasioned by having remained too long in adoration before the Blessed Sacrament; but God willed that she should recover. As to Mary Teresa, that she continued to live at all seemed a miracle; she lived to suffer, and not to be cured. She now saw fully accomplished that wish which she had formed a few days before the accident when writing to her children at Lyons. 'Ask our good God to give your Mother a more *determined* illness, so that she may be able to surrender her trust to another; for now she does nothing well, neither her duties nor her purgatory.' In fact, this terrible event forcibly made known to her children the heavy responsibility which their Mother had until now borne alone with a courage far beyond her strength. From her bed of suffering, which she now left but rarely, and never without heroic efforts, Mary Teresa assisted, as from a half-opened tomb, at the continuance of her work. Nevertheless, with the indomitable energy of her nature, she quickly recovered, amid cruel tortures, the presence of mind requisite to preside, at least from her bed, over the government of her two houses. Nine days had not elapsed since the fire when we find her dictating a letter to her community at Lyons, in which she appears more than ever forgetful of herself, and wholly rapt in God. 'O yes, we have been placed in the crucible, but God has made Himself manifest in an impenetrable manner, and He is specially blessing the institute;* I feel that He is likewise helping my poor soul : mingled with the fire and suffering, faith and life are strong within me. God bless you, my very dear children ! Continue to preserve the trust confided to us ; neither fire nor robbers can take it from us, but only our own infidelity.' Again, in the material losses caused by the fire, very sensible losses for the poor house,† she makes use of

* Several remarkable conversions, for which the community had long prayed, took place during the days immediately following the fire.

† A charity sermon, preached by Father Lefèvre in the Church of St. Thomas Aquinas, on occasion of the fire, obtained for the community the means of repairing their loss. Meanwhile the Blessed Sacrament was preserved in an oratory, and the daily and nocturnal adoration was never interrupted.

The reader will, perhaps, take an interest in an analogous incident which belongs to the terrible year 1871. During the siege of Paris—even during the bombardment, which thrice threatened the Convent of the Reparation—the adoration continued without interruption. Several churches being unable to carry out, in their turn, the exercises of Perpetual Adoration, the chapel of the Reparation was appointed by the diocesan authority to supply their wants and obtain for the adorers the benefit of Exposition of the Blessed Sacrament. Under the reign of the Commune, amid the incessant alarms caused by the perquisitions and trickery of the municipality, the Blessed Sacrament still continued exposed in the little chapel. On the 24th May the sisters were informed that the Federalists were about to take possession of the convent and fortify it. They then determined to ask the chaplain to remove the Monstrance. At the same time the regular troops entered the monastery from the Rue Gay-Lussac, and thence, by a breach, penetrated into the Convent of St. Michael, whence they at last issued by a private door into the Place du Panthéon, thus turning the barricade which had so long stopped their progress. Thanks to this circumstance, they were in time to prevent the formidable explosion which would have buried the whole quarter under the ruins of the Church of St. Geneviève. The arrival of the soldiers likewise saved the Convent of Reparation from the fire which several pretended refugees, who were quartered there, were ordered to light at a given signal: petroleum was found in their possession.

We will give one more incident. In a nocturnal perquisition, undertaken by a detachment of National Guards, a word from the Superior caused them to respect the Monstrance. The Federalists passed through the chapel in silence ; one raised his kepi; another genuflected. Two sisters were kneeling in the choir, and continued their adoration without them to raise the hearts of her children to God. 'Let us think before all else of our spiritual temples. How can material glory, which can be destroyed in less than an hour, glorify the All-Powerful God? He demands an immortal sanctity. Become holy, my dear children, I beg of you. I give you my blessing with all the plenitude of grace springing from the union with Jesus crucified.'

In another letter, the second that she was able to dictate, she explained to her children how it was that, in the moment of peril, although seeking for a means of escape, she was still entirely resigned at not finding one. 'I was especially struck by this thought: *God alone is all.* Life is of little consequence if one can place it in the hands of God. I then thought that I should do better to remain where I was, and prepare myself to die well, than to exhaust all my strength in seeking a means of exit.' A few weeks later, in spite of her burnt eyelids and maimed hands, she took up a pen to write herself to her absent children at Lyons. 'My very dear children, it is myself, be not afraid. My writing is changed, my face and my hands are different, but my heart is still the same. I shall be your Mother a little time longer in this valley of tears, and then I hope that this baptism of fire will enable me to go and prepare a place for you in the realms of glory. May the hands of Jesus crucified bless you.'

Notwithstanding her energy, during the first half of the year 1856, she was in a state of utter helplessness. For a long time her eyes were a source of great uneasiness; the contraction of the upper eyelids caused a swelling, which threatened complete loss of sight. But towards midsummer she became sensibly better, and was able to resume the superintendence of business. Without alluding to the spiritual government which was always her principal solicitude, exterior cares were not wanting. From all sides she received proposals for foundation;

---

turning round. On leaving, one of the men slipped into the hands of the portress a note, addressed to the Superioress; on it were these words: '*Pray for me.*' Thus does God recompense by signal favours the fidelity of the Réparatrices to their *Perpetual Adoration.*

from Poland, Lyons, Geneva. She objected to Poland, saying that the institute could only be established there under the protection of the aristocracy of the country, whose sumptuous tastes, brilliant qualities, and natural elegance, she feared, might corrupt her poor Nazareth; it would be better, she said, to send there religious of a more ancient institute and a more formed spirit, one especially whose aim is the sanctification of the upper classes. She preferred London, as her great desire was to raise a Eucharistic sanctuary in the land of heresy: but, taking into consideration the weakness of her infant family, she feared for it '*the invasion of ease*' in that country which cannot understand any deprivation of the comfortable. She was still more inclined to Geneva, on account of the '*Swiss simplicity*,' which seemed to her better calculated to receive the spirit of Nazareth. Of these three foreign foundations, not one was realised; and the projected establishments at Langres and Nantes likewise fell through. In all these crises Mary Teresa maintained great reserve, seeking no advances and receiving those made to her with extreme prudence. At the time of which we speak she received many petitions; but in the following year a foundation analogous to her own roused the sympathy and concurrence of those who understood in a different manner from herself the realisation of the common idea.*

But if she did not acquire new houses, she at least gained worthy children to the Reparation. During the year many good postulants were received, and it was likewise arranged that the novices of Lyons, and of any other house that might hereafter be established, should make their novitiate at the cradle of the institute, so as to insure unity of spirit.

During the same year another addition was made, though

* This relates to the Congregation of Marie Réparatrice, founded by Mme. de Hoogworst. The following is what Mary Teresa wrote of it to Brother Francis, the confident of her inmost thoughts: 'This foundation does me good; I understand that, if we are both from God, He wishes to glorify Himself by two foundations as different in aim as those of St. Francis and St. Dominic; and that the only means of attaining the aim He has shown me is to remain as firm in my path as that of this lady appears safer and, humanly speaking, easier.'

of a different kind. The house next to that occupied by the community in the Rue des Ursulines was put up for sale; the person who came forward to purchase it threatened to be a disagreeable neighbour. Mary Teresa recommended her children to pray and fast, and soon an unexpected gift enabled her to buy the house herself; the greater part of it she let to lodgers or to persons making retreats. The community thus became lessees of the house they inhabited and proprietors of that in which they did not live. Later, in 1860, as expropriation was imminent, Mary Teresa deemed it prudent not to renew her lease on No. 12, and the community removed to the newly-bought house whilst waiting for the construction of the new monastery. Thus does Providence take charge of those who abandon themselves to His guidance.

The reader is perhaps astonished to see *the poor burnt creature,* as she called herself, find strength to attend to such delicate and laborious business; but he will be still more so at finding her fatiguing her bruised body by undertaking a journey to Lyons; but she had long accustomed herself to stop at nothing short of the impossible. On returning to Paris she resolved to prepare herself for the anniversary of the fire, by a long retreat. She spent the Octave of All Saints in complete solitude, taking for the subjects of her meditations the eight beatitudes. We have before us a voluminous collection of her reflections, written entirely by herself for her confessor; and we cannot look without emotion on these pages, each one of which bears witness to a victory of energy over acute physical suffering. But what is still more worthy of admiration, is the doctrine contained in these meditations. We do not fear to be mistaken when we say that nowhere have we found a more profound analysis of the subject, or a truer sentiment of evangelical perfection. The innumerable writings of Mary Teresa on spirituality are full of scattered treasures; but this is a body of mystical teaching so complete and sublime, that we fear to depreciate it by making extracts. We hope to see it published in a collection of her works at some future time.

The farther we advance in the life of Mary Teresa, the

greater difficulty we experience in choosing materials from the abundant documents in our possession, which are sources of great edification, but form but little matter for narration. The institute was founded, and had gradually developed under the vigilant eye of the Mother, who, in proportion as suffering and weakness obliged her to retire from active life, confined herself, as far as possible, to a passive state of victim; so that now, more than ever, we must study her soul. This we are enabled to do by means of her letters, the number of which decreased, but in which external affairs are henceforth constantly compelled to give way to spiritual lessons and exhortations; her written statements for her confessor, which are more detailed than formerly, and which accurately describe the vicissitudes of her spiritual life; and, finally, her mystical writings, which flow from her pen as if, aware of the approach of death, she was anxious to embody the *spirit* of her foundation, and thus insure to her children a religious inheritance. In order to avoid unnecessary repetition, we shall be obliged to pass quickly onward; but also, so as not to deprive the reader of the edification to which he is entitled, we will give an abstract in the last chapter of the most characteristic features of the spirit of the holy Foundress.

The year 1857 opened with a singular event, the sacrilegious murder of Mgr. Sibour. Mary Teresa experienced a feeling of great grief, and ordered prayers and fasting in both her houses. It was under such circumstances that her vocation, as a child of Reparation, revealed itself in all its energy. Nothing moved her save the honour of God; she was not one of those whose horror of the crime exceeds the hatred of the sin that the crime involves. The simple account of a sacrilege in the sanctuary overpowered her; on hearing of such an event, which had lately occurred, she wrote, 'The fire I endured was mild compared to this mortal anguish, to these tears without consolation. I now understand how it is that one must either *suffer or die*; for without suffering life would become too burdensome.'

Except the sad emotion caused by this tragic event, this year was signalised by no remarkable incident in the history of the

Foundress or of her institute. It terminated by a happy event, the definitive approbation of the two Archbishops of Paris and Lyons to the existence of a Superior-general for the whole institute. Mary Teresa attached great importance to this point of the Constitutions, being persuaded that, unless provided with a common centre of authority, a newly-formed society could not extend itself without being exposed to dissolution. On the 1st February following new elections were made, which terminated by the existing Superiors maintaining their office. The poor invalid was obliged to resume the burden, and again drag herself to Lyons, whither, she said, she was called by the needs of those souls whom the letter kills and the spirit does not vivify. It was, in fact, during this visit that she gave to her children a series of conferences on those words of our Lord, *The letter kills, but the spirit vivifies.* She applied them successively to the peculiarities of the Christian life, to religious perfection, and to the vocation of *Réparatrice* with such sublime views, such pure doctrine and vigour of expression, that we are of opinion that this little collection may worthily take its place among the writings of the great masters of asceticism. Energy and affection are inseparable in those hearts that God has honoured with a spiritual paternity or maternity. The accents of St. Paul should be on the lips of all who, like him, generate souls to Jesus Christ. 'I have been told,' wrote Mary Teresa, at the end of a magnificent letter, on the feast of St. Michael, 'that I feed my children on blood, instead of milk. O yes, I desire to regenerate them in the sacrifice of Jesus crucified, my Spouse. My breasts, like Mary's, are pierced with swords which have passed through the heart of our Divine Love; and she who wishes to drink at this source, as a true child of the Reparation, will find this blood not bitter, but sweet as the Living Bread. Adieu! May St. Michael trample on the dragon in each of your dear souls!'

Notwithstanding her zeal for the sanctification of her children, she felt herself more strongly called than ever to solitude. Her confessor reproached her for not sufficiently corresponding to this inspiration; he ordered her to begin to relinquish her office by retiring to her cell, with a sister who should serve as her secretary, carry her orders, receive in her stead all morning visits, and, though usually preserving silence, should, at certain hours, give her an account of all that she had done in her name. This plan seemed to succeed; and by means of the repose thus obtained, the poor invalid began to recover her strength; but, above all, her soul dilated in solitude. For the first time during many years she could abandon herself without scruple to the divine action, and thus prevent the interior reproaches of the Divine Spirit, who complained of her resistance. '*When I stop you, desist*'—such were the words that an interior voice had one day spoken to her; but how was it possible to stop when urged on by duty? But this time she did stop, and found repose. With regard to her body, to consent to live amounted in her to a merit. She wrote to Brother Francis as follows: 'The thought of a longer sojourn in this exile than I had anticipated has caused me a little sorrow. But, O brother, how quickly one comes to terms with this thought of death; and how bitter would be the thought of time did not Jesus dwell and reign on this earth, where time, in and for Him, participates in the qualities of eternal things!' And again, 'It is for my sanctification that my friends should pray; they may likewise ask for the preservation of my life, *provided that they do not beg for my cure*. It is fitting that one called to Reparation should desire the last years of life to be years of true immolation. It is just that what she requires of her children should be left them as an inheritance by their Mother.'

Nevertheless even this semi-retreat did not satisfy Mary Teresa; she enjoyed the tranquillity afforded her by her new position, but experience soon taught her that it was not equally beneficial to her community: the sisters who were appointed to represent her could not resolve to act without her sanction, so that the authority delegated by the Mother was found to be executed by no one. After serious reflection, she at length adopted a decisive course of action, viz. that of entirely abdicating the government of her congregation by the election of a new Superioress. Cardinal Morlot was the first person to whom she spoke on the subject: in his dealings with Mary Teresa in the preceding year, on occasion of the drawing up of the Constitutions, this venerable prelate had conceived a high esteem for her piety and judgment; animated likewise by the spirit of faith, he treated with great consideration the interests of religious communities, being of the same opinion as the Saints, that the glory of God is concerned as much in them as in the most important enterprises. So when the Foundress laid before the pastor of the diocese her design of abdicating her position, she found that she had not presumed too far on the goodness and attention of the prelate. The reader will be able to judge of this for himself by the reply, which we now lay before him:

'Paris, 14th Feb. 1859.

'Rev. Mother,—Since I received your letter I have considered long and earnestly the proposal which you communicated to me, and I have begged of our Lord not to permit that I should answer you otherwise than in accordance with His inspiration. From the first I was touched by the motives which urged you to make this communication to me, and since that time their importance has not diminished in my eyes. If you still are of the same opinion, and if nothing has occurred to lead you to alter your intentions, follow out your plan in the manner you think best. If God preserves you in this world, you will not be useless in it, neither to yourself nor to the holy work in which you have been called upon to coöperate in so direct a manner. You will perfect the work of your sanctification, whilst at the same time edifying and assisting your children by the practice of the virtues of your holy state, in suffering, patience, and in the true spirit of sacrifice, immolation, and expiation which is the spirit of your institute.

'I recommend myself especially to your remembrance and your prayers Arrange with the Superior so as to regulate all things in a fitting manner.

'Accept, reverend Mother, this fresh assurance of my affectionate esteem.'

We have thought it interesting to give this letter in full; it does no less honour to the charity and piety of the venerable archbishop than to the sanctity of her whom he treated with such respect. Nor did the cardinal confine his goodwill to these expressions; the time was come when Mary Teresa and her first companions should consummate their religious consecration by perpetual profession. Mgr. Morlot came himself to receive their vows and encourage them to the sacrifice. He spent the whole morning in the house; and, after the ceremony, to which the poor Superioress had to be carried, he visited the invalid on her bed of suffering, and spoke with her for a long time on the interests of God and of the great work she had founded.

Fortified by the approbation of her pastor, Mary Teresa did not delay the execution of her project of retirement. It was a great blow to the community; but the Mother, who knew her children's hearts, had reserved this communication for the great Octave of the Reparation, which takes place every year during the Carnival. The sacrifice which she required of them was thus accepted in the spirit of expiation, and a few days later the new government was constituted and accepted by the chapter. Mary Teresa still kept the title of Mother-general, but named a coadjutrix, who should inherit all her rights and powers. She had very unwillingly yielded to the instances of the counsellors, who were determined to leave her a title that no other during her lifetime could bear. But her strong mind could not long consent to so uncertain a position; and she at length begged that new elections might take place, and a real Superior-general be chosen, thus giving to her retreat a more definitive and absolute character. She could not have demanded of her children a harder sacrifice, but she had full authority over their hearts. The elections took place on Tuesday in Whitsun week, the very day that, ten years before, Mary Teresa had made her profession and witnessed the clothing of her first novices.

It must not be imagined that Mary Teresa, in thus seeking repose, yielded solely to her love of rest. She had the most serious reasons for believing that such a step was necessary, both for her own soul and for her institute. She had all the feelings of a Mother, but she felt that, as Superioress, she could do little for them. At the commencement of her undertaking, when the reunion of pious young girls whom Providence had placed under her charge had not as yet assumed the form of a religious institute, she had felt at ease; but from the day that she had been obliged to exercise regular authority over them she had begun to groan under the burden; a violent conflict had arisen between the duties of her office and the imperious exigencies of her supernatural life. 'As long as I bore the title of Superior,' she wrote, 'I felt that it was only provisionary; that it was not my special vocation to be in authority; the opposition which the foundation received led me to retain it, and I have been obliged to lead a life contrary to the one God had marked out for me, and which He *wishes should be solitary and hidden.*' We have already remarked that Father Julliard fully shared in these views. 'He would willingly wall up the door of my cell,' she said. Thus the exterior voice of obedience agreed with that of the interior to quench all resistance. Besides, the welfare of the institute seemed to her not less at stake than her own in the reduction to practice, before her own eyes, of those rules which were destined to perpetuate its spirit. Since illness prevented her from doing anything herself, it was better to see how things would go on without her. 'If our provisionary position had continued,' she wrote, 'the actual authority in our houses would have been lost; there would have been a practical abdication of every office; and when the critical moment had arrived, an unhappy conflict of divers or contrary opinions might arise, all depending on my presumed intentions. If, on the contrary, all is effected in my lifetime, I shall be able, with one word, to pacify all differences and solve every difficulty.'

It was not without much trouble that her children, notwithstanding their desire to obey, accustomed themselves to the new order of things. 'The Superiors,' wrote Mary Teresa, 'cannot convince themselves that they are Superiors, nor the sisters that I am one no more.' But soon the impetus was given; and Mary Teresa was at length able to enjoy that interior repose which gave her the freedom to pray, to suffer, and to love.

CHAPTER XIV.
1859, 1860.

Serious illness.—Foundation at Chalons.—Increasing ardour of Mary Teresa's feeling towards the holy Eucharist.

NEVER, in fact, had love and suffering more violently disputed the possession of their victim. The year 1859 passed for Mary Teresa in an alternation of dangerous crises, which seemed to announce approaching dissolution, and interior trials which transported her in an instant from the abyss of desolation to raptures of happiness. In the month of May a sudden increase of illness led her to think that death was at hand. In this belief she wrote as follows to Brother Francis: 'The grace above every other grace is that of being delivered from this terrestrial prison. When one draws near to that ineffable moment, obscure according to human reason, but so luminous to faith, one has but this fixed idea: Here is death; there life! and it depends on my fidelity whether destruction will bring about the plentitude of joy or the plentitude of sorrow. Ah, before that hour arrives, one can form no idea of the anguish and yet the peace of one's last hours even in that dim light of eternity. All is destroyed for the soul before the destruction of the material being, when the conviction of approaching death and a look of faith, concentrated in God alone, entirely engross the mind. One then feels a unique, Love whose attractions are a consuming fire, but which is nevertheless exceedingly painful.'

Her soul shrank from the thought of purgatory; yet, in her desire to purify herself in this world, she was not actuated by fear alone, but also by love. 'Yes, I wish still to live and suffer; for in this purgatory on earth I can communicate every morning, and I rely more on the Incarnate Love than on suffering itself for the payment of my ransom.' Another time, completely penetrated with her union with Jesus the Victim, she compared her life to the Eucharistic Sacrifice, and did not wish that the time of immolation should find her simply resigned: the joy of thanksgiving was still wanting. 'Pray for me, brother, *my Mass is drawing near;* may everything be done in faith! May I say, It is just and reasonable, equitable and worthy of our vocation to return thanks to God on arriving at Calvary—Hosanna in the highest heavens! May my heart be above, in proportion as my body is attracted to the dust of the earth whence it sprang.'

Then the crisis passed, and a slight improvement in her health withdrew her for a time from the consideration of the near approach of death to fix her thoughts solely on the tender cares of love. On the feast of Corpus Christi her soul melted at the thought of the desertion of the Eucharist. Being unable to bear this sorrow alone, she took up her pen and wrote to her dear son, Brother Francis, then at Rome, where he at least must have had reason to rejoice; though at Paris his poor mother had only torrents of tears to offer to the Living Bread as a festal bouquet. 'Ah, if the body of God were present in the depth of every heart, how would not all these beings, created and redeemed by Him, be drawn to the centre of life with unbounded self-sacrifice? On the contrary, everything is a pretext for leaving Him alone, unglorified and unloved; the country house to be visited,[*] the oxen to be tried, the bride to be married, the interest of *self* to be considered,—everything serves as an excuse for remaining away from the divine feast in which the soul participates in the wedding of the Bridegroom and Bride. Give me, they say, signs that it is the will of God that I should devote myself to love, praise, and glorify Emmanuel; otherwise I shall seek for life on the high-roads.'

Then, thinking of the vocation of the priest of Reparation,

---

[*] Paraphrase of the parable of the wedding-feast, Matt. xxii.

she exclaimed, 'O my good brother, what patience you will require! If God does not inflame your heart with the fire of pure love, you will be able to accomplish nothing! If, on the contrary, this fire is lighted within you, O blessed martyr, then I warn you of sufferings, to be compared, as far as is possible, to those of Christ, and neither a scaffold nor a sword will be needful to torture you. Ah, I knew not what I was desiring when I asked to be delivered from the love of creatures and of self, to live henceforth only on that love which is the sap of the Heart of Jesus Christ! As yet I have but sparks, and yet what a passion!' Then she has not only to answer for her own love; it appeared to her as if Jesus questioned her concerning the fidelity of her children. 'Brother, when I hear a voice within my heart saying, "Mother, poor Mother, do these children, whom you have given Me for Eucharistic spouses, love Me more than others?" O, I assure you that I sometimes almost die of grief and fear to make these elect souls understand that Jesus is rather offended than glorified, amid this display of honour, if they do not live in Him and for Him.'

This zealous thought reminded her that her children had no fathers of their own, consecrating their priesthood to direct them in the path of Reparation; and this remembrance renewed all her sorrows. 'No sooner was Mary trusted to witness the immolation of her Son than God confided her to the care of the beloved Apostle. But now the guardianship and education of souls who desire to immolate themselves with Jesus and Mary appear only as accessories to the life of a priest. . . . We must, then, remain in these *mixed paths*, in which a true guide is not considered necessary. We must have the appearance of a special vocation without its Life! For the vocation of Reparation requires the angel who offers the chalice as well as Him who causes it to be accepted. We are not stronger than the Man-God; we have the right to say to the apostles of Jesus, Watch and pray with us!'

These vicissitudes of her physical and moral life occupied the whole year. With her accustomed vivacity, she herself characterised this singular state in a letter to her friend Clémence. 'If you only knew the strange existence of that person who, for fifty years, has been constantly on the move! I resemble a being, half animal and half vegetable. The vegetable is a prey to drowsiness, from which it is suddenly aroused by the sufferings of the animal; then, amidst all this, the soul is like marble or like fire, according to circumstances. But Father Julliard says that all is as it should be. Nevertheless, I assure you that I have much trouble in silencing the interminable reasonings of that Miss Theodelinda whom you knew philosophising upon everything.'

But whilst she was thinking that she had nothing more to do than prepare for death, by accepting suffering, God suddenly restored her to a kind of health and an unexpected strength to work for His service. In the commencement of 1860, she felt her strength return, and declared herself cured, 'so far,' she said, 'as one can be after being burnt.' Her reviving activity was not long without the means of satisfying itself; for it was at this time that the impending expropriation and the termination of their lease obliged the community in the Rue des Ursulines to remove from No. 12 to No. 14, the house which they had recently bought. But an affair of still greater importance was about to call for all her care. A branch of the institute was greatly desired at Chalons-sur-Marne: since the preceding November the Foundress had received serious proposals from that town. Such business as this was not included in that which her abdication allowed her to leave to others; so she found herself compelled again to take part in active life. She at first carried on the correspondence by letter, with that firmness, prudence, and faith which, setting aside both natural eagerness and pusillanimous fears, seeks solely the will of God, and does not hesitate in its accomplishment. Difficulties were not wanting; but the zeal of those persons of the town who desired the foundation in their midst, together with the zeal of Mary Teresa herself, succeeded in overcoming them. In the month of March 1860 we find her at Chalons, where she and her children were received in the hospital-house of St. Joseph, whilst waiting until the Reparation should have a roof of its own. Mary Teresa was particularly happy to see the work of faith and expiation transplanted to a country so long left desolate through religious indifference. The Bishop* (Mgr. Bara) likewise showed her a paternal benevolence, which his successor (Mgr. Meignan) has never ceased to continue to her children.† Finally, the pious persons who had solicited the foundation, and all those with whom she came in contact by means of the undertaking, welcomed her with such cordial kindness and simplicity that it was quite apparent that faith alone could have formed in an instant bonds so strong and yet so gentle. During Mary Teresa's last years the house at Chalons was to her as a peaceful port where her troubled soul could seek repose and consolation. Even her body derived good from it; it was there that she regained strength enough to practise almost entirely the rule of her institute and even to recommence the exercise of voluntary penance.‡

For all else she could scarcely perceive that she had quitted her monastery. Immediately on arriving at Chalons, she had begged and obtained the favour of carrying on the night adoration in the chapel of the Convent of St. Joseph. With the four sisters she had brought with her, and a secular sister, she accomplished this task; from eight P.M. to six A.M. they replaced each other every two hours before the tabernacle.

One of the sisters, unable to bear such fatigue, fell ill. The

---

* At the time of the first steps and Mary Teresa's preparatory urney to Chalons, in 1860, the Bishop was Mgr. Prilly, of holy memory. jo Long preoccupied with the thought of Reparation, he had earnestly pressed the idea of a foundation, and with his dying hand had written to request it. His coadjutor, who succeeded him a few weeks later, had the consolation of accomplishing the wish of the holy old man.

† We have ourselves heard the Bishop of Chalons say that he considered the foundation of the sanctuary of Reparation in his town one of God's greatest blessings on his diocese.

‡ We learn from the account Mary Teresa gave to her confessor of her manner of spending the day that at this period she took the discipline every evening before going to bed. Her written account of the following year shows us that she had continued this penitential practice during the whole year.

night adoration was then stopped, after having lasted nearly a month. But this illness served to reveal in a still more striking manner the charity of the pious nuns of St. Joseph. When the time arrived for them to take possession of the house they had acquired, and fitted up as that of the Reparation, Mary Teresa would not leave the friendly roof which had sheltered her without exhorting her children to gratitude. On her knees in their midst she pronounced this prayer, which we think savours not a little of the spirit of St. Francis of Assisi: 'Lord Jesus,' she said, 'bless and protect for ever the benefactors and superiors of this house, in which we have been received with so much charity. In the name and for the glory of Thy Divine Son, O Holy Father, bless also the little children and all who inhabit this holy house.' Then all kissed the ground, and the same prayer was repeated in the other rooms. Thus does the charity of the Saviour render His children debtors one to the other.

On the feast of the Dolours of the Blessed Virgin, everything being nearly arranged in the new house, the Bishop blessed the chapel, numerous associates were enrolled, and the perpetual adoration began to glorify the Eucharist in a new sanctuary. The sisters whom Mary Teresa had summoned from Paris and from Lyons to commence this new work were worthy of sharing in this labour of love; they had renewed the wonders of laborious poverty and joyful privation which had signalised the first foundation. Their Mother took pleasure in praising them when writing to her confessor.* 'All

* Father Julliard had just died, and the confessor who then directed her was Father Freyd, of the Congregation of the Holy Spirit. We shall be fully complying with the intentions of Mary Teresa by relating her feelings at the death of the holy Marist: 'The close tie which bound our souls never led him to derogate from his rights as a director. Dead to natural affections by means of the labour of religious and contemplative perfection, his heart had attained to that degree of charity which alone can coöperate in the foundation of the works of God. . . . The annals of our family will be unable to mention my name without adding to it that of the benefactor of my soul, who continues to be my protector in heaven, where his hidden virtues, his love of immolation, and his sufferings are now amply recompensed. Contrary to all expectation, I was able to leave

these dear souls, who have united themselves to my poverty to establish Jesus our Victim on this little Eucharistic throne, seem to participate, in some measure, in the happiness of heaven. Everything is done with the joy and liberty of the children of God; and as charity bears a load without being overburdened, so we feel no fatigue after whole nights passed in laborious works. The penance of Lent, augmented by the most complete privation of even necessaries, appears quite welcome to these souls of good-will. Not one has ceased to fast and abstain, if we except the unworthy servant whom God has given them; and even this latter has put on one side many little comforts.'

Even so early as the following year the good effected by the foundation of Chalons was manifest. Mary Teresa wrote thus: 'Of the three communities this is without doubt the most edifying; our little traditions are established here perfectly. The sanctuary is delicious, and crowds of pious souls and visitors flock hither to honour and pray to the Divine King. What especially delights me is to behold the little children, when school is over, come to see the good Jesus and make their genuflections, as they see the sisters do, whilst some of them kiss the floor, having seen our sisters do so after prayers in the evening. These little blessed ones at least have no prejudices; they will grow older, and make their first Communion with the instinct of adoration and respect for the Holy Host. I heard one little fellow say, pointing to the Blessed Sacrament, "Mamma, does the good God then always remain there?" The

---

my bed of suffering to assist at the last moments of that short but beautiful life; and I heard issuing from his heart the aspirations of praise and confidence which are the forerunners of eternal bliss. I then felt, in that hour of separation which deprived me of so great a good, that love is strong as death, and that those who leave us in the holy grace of God participate in the riches of the Father of the family, and there obtain succour for the indigent in this valley of tears. On the day of the death of that good father I received a grace of *strength;* I understood that the very difficulties in which he left me could be solved by God alone. Forgetting my own self, I invariably fixed the eye of my soul on the sole object, viz. personal sanctification and the greater glory of God.'

faith of his Baptism made him already communicate spiritually with the Jesus of little children.'

Unfortunately the financial difficulties which had marked the commencement of the foundation were far from being at an end. Indeed, affairs soon became so critical that Mary Teresa feared that she would be obliged to abandon the foundation. 'How sad it would be,' she wrote, 'to have to leave this solitude! Pray earnestly that I may not be compelled to dethrone our Master in this cold country, which stands so much in need of His divine warmth!'

The Divine Master took compassion on the loving anxiety of His spouse, and the institute was enabled to live on from day to day, in absolute poverty, but likewise in great confidence. An extraordinary incident justified and recompensed their filial self-abandonment. One day, on opening the money-box, which should have afforded the means of providing the lights,* Mary Teresa found only a few pence. She was greatly touched, and, kneeling down, she burst into tears, asking pardon of our Lord for the indifference of Christians towards the Ever-blessed Sacrament. 'My Beloved,' she exclaimed, 'if I have exposed Thee to contempt, instead of advancing Thy glory, I would far rather that Thou shouldst destroy me.' We borrow these details from her confidential account of the circumstance to her confessor. She proceeds thus: 'Nevertheless I began to pray, as God inspires me to do when He wishes to hear me. My soul cried out, "*Help for the external glory of the Blessed Sacrament!*" I humbled myself in my unworthiness; but I reminded God that He is all-powerful—that, if this undertaking were His own, He might assist me in the same way as He had assisted His Saints, and I enumerated the miracles of multiplication which I remembered; I am almost certain that I thought of the widow of Sarepta; though the object I had in view was

---

* This is the great burden of the communities of Reparation; the rubrics of the Church require, in presence of the Blessed Sacrament exposed, at least six wax candles always lighted. The perpetual maintenance of these lights, together with the cost of the lamps, the tapers during Mass and Benediction, amounts annually to considerable sums.

not the increase of oil, but of the pence to buy more.' A few days later, one Saturday evening, the sisters went to fill the cruse of oil to trim the lamps: the cask was empty; they turned it over, but were only able to obtain a few drops; they asked each other how they could possibly feed the lamps until Monday, as they could not buy oil on the Sunday. But what was their surprise when, on the following morning, a sister went down and filled the cruse without any difficulty! For three weeks the oil continued to flow from the cask without diminishing, each time that the smaller vessel was filled from it. At the end of that time, the sacristan having been changed, she who succeeded to the office found the provision exhausted after the lapse of two days; by raising the cask she could only fill a few glasses. Then, with child-like simplicity, she prostrated, saying, 'Lord, I know well that I am not worthy, like my sisters, to obtain Thy graces; but it is for Thyself that I pray to Thee. *Thou hast need of the oil.*' Immediately the cruse filled, and for another week the miraculous cask continued to furnish with the necessary oil the seven lamps which burnt day and night before the altar.

The accounts of the procuratrix confirmed the miraculous character of this incident; for, a few days before the event, she had told the Superior that it was time to renew the provision of oil, the ordinary interval that elapsed between each purchase having already passed.

Mary Teresa possessed in the highest degree the virtue of discretion; and, if I dare say so, modesty concerning the supernatural. 'I fear,' she said, 'in this century of little faith, to cast pearls before stupid incredulity.' For this reason she preserved an absolute silence on the subject of this miraculous multiplication, and her children followed her example. She disclosed it to her confessor alone; and it is from her account in a letter to him that we have produced the history of this favour, for the consolation of believing souls.

Mary Teresa spent the greater part of the year 1860 at Chalons; two visits to Paris were but short interruptions to her abode in this place, where she seemed to acquire fresh life. Whilst she was devoting herself to the care of her new family, one of her children was sinking, far away from her, from decline; and it was in the following words of admirable simplicity that she exhorted her to prepare for her passage hence: 'Poor child, how happy you are to approach the limits of this miserable world! for, with the exception of Communion and Reparation, there is nothing in it that can satisfy a heart created for the one and eternal beauty; and, my beloved child, I say to you with confidence, "Depart, Christian soul; go and prepare for us a place. I bless you from my heart. I forget the sorrows which have sometimes obliged me to cause you to shed tears. Remember me before our Lord; speak to Him of my needs, for they are immense, for the accomplishment of my mission. How happy you are! I also had reached the port, and behold, I am now recast on this sea, full of shoals. But may God be blessed! Let us love Him: you in glory and beatitude, your poor Mother in humiliation and suffering. Adieu, my beloved child! May Mary in triumph conduct you, and the angels bear you away! May St. Michael allow no trouble to approach you!"'

Let us compare this strong and serene affection with the affection that the world conceives and practises: a pusillanimous love which, when separation is imminent, lives on reticence and condemns the poor departing soul to concentrate in herself all care for her eternal safety; one cannot help exclaiming, Christian affection is more true, more profound, more helpful!

The fifth anniversary of the fire found Mary Teresa still at Chalons. This date never passed without making a lively impression on her soul at the remembrance of that favour which had rendered effective her consecration as victim. This time, far away from her children in Paris, she communicated to them her impressions in an admirable letter which we wish we were able to produce in full. 'For us also, my sisters, a day came which showed us plainly that our mission is not only to preserve the fire of love, but also to be devoured by it without dying. . . . This day is great amongst all the days consecrated to our vocation, and we wish to perpetuate the remembrance of it as we do the memory of our Baptism. In this material fire the vocation of Reparation was to be baptised; for it was in the immaterial fire of love and suffering that it sprang from the Heart of Jesus. . . . My dear children, on this anniversary, whilst contemplating the holocaust of the Sacred Species, and calling to mind the signal graces which your Mother has received, plunge yourselves generously into those two furnaces of life to your souls—*love* and *sacrifice*. Be not afraid; the flames of these furnaces are certainly piercing; but if one issues from them annihilated, if the functions of this purification leave burning stigmata on the senses, there nevertheless comes a moment when, beneath the Eucharistic annihilation, one discovers the spring of living water which refreshes our burning thirst and, like oil, heals all wounds. Fear nothing; enter this fire; you will there see unveiled the power and goodness of your God towards a creature whom He wishes to make His servant. . . . My God! my Saviour! . . . my Spouse of fire and blood! from those heights where Thou awaitest them draw to Thyself these beloved souls, draw them so that they may not be able to resist. Enveloped in the flame of Thy Love, grant that they may declare themselves vanquished, and say, "The divine Hand has cast us into the furnace and closed all means of escape; *there is now no time to withdraw.*" . . . Souls of my soul, O my children, think seriously on your last end on this day which reminds you both of death and life, of destruction and immortality! Jesus, on leaving this dust which you look upon with such respect,* still remained glorious on the throne of His Father: let us retire from this body of clay to take up

---

* She here alluded to the fire which reduced the Sacred Species to cinders, which were preserved by the community as a relic. According to the Catholic doctrine, the Real Presence ceases on the destruction of the Species; but what remains of the destroyed Species may be honoured as a remembrance. It is to be remarked that, throughout these delicate proceedings, Mary Teresa never departed from dogmatic exactitude.

our abode within the inaccessible sanctuary where dwells Jesus our Love!'

A soul consumed to such a point by the fire of charity could not long bear her exile. Mary Teresa had still two acts to perform in this world: to accomplish a great mission, and to accept a great trial. Two years sufficed for this, and then she entered into her rest.

CHAPTER XV.
1861-1863.

Building of the new monastery.—Laying of the foundation-stone of the chapel.—Difficulties raised at Rome concerning the approbation.—What Mary Teresa suffered on this account.—Interior trials.—Last illness.—Sentiments during her last days.—Her death and burial.

THE great act which Mary Teresa had still to perform before passing into the other world was the strengthening of her foundation by building a chapel and monastery in the very cradle of her institute. In order successfully to carry out this project she was obliged to leave her retreat, where she had spent eighteen peaceful months, and resume, together with the the title, the labours and anxieties of Superior-general.

The reader will remember that the little convent in the Rue des Ursulines had been menaced with expropriation, caused by the projected formation of the Rue Gay-Lussac. Foreseeing this event, the community had removed from No. 12; but even in their new house they were not secure from the axe of the demolishers; though, being the proprietors, they could claim from the town an indemnity or exchange of land, which would enable them to establish themselves definitively and to begin to build. Such were the serious designs which Mary Teresa, on her return to Paris in the beginning of 1861, submitted, with her usual confidence, to the wise and benevolent judgment of Cardinal Morlot.

After serious reflection this latter not only authorised, but counselled and strongly encouraged, the acquisition of a small plot of ground situated in the Rue d'Ulm, No. 36, behind the garden of the little convent. The sum of 8000*l*. was needed—the expropriation money would suffice at least to pay for the ground; but the amount of the indemnity being unknown, if they were badly treated in the matter, there was a risk of their being left to pay all the building expenses. Under these circumstances Mary Teresa, who was always inclined to confidence, was nevertheless guided entirely by obedience; fearing on the one hand to tempt God, and on the other to appear to doubt His power, she sought from the lips of His representative the indication of His will; then she walked on the waters with the faith of St. Peter, knowing, she said, that God could as easily find, when necessary, 8000*l.* as one penny. Now the Cardinal had on this occasion spoken in a decisive manner: '*Your chapel is your work itself; you must not hesitate.*'

She did not hesitate, and Providence seemed, by an unexpected help, to reward her faith. The indemnity could not be obtained until after the conclusion of the treaty with the town. Meanwhile, to obtain the deed of sale, it was necessary to lay down at once 480*l.*, of which not one penny had yet been collected. A few days before the appointed time a religious brought Mary Teresa the sum of 400*l.*, and what is truly admirable is that it was not the gift of a wealthy benefactor, but the heroic sacrifice of a poor lady, who thus surrendered at once half of her small fortune (her capital amounted only to 800*l.*), to make reparation, she said, for the faults of her life. Other offerings received about the same time increased the sum to more than was absolutely required, and the ground destined for the sanctuary of the Reparation thus became the property of the spouses of Jesus Christ. The deed was signed in the month of August 1861.

The effort which Mary Teresa had been compelled to make for several months in order to bring this business to a conclusion had exhausted the strength which she had obtained in her late seclusion. She had to pay for this excessive activity by six weeks of illness, utter weakness, and terrible suffering. Many secondary causes added to the principal one to torment her. Still penetrated with the thought of approaching death, she desired to see her three communities established on such a footing of regularity as should insure their surviving her. But the construction of the spiritual edifice was not the least laborious. Heaven, always jealous of the noblest souls, had recently deprived her of two more of her dear children, and two who were especially useful to the institute. Novices abounded; but the older sisters were few in numbers: there were scarcely sufficient to fill the important offices of the mother-house and attend to the direction of the two provincial houses. Finally, to increase her anxiety, a tiresome law-suit threatened not only the interests but the very honour of the congregation and of the Church. The heirs of one of the deceased sisters boldly claimed a large donation made by her before her entrance into religion, and brought an action against the Foundress for embezzlement. On hearing this Mary Teresa trembled, but was not troubled. A glance at her Divine Master, who also was accused, defamed before men, and dragged before the tribunals, restored peace to her soul. For eight months she bore this cross, pleading her cause with her children in fasting and tears before the Eucharistic throne. At length, in the month of August in the following year, notwithstanding the rage of the adverse party and the eloquent hatred of an illustrious advocate, the decree of the court dismissed the complaint, and brought to light, together with the justice of their cause, the delicacy of the proceedings of those persons whose very honesty had been called in question.

The building continued. The monastery had been commenced immediately upon the acquisition of the land. Various circumstances caused the erection of the chapel to be deferred for several months. The Holy Father had sent the foundation-stone from Rome, in testimony of his sympathy with the institute and his esteem for a pious lady, the faithful friend of Mary Teresa, who had pleaded with him the cause of the poor sisters of the Reparation. This stone had been taken from the ancient Basilica of St. Clement, recently discovered at Rome, beneath the basilica dedicated to that Saint in the twelfth century. The precious fragment was laid on the 22d July 1862. Mgr. Chigi, Apostolic Nuncio, presided at the ceremony, and received the vows of a young sister whose family was connected with his own—Elizabeth Marescalchi, in religion Sister Mary Veronica—who was one of the most dearly loved by Mary

Teresa, one of the most faithful heirs of her spirit, and whose premature death but too soon revived the sorrow of the Sisters of the Reparation, still mourning for their common Mother.*

This latter was not destined to see the edifice completed, the foundation of which had thus been laid by Pius IX. Her measure of labour was full; it only remained for her to fill up the measure of her suffering, and then die, as she had lived, a victim.

This great trial came from the side on which she least expected it, viz. from Rome. We are about to speak candidly of the difficulties which embittered the last days of a life chequered by so many trials. We can solve the sad problem which placed Mary Teresa between the intimate feeling of her vocation and the still more imperious feeling of obedience to the Holy See. Thanks to God, the opposition between these two feelings was but apparent, and the sanction given by the Holy Father to the institute, within two years after the death of the Foundress, shows clearly that the difficulties in question were merely, in the hand of God, the instrument He made use of to complete in His spouse the work of suffering and the merit of immolation.

The reader will recollect that since the Laudative Brief had been granted to the institute in 1853, experience had suggested many modifications, and had obliged the Foundress to alter several articles in the future constitutions of her order. Since the foundation at Chalons especially she had actively carried on this work under the kind superintendence of Cardinal Morlot. Such was the state of things in the end of the year 1861. At this time Mary Teresa's health was a subject of great anxiety. A crisis, which might be her last, renewed her maternal solicitude for the future welfare of her congregation. Undoubtedly it would have been a great consolation to be able to leave to her

---

* Sister Mary Veronica died in September 1869, the feast of the Seven Dolours. The remembrance of that angelic soul carried with it, in those who knew her, a grace of sanctification. Notwithstanding the utter weakness to which her long and painful illness had reduced her, her Superioress wished her to retain to the last the post of Mistress of Novices, being persuaded that the very sight of that holy soul, and the affection she inspired, would be an eloquent lesson of religious perfection.

children a pledge of life and fecundity in the approbation of the Holy See. In her intimate correspondence with the pious friend of whom we have spoken she revealed her heart's secret desire, which, however, she never put into words; and, perhaps, had the question been asked, she might have hesitated to take the initiative in a formal request for approbation. But Mme. de —— set out for Rome. Being a loving and devoted child of Mary Teresa, it was not without heartrending feelings of sorrow that she separated from that Mother at a time when she feared never again to see her here below; but she was actuated by the sincere desire of again being of use to her, and of consoling her last days; and it was this filial desire, together with her devotion to the Institute of Reparation, that inspired her to enter on that enterprise the result of which we are about to relate.

On her arrival in Rome this lady, who was already known to and greatly esteemed by the Holy Father, soon succeeded in obtaining an audience. On the appointed day she recalled to mind all the dear recollections that she had left behind in the house in the Rue des Ursulines in Paris; she already, in anticipation, begged the blessing of the Holy Father for the Mother, her children, the present and future of the institute. Full of these thoughts, she took up her pen, and, as if urged by a mysterious instinct, she wrote a long petition, describing the history and character of the institute, and in which she expressed the desire to see it soon consecrated by the approbation of the Holy Father. Assuredly it was not her intention, when writing these lines, to make an express petition for approbation, and still less to precipitate a matter destined to follow a regular order in the Court of Rome; she simply obeyed the promptings of her heart; and although she had glided the word 'approbation' into the body of the petition, she nevertheless concluded with these simple words: 'I beg his Holiness's especial blessing on this undertaking, on this ground prepared for Jesus, and on all those souls who have consecrated to it their hopes and offerings.' This action had been so spontaneous on the part of Mme. de —— that she was still writing when word was brought her that the carriage was ready to take her to the Vatican. Once in the presence of the Holy Father, she spoke little but of the object on which her heart was fixed; then, with a confidence which afterwards greatly astonished her, she took the petition and presented it to the Pope. Pius IX. glanced over it with a benevolent expression, and then put it into his pocket. The audience terminated thus, and Mme. de —— retired, fully persuaded that she had done nothing further than obtain a benediction for the institute and for its Foundress. This belief she expressed the following day when writing to Mary Teresa, telling her of her visit to the Vatican. What then was her astonishment when, a few days later, the Pope sent a prelate of his court to collect particulars regarding the institute. She feared to have said too much; but there was now no time to draw back, and she was obliged to answer the Pope. Mary Teresa, hearing of what had occurred, saw in this unexpected turn of events an indication of Divine Providence. Confirmed in this idea by her ordinary counsellors, she hastened to reassure her dear child respecting the initiative she had taken, and to prepare the plan of her institute; that is, a summary of the constitutions, containing only the essential indications of the object, spirit, and observances of the family of the Reparation. This was, in fact, all that the Holy Father required; but Mary Teresa had flattered herself with the hope that, when once in possession of this plan, the Pope would examine and decide for himself. Her faithful friend, better able to judge of what would happen, warned her in vain that such a privilege could not be expected; that, whether she so willed or not, the case was about to become one of the many submitted to the decision of the Holy See. It was some time before Mary Teresa renounced the hope she had conceived; meanwhile the plan of the constitutions arrived, and the Holy Father handed it over to the secretary of the Congregation of Bishops and Regulars.* Thus the business was begun almost without the knowledge of the parties interested.

* A Roman congregation, whose business it is to examine into all affairs concerning religious orders and their connection with the episcopal authority.

It is not our intention to give a detailed account of the negotiations following this primary step. We will merely say that one of the persons employed in the investigation of the case evinced more curiosity than benevolence, continually demanding fresh documents, and introducing many others which were foreign to the constitutions, and sometimes even to the spirit of the institute. For instance, Mary Teresa had formerly had spiritual relations with Sister Saint Peter, a Carmelite at Tours, whom we have before mentioned, and it was intended to make her responsible for the writings of Sister Saint Peter. Certain litanies and other formulas, which were not irreproachable considered from a liturgical and theological point of view, had been communicated to the Foundress, and sometimes used by the community: from these a statement was drawn up, which pretended to represent the spirit of the institute. Certainly Mary Teresa was far from wishing to dissimulate anything that might enlighten or decide the judgment of the Holy See; she unreservedly accepted it in advance, and never stayed to examine the intermediate steps of the proceedings. 'If you knew, dear child,' she wrote to Mme. de ——, 'how indifferent I feel concerning the decision which will be passed. Doubtless the supreme pastors will make use of agents, but I will never place my hope on secondary causes.' Nevertheless, notwithstanding the simplicity of her obedience, she could not give up her interest in her institute, nor see without sorrow that it was considered replete with the very abuses she had sought to avoid, and with the excesses which she had blamed.

Her pious friend eagerly wished that the Foundress might be able to undertake the journey to Rome, as she never doubted that her presence, her loyal explanations, the authorised commentary which she alone could make on the written documents, would have dissipated every cloud. A temporary improvement in her health rendered this journey possible; but her Superiors did not think fit to allow her to undertake it. She sent in her stead Father Francis, who was too intimately united to her thoughts and her heart not to participate in all her sufferings, but whose character was not sufficiently conciliatory to overcome the prejudices already conceived against the order.

About the same time the canonisation of the martyrs of Japan attracted to Rome bishops from the whole world. This was a favourable circumstance, and one which, for a short period, raised the hopes of the Foundress. The testimony of Cardinal Morlot was such as might have been expected from his paternal benevolence. Mgr. de la Bouillerie likewise consented to be the advocate of the sisters of the Reparation.* But the favourable impressions produced by these precious recommendations did not long survive the actual presence of the prelates. Father Francis, by his rather untempered zeal, only aggravated the difficulties by prejudicing the person who might have brought the affair to a successful conclusion. Recalled to Paris, at the request of Mary Teresa, whom a terrible relapse rendered unable to fulfil her numerous duties, he left matters in a very unsatisfactory state. And yet it was too late to put a stop to the proceedings. Mme. de ——, who still remained at Rome, and whose prudence would have advised other measures, was powerless to mend matters which she would have prevented. On her last visit to the secretary of the congregation, she was received rather harshly, and was informed that *official observations* would be sent to Paris concerning the spirit and observances of the institute. With this sad news, she returned to France in the early part of June 1862.

She found Mary Teresa in a state of indescribable suffering; her fever was so severe that all the nourishment she took, even the simplest drinks, consumed her internally, like a poison. Morally her sufferings were not less acute; the trial of which we have spoken did not seem to be drawing to a close; nothing

* The following is the letter that he wrote in their favour: 'The holy work of the Adoration of Reparation began in Paris when I lived there in the capacity of vicar-general of the diocese. I encouraged it as far as lay in my power, and since then I have been happy to hear of the development and progress of that pious institute. Several houses have been established in France, and everywhere they have become precious centres of devotion to the Divine Eucharist. In all confidence, I now solicit the approbation of the Holy Father in favour of the Institute of Adoration of Reparation.   '✠ Francis, Bishop of Carcassonne.'

seemed to warrant the idea of its happy termination; on the contrary, it appeared as if the poor Foundress were about to be overwhelmed by a cleverly-contrived calumny. The difficulties which had arisen at Rome caused her to regret deeply having allowed the business to be brought forward. The observations addressed to her renewed all her former doubts regarding the rectitude of her path. Without knowing the precise object of these observations, a secret instinct warned her that they bore a relation to her last and heaviest cross; and her soul, already so rigorously tried, experienced that interior bitterness which precedes great tribulations.

The year 1862 was thus brought to a close; and with it came an event which plunged the Church of Paris into mourning, but which Mary Teresa had especial reason to deplore—the death of Cardinal Morlot. In him she lost a father, a stay, a counsellor—I had almost said a friend; the community lost its most powerful protector. Almost the last time the venerable prelate had been out was on a visit to the poor convent; he had remained for long by the mother's sick-bed; he had blessed and encouraged the sisters in the exercise of their holy vocation, and had left them strengthened by the grace of his presence. God permitted that so precious an assistance should be taken from them at a time when it was of the greatest importance. In the beginning of the year 1863 the observations, so long announced, were at length forwarded to Paris, addressed, not to the community, but to the vicar's capitulars. The fears expressed by the Sacred Congregation concerning the tendencies and practices of the institute were shared in by the depositaries of the diocesan authority; and when, a short time later, the observations were officially communicated to the Superioress, she found herself alone to face the distrust of which she was the object. But I err; she still possessed a precious support in the person of Canon Dedoue, whose wise direction and enlightened devotion have never been withheld from the institute, neither during her life nor after her death.

It would be a mistake to imagine that these observations threw any blame on the institute itself; the facility with which, two years later, the approbation fell, *like a ripe fruit*,* into the hands of the new Superioress, would alone suffice to discard such a supposition. But in the 'Observations' we are able to trace the prejudices of the person who collected the information. The name of Réparatrices was deemed ambitious. The cause of this criticism was the abuse that certain false devotees had made of the title. In her writings and throughout her whole life Mary Teresa had amply proved her horror of these false devotions. Nevertheless she did not care to defend herself on this point. She had several times during the preceding year written to say that she was ready to renounce the name. It seemed likewise to be desired that her institute should place itself visibly under the protection of Carmel; nothing could have better responded to the earnest desire of the daughter of St. Teresa; but was it not the Carmelites of France who had obliged the infant third order to separate from them?

A second observation related to points of dogma. In the scattered leaves which had been transformed into authorised documents were found chance expressions and badly-worded advice relative to the devotion of Reparation. In them the sisters were exhorted, when preparing for confession, to join to repentance for their personal faults, a sorrow for the faults of all men. It was feared that these words contained an invitation *to confess faults which they had never committed*. The incredible excesses into which some persons had fallen, who had made piety an affair of imagination, justified this distrust on the part of the Roman authorities; but the danger of error existed only in the formula; if notes, written on the spur of the moment, with the freedom and negligence of conversation, had not been endorsed in the file of papers submitted for examination, such a suspicion would never have been cast on the spiritual doctrine of the Réparatrice order.

After dogma, the observations passed on to liturgy; the proper office of the children of the Reparation was interdicted, and its place was supplied by the votive office of the Blessed

* These are the words of a person who witnessed the measures which, in 1865, ended with astonishing facility in a decree of approbation.

Sacrament, taken from the Roman Breviary. Mary Teresa willingly made the sacrifice of this prayer composed under the auspices of Cardinal de Bonald; but she suffered, in her gratitude and affection, at the sight of the blame which thus seemed cast on her venerated protector.

The final observations showed still more clearly what an erroneous idea the papers which had been sent in had given of the institute they were intended to make known. The sisters were accused of interfering in the *spiritual direction of men*, the Superior of usurping the rights of a confessor. The first reproach was intended for the *association* which comprised members of both sexes. Certainly the Sacred Congregation, hearing of nuns who pretended to direct men, had a right to protest; but what can we say of one who persisted in seeing spiritual direction in the simple union of prayers which exists between the associates and the sisters of the Reparation? With regard to the Superioress's share in the direction of the sisters, it was easy to make sure that it was confined to the minimum of the right which the Constitutions granted to all ancient orders; but, by a wrong use of the word, people were led to believe that the abuse existed.

Such were these so-called 'Observations,' all bearing the sign of wisdom and the stamp, in their expression, of a paternal indulgence. They certainly did not contain, in any degree, a reprobation of the institute; and the criticisms contained in them were applied to defects which could not even be traced in the constitutive plan presented to the Holy Father; they related to details which might have been separated from the case, and which a more charitable examination would at least have interpreted, not according to the whims and exaggerations of persons ignorant of all that concerned the institute, but according to the approved spirit, the writings, and the conduct of the Foundress.

The conclusion was, that, before obtaining the approbation, the institute should make itself better known. And, in fact, when it was better known, the approbation was immediately granted. But for the time being the 'Observations' remained as a direction which it was necessary to accept and follow. Nevertheless, upholding, with a firmness full of submission and respect, the interests of the community confided to his care, the Superior drew up *explanations*, destined to rectify the equivocal language which had called forth these reproaches, and to explain, on other points, the full and entire adhesion of the Foundress and her children to the counsels which had been given them. These explanations were presented to the new Archbishop of Paris, Mgr. Darboy, who, being ignorant of all that had taken place, refused to interfere in the matter, but whose benevolent protection was soon after secured to the Institute of Reparation.* Thus it became necessary to send these *replies* direct to the Sacred Congregation; and the affair of the approbation, which for eighteen months had been laboriously carried on amid difficulties which might easily have been avoided, was now lost in silence and oblivion; but to be renewed two years later, and brought without effort to the most prompt and successful conclusion.

But though the future and the interests of the institute

---

* In 1865 Mgr. Darboy himself introduced the affair of the approbation. Mlle. Darboy, the sister of the prelate-martyr, had the delicate attention to make the community a present of a precious autograph—the pencil copy of the letter which he wrote on this occasion. The following is the text of the letter:

'George Darboy, by the grace of God, &c.

'The Superioress of the community of the "Adoration Réparatrice," desiring to secure for her foundation the blessing and encouragement of the Holy See, has begged us to second her address to our Holy Father the Pope.

'We eagerly comply with this request. Nothing can give us greater pleasure than to see a congregation flourishing and developing itself in our diocese, founded to adore our Lord Jesus Christ in the Blessed Sacrament, and to repair the outrages committed against His divinity. Moreover the means which it offers to its members in order to attain its end appears to us perfectly praiseworthy, and the rules, the draught of which has been submitted to us, can most usefully be put into practise.

'For this reason, wishing to make our Lord Jesus Christ known, loved, and served by means of a pious congregation, and desiring to draw down on our diocese new blessings, we venture to express the hope that his Holiness will be pleased to encourage the congregation of the "Adoration Réparatrice," and thus to give it increase and strength.

'Given at Paris, on the 9th day of June 1865.''

were in no degree compromised, yet the timorous soul of the Foundress had received a cruel wound. A calmer and more just view of what had occurred would undoubtedly have spared her this excess of sorrow; but who dare reproach her for having felt too keenly a trial of which her filial submission was the cause, and for not having reasoned sufficiently on a point which seemed to her one of faith? An expression of mistrust, issuing from the centre of Catholic unity, had reached the birthplace of the work of which she was the instrument, and this was sufficient to fill her conscience with alarm. To submit, to accept all these reproaches and changes, to lend herself to every disavowal in word and deed; in one word, to do far more than had been required of her,—all this she regarded as nothing. But to continue to live after the blame incurred at Rome, still to bear the name that had been declared ambitious, still to direct souls in that path which had been deemed unsafe,—no, no, she could not endure the bare idea. She would assemble her poor children, would recall to them her past life, her actions, her writings, her words; she would acknowledge herself to be the plaything of an illusion, and beg her children to seek, in an authorised religious order, a less suspected means of sanctification. Such was the first impression of her heart on receiving the observations. And it did not proceed from discouragement or anger: it was an excess, but a sincere excess of abnegation and contempt of herself.

'Father,' she wrote to her confessor, 'I had relied on that approbation granted by the most legitimate authorities. Strong in this belief, I have often poured forth my joy on this point to my children. And now, if, being their Mother, I do not commit to writing a retractation, if I do not take from them all that I have written for them, a tradition will remain in their hearts incompatible with the obedience due to Rome—something similar to that Jansenistical venom existing in certain orders during the sixteenth and seventeenth centuries. O no; may God preserve me from the greatest misfortune that can befall a Catholic soul!'

Thus, ever prompt in accusing herself, she exaggerated the

drift of the criticisms directed to certain details of her institute. The worst days of her spiritual life seemed to have returned, days in which all seemed to her illusion and the mockery of the devil. For long, obedience had reassured her, but now obedience seemed to require that she should condemn herself and her foundation; for she could not but acknowledge that the Réparatrice devotion, which had been declared to teem with perils, was the very foundation of what she had regarded as her vocation. Until then she had never ceased to inculcate it into her children. The last fifteen years passed before her eyes. What had she done during that time? Drawn poor souls far from the high road, and exposed them, along with herself, to be disowned by the Church. Was it to obtain such a result that she had suffered for so long, that she had sacrificed her repose, nay, even her Carmelite vocation? Why had she not abandoned all when she was first reproached by the Council of the Archbishopric of Paris? Then she would not have merited the reproaches addressed to her from Rome ten years later. She was told to wait for the definitive judgment; but how could she maintain, even provisionally, three communities in a form of life of which the Holy See had hesitated to approve? In the midst of such humiliating thoughts, and the anguish consequent on them, imagine the clear and firm mind of Mary Teresa, suspecting a mistake but too real, and yet rendering an invincible testimony to the uprightness of her views and the truth of her vocation; one will then be able to form an idea of the violent conflict which was rending her soul and depriving her poor body of the last remnant of life.

Fortunately, in this great crisis, as in every preceding one, spiritual direction came to the assistance of her conscience at the point of death, and the voice of truth made itself heard above the cry of anguish and of temptation. We do not know the secret of the consolations that her prudent and pious confessor,[*] so renowned for his filial devotion to the Holy See, instilled into her soul; but he was not in want of reasons to reduce to its right value the exaggerated uneasiness of his peni-

[*] Father Freyd, Superior of the French College at Rome.

tent. The formulas had been found too aspiring. Very well, then the formulas must be corrected; but nothing in the reproach condemned her conduct or her doctrine, nor could it have prevailed over the evidence of facts. Who, then, knowing Mary Teresa, could doubt the horror she had always evinced towards everything that attracts notice? How many times had she not resisted even God Himself, in order to avoid the manifestation of His graces! With regard to illusory devotions, she could not be suspected of weakness on that point,* she who had always refused, even at the expense of the temporal interests of her foundation, to join such alliances proposed by certain protectors, who were not sufficiently careful to avoid this danger. Was there question of dogma? Again, if any little expressions had been in fault, the expressions must be rectified; but why think that, on its account, the Church would condemn the Réparatrice idea? Does not the Church herself command prayers of reparation? does she not invite her children to unite their penances to the sufferings of the Redeemer for the conversion of sinners? If we wrong the mediation of Jesus Christ by associating ourselves to it, Luther was right in his opposition to the Council of Trent, and good works have no share in our justification. If the expiation of the just, vivified by the merits of our Saviour, cannot be offered for the sinner, the doctrine of the Communion of Saints must be erased from the Creed. Evidently this was not the meaning of the Roman observations;

* She one day wrote as follows on this subject to her community at Lyons: 'The doctors of the Church greatly fear that shade of illusory spirituality which leads some, under the pretext of becoming *Réparatrices*, to take the name of *victims*, and to think that to repair is to leave the common path. At their first *bobo* or grief they think themselves a Saint Katharine, and presumptuously set the smaller religious virtues on one side. You know how much I participate in this fear. . . . Prove this by avoiding self-seeking in your interior life as you would avoid the plague. Enter more and more into a true and solid abnegation ; *be good daughters;* have a good spirit, truly Christian, which clings to a true practical self-renunciation, and flees from those paths in which one loses oneself *first in the clouds, then in the senses.*'

And again: 'What is required of us is to change some words, and perhaps more simple ones might be less liable to turn weak heads and ambitious natures.'

and if not, these latter were but the just and wise criticisms on a few expressions found in unimportant writings, and the institute had only to wait in peace for the ultimate judgment of the Holy See on the order, which would end in its favour.

We do not doubt that Mary Teresa found, in these suggestions of her spiritual father, the solution of her scruples, at least so much so as to induce her to bear her burden to the end. If we possessed no other proof, a simple comparison of dates would be a sufficient one. This affair at Rome, begun in January 1862, and abandoned in May 1863, coincides with the date of the building of the monastery, with the laying of the foundation-stone of the chapel—in short, with that period of activity which immediately preceded, in the life of Mary Teresa, the recollection of the last hour. It may with truth be said that never was she more actively a Foundress than at the time that her Foundation became the object of the most cruel suspicions. Thus does divine jealousy unmercifully pursue great souls, never suffering them to repose in their work, and loading them with humiliations at the very time that they are working most efficaciously for His glory. And when the trial does not proceed from without, but from the house of God; when, besides the persecution of her enemies, the soul has to endure the suspicions of friends, the mistrust of the Father of the family; then it may truly be said that the rigour of the divine treatment is at its height; and in order to explain it, we must recognise in the soul who experiences it a sanctity sufficiently rare as to merit to pass through the crucible.

So also we must not be astonished to see the passionate lover of the glory of Jesus Christ end her career in a state of painful dejection. Of late, in that repose of mind which her temporary abdication had afforded her, all the youth and freshness of her heart had at times returned, enabling her to enjoy the spiritual delights of which the austerity of her life had so long deprived her. Now she fed only on bitterness, but she knew how to accept it in peace. She wrote thus to her confessor:

'I can no longer serve as a Mother to my sisters, and you

know that their affectionate hearts seek me as if by a natural instinct. I must, then, reinstall them, see that their new life is properly ordered, and then disáppear for ever. . . . . Father, I assure you that if such be the case, my poor soul will bid adieu to this world in the greatest peace. After considering my past life, and declaring my inspirations to be illusions, what more is left that can trouble me? I know that the Redemption is abundant, and I feel in my heart, amid the greatest anguish, a love strong as death.' Again: 'I can say, from the depth of abjection into which I have fallen, My heart is ready. Let God break me or restore me as He pleases. I desire and seek only a requiem on leaving this life; and in the next, that place in purgatory reserved to illusory good intentions. This disposition, sad certainly, does not diminish my courage. When I am able, I perform the duty of the hour; a crisis follows, and I remain in a swoon as long as God pleases.'

Nevertheless the terrible disease against which her energetic constitution had struggled for years, increased daily in violence; everything seemed to sanction the belief that the last change, so many times expected, had at length arrived. She now felt more absorbed than ever by a numbness which deprived her of every faculty save that of suffering. 'I desire,' she said, 'to remain faithful to the triple oath which has bound me to be a servant of God unto death; to beg, to obey, to suffer, such is the foundation of my edifice. I should be a vile beggar, a poor slave condemned to hard labour; a victim, abject in body, in mental powers, in everything. . . . My being is without strength, without life. I am truly ready to be cast into that place where the dead are sown, where they wait for the harvest of Christ. . . . But how is my soul employed amid this sleep? She believes and communicates; she hopes and confesses; she loves passively, by delivering herself up to the accomplishment of the merciful justice and will of God. Beyond this, ask nothing of me, you who are my masters! I assure you that it is a great thing to do so much; if more were required of me I should become mad. But why do I speak? I show myself too much. . . . The dead should not issue from their graves. . . .

Lord, let the angel of death, who has so often approached me, place upon me a heavy stone which will retain me in the abyss into which I have fallen. Grant at least that I may there repose in the peace of those who are judged, and that I may no more trouble the living with my complaints. . . . Silence ! . . .'

If the reader be troubled or scandalised at this passage, we refer him to the *Lives of the Saints*. There is scarcely one who, at some time or other appointed by God, has not experienced that supreme anguish of a soul who finds herself lost in darkness, ignorant whether she is worthy of love or hatred. It is not despair ; for in the depth of these desolate souls there exists a firm faith, an unconquerable love ; never have they been more ready to suffer martyrdom. But God hides Himself, He seems to have withdrawn His consolations ; and a last resemblance to the crucified Saviour forces them to cry out, ' My God, my God, why hast Thou forsaken me ?'*

Towards the beginning of July the invalid grew worse ; the doctor declared that an abscess had formed below the brain, and that it was time to administer the Last Sacraments. Mary Teresa had always entertained a particular devotion for the Sacrament of Extreme Unction. She received it from the hands of her confessor Father Freyd with sentiments of sweet contrition. She then relapsed into that state of apparent torpor which in her did not prevent union with God, and from which she recovered at times ; thus enabling her to commit to writing, under the direction of her confessor, the impressions of her last days. She unceasingly conversed with the angel who, she imagined, was sent from God to receive her soul. ' How beautiful,' she would say, ' is that angel of death, commissioned by love to purify our life and sing the canticle of our deliverance ! That angel is the greatest friend of man ; his action is admirable, powerful as justice, sweet as love ; his mission is more beautiful than that of any other of God's messengers. . . . Beautiful angel, who hast in thy hand the sceptre destined to govern this

* The *Life of Father de Ravignan* affords a striking example of this action of God. His pious biographer, Father de Ponlevoy, has given a touching picture of the interior trials which prepared him for death.

miserable nature, wield it, and strike! Strike my heart in its inmost affections, Thou who art so pure! Strike my mind by delivering it to abjection!... Strike my body and all its senses by sickness, suffering, oppression, weakness! Finally, celestial envoy of love, obtain from our God that the last stroke you have to give may carry me away to heaven!'

Physical sickness continued its ravages; and feeling that death was at hand, she exclaimed, 'The angel of death has returned; he no longer holds the burning coal of suffering; his work is finished, at least on this earth; my senses could not bear farther annihilation without death.'

'He is sadder, but more beautiful than the first time, when He was beginning His work of destruction and purification. His terrible energy then impressed on my entire being a generous activity which served as a counterbalance to suffering, and comforted me in my agonies. I felt the realisation of those divine words: "And there appeared to Him an angel from heaven, strengthening Him; and being in an agony, *He prayed the longer*."

'There is in the accepting of the chalice a spring that exhilarates. But after drinking it to the dregs one lowers one's head, complaining lovingly of abandonment; and there come those who doubt, who deride, and present vinegar and gall. . . .

'The angel of death has returned, and day and night he is beside me, awaiting the signal for departure to free my soul from its clothing.'

All is not sadness in this expectation. The poor agonising soul still feels rays of joy.

'Sometimes He places a spark on my lips, and a song of praise, rapid but penetrating, issues from me and makes me acquiesce in the designs of God. Generally, the angel looks at me with profound calm. Everything within me seems to stop. I no longer hear the pendulum of life; it appears to participate in the eternal silence. At the commencement, when in this state, I was afraid of annihilation; but now a secret intelligence, which has no name in the inferior regions, reveals to me what God is and heaven. . . . These divine movements are rapid as thought; they do not dissipate the mortal sadness and abjection of the cross; but they fill my heart with hope and love.'

With a singular strength of mind she, as it were, assists at the departure of her soul and the dissolution of her flesh. 'Poor flesh! it also is silent, dried on the bones which bear it still; it already expects the resurrection; and even the worms anticipate their rights. This last struggle between animal life and the life of the mind is a strange study, not unworthy of the children of God, since Job desired a graver's pen to write it. Amidst this abjection of corruption which devours the flesh, and this resistance of the mind which calms its revolts by submitting them to faith, a holy pride fills the heart; one feels assured that one's faith is not vain, and that the divine food truly produces its germ. He who eats the flesh of the Saviour and drinks His blood shall not die, but shall pass from the Eucharistic life to the plenitude of the life of God.'

At length, after long listening to and contemplating her celestial companion, she addressed him in a final prayer: 'Remain there always, beautiful angel; do not leave me until you have deposited me in the bosom of God. You are my friend. By your contact, which brings on weakness, suffering, or tears, remind me of your presence! . . . The angel of death is there. He awaits me. . . . We do not sin when thinking of our last moments. . . . To die. . . . I shall soon die. . . . '

In this manner six weeks passed away after she had received Extreme Unction. On the 28th August it was decided to remove her to the new monastery, which had just been completed. It was the promised land, and God permitted her to die in it. She was carried on a litter, borne by her dear son, Father Francis, and one of her sisters; the Sister Assistant held an umbrella over her head, and another sister followed this modest and touching *cortège*. On entering her cell the invalid said to the assistant, 'O, how happy I am to be able to close my sacrifice here. I feel greatly consoled at having fulfilled the will of God. I feel that in coming here I am doing His will. . . . I hail this dwelling of the Lord with joy. . . . My children, preserve very faithfully the work of God.'

Thus, on the very threshold of eternity, she again obtained the sweet assurance of having accomplished her mission ; after so many crucifying doubts, she expired in confidence ; it was the commencement of her reward.

In her cell had been placed a small altar, decorated with great care. The assistant asked her if she was not pleased to see it. 'My child,' she replied, 'after once accepting to live in the state in which I now am, I should no longer see anything, feel anything, nor take pleasure in anything.*

The following day passed in great calm ; but on Saturday morning, finding their Mother worse, all the sisters repaired to her cell. Like St. Francis of Assisi, Mary Teresa wished to sing on her deathbed ; but her voice failed. At the suggestion of Father Francis her children responded to her pious desires by singing the hymn of the Compassion of Mary, the *Stabat*. The singing was interrupted by the arrival of the Rev. Father Freyd, who spoke for some minutes alone with the dying Mother ; the latter then asked that the Litany of the Saints might be recited. When it was over, all the sisters ap-

---

* It was doubtless in order to maintain to the last the calmness of a soul separated from all things, that she previously informed her family of the approach of her last hour.

'My dearly-loved Sister and Nephew,
'I have desired and asked for you the blessings of the Lord. I still pray at my last hour that divine Providence, who has promised to bestow a hundredfold on those who seek the kingdom of God and His justice, may bless the temporal goods of your children and grandchildren ; and I beg of Him to preserve in our family the honour of intact probity, of justice, and Christian delicacy.

'. . . May your children and grandchildren seek in our houses prayers in all their necessities. Knowing my children as I do, I think I may promise you that you will always find their hearts devoted and attached to yours by unchangeable feelings. I am also so confident of your love for me that I feel sure that wherever there are Sisters of the Adoration Réparatrice they will always find in you friends, protectors, and defenders of their rights and interests.

'May the Lord Jesus in the Ever-blessed Sacrament receive into His fatherly Heart my wishes and prayers, and grant to my two families length of days, a numerous posterity, peace in this world, and happiness in the next!'

(Taken from a letter of the 12th December 1858, which was not to be forwarded to her relations until after her death.)

proached the bed to receive the blessing of their Mother, who, summoning up all her remaining strength, addressed them in a few words, of which the following is the sense: 'My dear children, I ask your pardon for all my faults, my want of charity, and omissions. I long to expatiate them in purgatory, or repair them in heaven by procuring for you many graces. Adieu, my beloved children! My last wish is that you should always be children of St. Teresa of Jesus. Adieu, my children; be generous, very generous. God requires generosity. He has given us everything that we have; we must not think of ourselves. . . . Adieu, my beloved children; your love and devotedness are as a lively flame in my heart; love is strong as death. . . . I bless you from my inmost heart.'

She then wished that the professed sisters should, two by two, kneel at the foot of her bed and embrace each other, pronouncing these words: 'He that loveth Me keepeth My commandments.' This, she said, was to atone for all the faults against charity, *which were henceforth to be remembered no more.*

On the following day, Sunday the 30th August, she sent for the sister-assistant. 'My child,' she said, 'I feel that I am about to die. The anguish of death is upon me.' The agony lasted during four hours. Towards ten o'clock her countenance was suddenly seen to change and assume a beatific expression. Her eyes were fixed on heaven, and she said three times in a faltering voice, 'I see—I see—I see!'

And what remained of her mortal life was sweetly absorbed in the eternal love of God.

Whilst her soul rejoined in heaven the souls of her children who had gone before her, her body was laid beside their remains in the vault of the Institute of the Reparation in the cemetery of Montparnasse. Her children ardently desired to preserve her remains within the sanctuary which she had prepared for the glorification of the Eucharist; but the backward state of the building and the difficulty of procuring the requisite authorisation compelled them for the time being to relinquish their project. Providence, however, soon intervened, in a manner worthy of notice, to recall from exile the bones of the Foundress. Within five months after her death proceedings, not originating with the community, were set on foot, and every obstacle was overcome with surprising facility. In the foundation of the new chapel a crypt had been formed immediately beneath the spot where the Eucharistic throne was to be raised; the body of Mary Teresa was translated there on the 26th February 1864. There it now rests, on the spot she most envied when alive; there, since the opening of the new sanctuary, her remains serve as a footstool to the altar of the Adoration of Reparation.

CHAPTER XVI.

Principal characteristics of the sanctity of Mary Teresa.—A few instances of her virtues: her faith, love of God, poverty, humility, love of suffering.—Her own idea of her foundation.—Conclusion.

WE have concluded the narrative of a life in which the action of God's grace is so evident that it should strengthen the faith of the weakest soul. It is not our intention to imitate the ancient hagiographers, who were accustomed, after relating the actions of the Saints, to give a methodical statement of their virtues. Nevertheless, we should not consider our task accomplished were we to neglect to place before our readers the most striking characteristics of this beautiful and remarkable life; and in order to establish some link between these scattered elements, we propose to classify them under two principal heads, viz. what relates to the Foundress herself, and what regards the work that she was raised up to accomplish. Her chief characteristics were greatness of mind and generosity of character; her intellect opened spontaneously to truth and her heart to devotion.

In her youth we saw her thirsting for knowledge, but still more eager for self-sacrifice. This exuberance of life formed, throughout the whole of her mystic career, the foundation of her most painful sacrifices. Divine love is jealous, and will not permit nature to attribute to herself any works of grace. This was the reason why this upright and clear-sighted soul had to undergo the trial of a strict and badly-understood direction, so that she might find in the darkness in which she was plunged that interior death of self which prepares the soul for great lights. But her heart especially, that heart so ardent and tender, was to be crushed in a thousand ways before it could become the confidant of the Heart of Jesus Christ and the channel of His gifts. We think that on this point the life of Mary Teresa may be compared to that of those great Saints on whom the cross of the Divine Master was most visibly impressed. Contradiction followed her everywhere, allowing her no rest. When a child she wished to love God, and was opposed by her family; on reaching girlhood she was conquered by grace, but it was now her confessor's turn to constrain her in her spiritual yearnings. Did she devote herself to works of mercy, an imperious attraction deprived her of the power of action; did she become without her own knowledge contemplative, she was forced to doubt herself and struggle even against God. At length, after innumerable contradictions, she thought that she had reached the desired port of Carmel; but instantly a new vocation displayed itself to her, snatched from her her dreams of a hidden life, and cast her trembling amid all the difficulties of an undertaking which was, humanly speaking, impossible. Then it was that she exhausted every form of sorrow. Foundress in spite of herself, she is accused of ambition; forgetful of herself, even to excess, she is reproached with ingratitude; struggling against supernatural graces, she is yet set down as a visionary; in turn the plaything of God and men, she gropes along a path strewn with thorns; her progress upward is rapid, but it seems to her that she is always going back. Her institute grows under her hand, but everything conspires to make her imagine that she has caused its destruction; fifteen years suffice to insure its development and stability in an almost miraculous manner, and during these fifteen years she never ceased to bear in her heart the crucified feeling which obliged her to join with all those who condemned her against herself.

Thus does God appear to take pleasure in breaking the instruments of which He makes use; in reality, He does not crush them, but contents Himself with bending them. Ruled by divine action, the creature no longer feels that she lives, though more alive than ever. Her faculties develop; the gifts of intellect, the treasures of the heart, the charms of a happy nature, all are employed in the service of grace, and the words of the Saviour are verified in the person of the Saints: 'He that loseth his life for My sake shall find it.'*

From this point of view, it is interesting to seek in the life of Mary Teresa manifestations of human nature peeping out amidst this living death. This we have been able to do from time to time, and the reader will recollect having more than once found in this story the artist, the poetic soul, the faithful friend, the cheerful bright companion, the loving daughter, the affectionate mother, when he expected to meet only a grave and austere person, moulded by penance and saddened by the sins of the whole world.

There remains but little for us to add to this portrait, which has developed itself during the course of the narrative; and if there be still something to be told, it is less the natural gifts belonging to that soul than certain details of her Christian virtues.

Her faith enabled her to understand the promises of our Lord to true believers in an extraordinary manner. Mary Teresa experienced temptation against faith, but never the hesitation of those souls who believe only by halves, and who treat God with only half confidence. An education scarcely Christian, and Jansenistic in its few Christian tendencies, had developed in her a reasoning spirit which led her to distrust everything supernatural; but in her inmost soul the faith of her baptism protested in favour of the rights of God, and when once pride of intellect had yielded to divine grace the supernatural took possession of her soul and maintained the mastery. Then miracles of faith were worked in her; nothing astonished her, nothing troubled her, when what she desired depended upon God alone. She feared only the obstacles of infidelity, which she called the only ones that can arrest the action of Providence. At a time of great financial difficulty she wrote as follows: 'This morning our Lord obliged me to accept all by leaving me in that state of abjection foretold in the Gospel to him who begins to build a tower without having the necessary materials to finish it. If the tower spring from me it will

* Qui perdiderit animam suam propter me, inveniet eam (Matt. xvi. 25).

crumble away; but if from God, He can preserve it.' It is a known fact that in those critical moments, when the very existence of her institute was at stake from the lack of indispensable means, assistance never failed to come to her aid in the most unexpected ways. Doubtless we must give due credit to those generous benefactors whose assistance more than once preserved the institute from ruin, and whose faithful friendship, outliving the Foundress, still continues to provide for the existence of her spiritual family in their many trials. But when we recollect that Mary Teresa was one of those persons who seldom asked and sometimes refused to receive; that, moreover, her old friends were not able to render much assistance; and that although gratitude afterwards united her by the closest ties to her new benefactors, yet that the greater part of them were entirely unknown to her when they came forward to her assistance, it is impossible not to recognise in the circumstances which brought them together the reward promised to that faith which never doubts or wavers.

This view of '*God alone*' in the conduct of events rendered her almost indifferent to the attacks of which her foundation was the object on the part of man. One day she was told that a celebrated religious, who had formerly rendered her a service, was taking part against her in an affair which interested her community. 'If Father ———,' she answered, 'served, when it pleased God, as an instrument to develop the work, what he will say at another time cannot harm it, unless permitted by God.'

In the same letter, she added: 'Do not trouble yourself about what is personal to me. I now feel too strongly how little I am worth to fear the loss of the good opinion of others; those who despise me will be perfectly in the right. I shall then no longer be what I so much dread, a *pharisee*, and in the acceptance of my abjection in the spirit of the *publican* I see a hope of justification which gives me courage.'

The same spirit of faith caused her to suspect all law-suits, in which she found too much human calculation, and the alleged motive of the glory of God did not reassure her when she had reason to fear that it served only as a pretext for earthly prudence. 'People,' she said, 'too often confound true acts of faith with *combinations of the glory of God according to human ideas.*' Neither did it afford her pleasure to hear that postulants had been won for her institute, if the will of God were not plainly manifest. 'Your zeal and the way you carry it out please me,' she wrote to Brother Francis, 'because you know how to concentrate it in the heart of God, and leave the Divine Spirit to breathe where and when He wills. O, how rarely is the creature called to make the first appeal to the heart of the elect! How true are those words of Christ: "No one can come to Me unless My Father draw him!" But they are especially true with regard to the Eucharistic work.' Finally, that faith, which had enlightened her in action, formed her consolation in suffering; and the remedy which in her own case proved so effectual she recommended to others. 'Every remedy is found in faith,' she often wrote; 'when my children can no longer draw strength from their sufferings, I make them meditate upon the Catechism; and when the eyes of their soul are once fixed on those divine elements of our origin and our last end, they again discover the bright star that leads to Jesus.'

It is likewise to this spirit of faith that we must ascribe her esteem, respect, and singular devotion for the Sacred Scriptures. Unacquainted, by the godless education she had received, with the sacred writings, she opened the Bible late in life, and at intervals; even then it was only in a prayer-book which contained but a part of the sacred books. She was not then better prepared than persons of the world usually are to taste that solid food which fortified the devotion of our fathers; but faith immediately revealed to her its great price. No sooner had she thoroughly become acquainted with the sacred text than she found in it all she needed for meditation or prayer. 'By a singular grace,' she said, 'notwithstanding my ordinary want of memory, all the texts of the Gospel and many others from the sacred writings came back to my mind without the slightest effort; and so abundant was this food that, even when I was not transported with love, I had real conversations with our

Lord; His Holy Spirit, I think, gave me these clear lights on the Divine Words. And even now, during my retreats, it is nearly always from the holy books that I receive practical lights on different mysteries or virtues. . . . I have often understood, or rather felt, that God is specially revealed in the Holy Scriptures, but that to understand them in their full meaning will be the occupation of eternity.'

Such were the foundations of Mary Teresa's faith; but faith is only the commencement of justification; charity is its crown and its plenitude. Did we intend to describe here the divine love in the soul of Mary Teresa, we should have to repeat what has already been said in the story of her life. We will merely add a few touches to the portrait. Mystical love was, we may say, the only passion of her life. It was in vain that, in her youth, she wished to resist the solicitations of the Holy Spirit, to enclose herself in the timid and reserved affection of the servant for a master; the wave of grace raised her in spite of herself and carried her even beyond filial love up to that One and Jealous Love which confers on the soul touched by God the title of Spouse. I say jealous love; the expression is not too strong if one recollects the delicacy and exigences of that Love. That conquered soul deemed it too little to sacrifice to God her repose, her comfort, her reputation; love required her to sacrifice even her zeal and holy desires. 'My child,' was once said to her during the time of meditation, ' my child, take care, you desire to serve too ardently; I wish you to love Me; but love will work in you as I please.' Hence the origin of that passive state which, in spite of herself, captivated the powers of her soul and paralysed even her body. To ordinary eyes it appeared a numbness and drowsiness; in reality, it was the victory of the Spouse triumphing over the resistance of His love, and compelling her, by physical weakness, to retire from converse with men and the duties of her station, to speak with Him alone. One day, when in the parlour, in conference with a pious lady, this supernatural state took possession of her; she struggled against it with all her might, both in order to finish what she considered a duty and not to let the divine action become apparent. At length she was overcome and sank down; it was thought that she had fainted, and she was carried to her cell; but her children, who knew her better, having left her alone, she remained during a great part of the day in a state of mental prayer, receiving the reproaches of her Master, and promising Him never again to fight against Him. When she could not, or did not, know how to yield in time, she fell into a state of the most complete prostration; those who then wished to recall her to life by external means inflicted on her, without knowing it, strange tortures; on coming to herself, she had to atone for her infidelity by long days of trial and spiritual desolation. When, on the contrary, she obeyed without resistance the interior call to solitude, she received in recompense ineffable delights, though these were often accompanied by great physical suffering; it was at such times that she received the greatest lights concerning her mission, and it was then that the Divine Spouse consoled her for the contradictions of men.

It was of this state that she thus spoke one day: 'My body troubles me less when I am prostrate on the ground and without witnesses.' It was this passive union which both attracted and yet terrified her, and which drew from her that cry of prayer and anguish: 'My God, my God, have pity on me! Strengthen me, if I must tread the miraculous path Thou hast shown me—the path of love and of suffering, . . . of celestial joys; . . . the path of sorrow even unto blood; the path in which a human being must deliver herself up to every kind of humiliation, to contempt; . . . a path in which we are disowned by the very souls we seek to save, . . . but a divine path in which we are united to the Saviour of men; a path in which one's supernatural being possesses the energy of the celestial spirits, in which we contemplate the adorable Face of Jesus crucified and reflect His virtues, His love, His glory. He who follows this path will be rejected by men, but he will be loved by the angels and saints. O eternal Love, Thou knowest how ardently I desire to walk in this path! My wish to love Thee has entered the very marrow of my bones.'

Thus love held her captive; but, when allowed, she broke

out into transports of zeal, into burning desires to communicate that Love to others, to gain souls to this Love, to surmount every obstacle which hindered Love. Her institute sprang from this desire; but she everywhere sought its accomplishment with unceasing ardour. She wished to see the undisputed reign of this Love of God established not only in her children's hearts, but in every heart that approached her. 'My child,' she wrote to a lady who had asked her advice, 'make a void in your heart, and Jesus will fill it. The creature hides the Creator; multiplied means hide the end. Supports are doubtless needed, but very few; means are needed, but they must be simple and adapted to the order of Providence. . . . Man has two wings to lift him up above earthly things; simplicity and purity of intention (*Imitation of Jesus Christ*). Meditate always on this, and a bright light will guide your steps. . . . What I desire for you is that you should make *the void;* the action of God is not free, for want of room.'

Without this perfect submission to the will of God, nothing appeared to her pure, not even the holiest desires. She wrote to a person who regretted that she had married: 'You desire to be a nun; all else is burdensome, wearisome, and leads you to despair. Very well. Say: I will leave everything for God, even my desire for a religious life. I will set myself to do His will, and with love and joy to bear the heavy cross of life in the world. Then I shall have left all, I shall follow Jesus daily, I shall be a saint; for a saint is a servant of God who abandons herself to Him to do what He pleases, neither more nor less.'

'Be calm,' she said one day to a young girl who hesitated concerning her vocation; 'I do not wish to *make you* a nun.' But the same fidelity which rendered her discreet in cases when the call of God was not manifest, or when unexpected duties became obstacles to a vocation previously certain, this same fidelity inspired her with a sad and even severe compassion for those souls who, through want of generosity, hesitated to respond to the advances of the Divine Spouse. One of her children, who became later on one of the holiest and best beloved, at first gave her this cause for grief, and Mary Teresa thus related her sorrow to her confessor: 'Seeing that I was moved, she suddenly said, "Mother, you think that I am on the brink of a precipice?" I answered, "My dear child, until now I thought that you shared with me the happiness I have possessed for thirty years, an ever-increasing happiness—the happiness of giving God an undivided love, and of being possessed by Him unreservedly. The thought of seeing the Divine Love within you depending on a creature fills me with sadness." ... Whilst speaking thus, my tears flowed abundantly, and my whole soul melted with love of our Divine Spouse. A holy jealousy tortured me; I desired to snatch that soul from the illusions of creatures.'

She denounced not less severely the conduct of those parents who interpose between God and the hearts of their children; she did not fear to show them in this resistance a source of sorrow and every kind of evil. She not only condemned opposition, but also useless delays. 'Let not a soul called by God,' she said, 'lose time; life is so short.' She once wrote to a mother as follows: 'Alas, what harm do Christian parents effect, without knowing it, by thus putting off the designs of God! A young soul tires amid these struggles; the devil takes advantage of it to raise temptations and troubles; and at length the soul approaches the holy altar, reserved towards God and cold towards those who, by imprudent prudence, have weakened the beautiful grace of fervour and faith in a vocation which she feels still exists.'

When she had to deal with pious parents who were capable of understanding the delicacy of Christian perfection, she wished that the vocation of their daughters should serve for their sanctification; she did not allow them to pursue into the cloister, by the cares of a too purely human affection, the dear victims that they had given to God. She was rigorous in her requirements; but at the same time she knew how to heal the wounds of the maternal heart and set a right value on the tenderest and most delicate feelings. 'My daughter,' she wrote to one of these poor mothers, 'for a long while you have educated your child for God alone; but later on you looked at her, and that look was one of the flesh and not of the spirit; you were proud of her qualities, and your nature was taken with it, for your maternal love had arrived at that point when *friendship* is mingled with it, a friendship which does not remain content with giving only, but wishes to receive. Then I saw you with sorrow fall into this natural temptation and leaving the path which God had traced out for you; that path that we must follow in company with the immolated Lamb, but in which there are halts which give a foretaste of heaven. O my poor dear child, you did not know the jealousy of the Divine Spouse when He has bestowed certain favours. . . . My child, I am old. I have lived long and very much in the affections; to my shame and regret I have often placed obstacles in God's way by feelings which were, in themselves, good and right. I know the struggles of holy love and legitimate but natural love; and I am convinced that you will recover from what you now suffer; but the only means is to allow Divine Love to gain the complete victory.'

Finally, she would have wished all who have influence over souls to work with equal fervour for the interests of God. In a private letter she complained that such was not always the case. 'They scarcely dare say that one must love God above all things. Directors are sometimes pusillanimous; they tolerate the rivalry of the natural affections against a divine and pure love. To repeat with St. Teresa *God alone,* or even *God above all,* seems a fanatical devotion.'

We need hardly add, for the history of her life is a superabundant proof of it, that this vigour was in her joined to a loving sweetness. 'Our state of victims should be neither sad nor stiff; neither cold nor bitter; no concessions to nature; but charity and sweetness in all our relations with others.' And again: 'Without love, a soul is at once independent and weak; the natural attraction to God makes her proud, and the philosophical knowledge of the abject miseries of humanity distracts her and leads her almost to despair.' 'When love possesses me, all within me changes; for love then is the only object that I need follow. All that increases charity in me is welcome; all that turns me from it is bad.'

Such were the marvellous effects of Divine Love in this chosen soul. It is then needless to inquire whether she possessed that *ensemble* of Christian virtues which are but the rays of love. However, it is interesting to note, in her life, the virtues for which she was most remarkable.

The spirit of poverty had in her preceded the religious vocation; had it not been her duty to keep a comfortable home for her parents she would soon have stripped herself of all that she possessed; but charity afforded her the means of living poorly under the appearance of ease. As she always gave more than she possessed, she was obliged to obtain, by continual work, the resources which she needed, and, by this laborious application, she discovered a fresh occasion of sanctifying herself by penance. This love of labour did but increase within her, after she had embraced religious poverty; she never ceased inculcating the necessity of it to her children : 'For us,' she would say, 'labour is a duty, not a recreation.' To gain her livelihood, to work in order to live, seemed to her to be the law of those who profess to imitate Jesus of Nazareth. But whilst working for daily necessities, she declared war unmercifully against whatever was superfluous. 'We must,' she said, 'be poor in reality and consent to be treated as the poor; let us not attempt to live in first-class style; our bread should be the bread of the poor.' One day, before her profession, when the community was but in its infancy in the house in the Rue d'Enfer, she required a tooth to be extracted. Instead of sending for a dentist, she repaired, miserably clothed, to the Hôtel Dieu, and there, amid a crowd of very poor people, she waited her turn to be operated upon by charity. She returned very joyful, and could not help expressing to Father Lefèvre the great delight she had experienced in passing for a poor woman. Another time, after long weeks of illness, she perceived that the tender care of her infirmarian had gradually accumulated in her cell many useless objects. She thus describes it in a letter: 'There were,' she said, 'books, holy pictures, boxes, flowers, furniture, and many other little things. I felt the greatest confusion at having opened the door to such superfluities, which hid my darling poverty, and I begged the procuratrix to take them away. Then, without any effort, I made a long meditation on the poverty of my dear Spouse.'

Poverty strips us of exterior possessions; it is reserved for humility to strip us of ourselves. This difficult virtue is the true touchstone of perfection. We do not think that the sanctity of Mary Teresa would have had cause to fear on this point. God Himself undertook to bend her pride by the severe guidance of her first director; but still more, by the austerity, rigorous in a very different way, of the interior path in which she was to walk. When the time came for her to undertake her foundation, she had arrived at that rare degree when the soul can say with sincerity that she despises herself; and this disposition continued to increase within her until her death, so much so that it sometimes led her into excesses. When we read the letters that she wrote during her last years, when we see in what light she judged her life and her past career, we can scarcely avoid feeling sad; we are tempted to ask God why He has joined so much bitterness to the practice of the purest virtue, and refused to His faithful spouse the sweet satisfaction of knowing that He accepted her sacrifices. The reply to this question will be found in the whole history of Mary Teresa: that period of her life in which she was, as it were, tottering in the path of love, was the very one in which she was loaded with the greatest favours; as her fidelity increased God gradually weaned her from the milk of children, and desired that she should consume herself slowly in the rigorous flames of a love so much more pure as it was more humble and more divested of all self-seeking.

' Nevertheless it must not be imagined that this disgust of herself amounted to despair. When her trials were the greatest she never doubted God's love for her, any more than during the most wearying contradictions she doubted the truth of her mission. 'My sin,' she said, 'is always before me; but it is no longer against me.' Often at the time that she felt herself overwhelmed by the feeling of her own helplessness and unworthiness, she gave the most striking proofs of that confidence in God which counts all obstacles as nothing. Broken down by humiliation, she recovered her boldness to serve the interests of her Master; she passed in one instant from the most extreme confusion to perfect confidence; or rather, there was room in her heart for both these feelings, which may appear to be opposed to each other, but which may easily be reconciled in a soul touched by God, through the fidelity which makes her docile to the divers influences of divine grace.

Poverty and humility form two branches of our Saviour's cross, love of suffering forms the third, and completes in the faithful soul the resemblance to Jesus crucified. But here it is needless to seek examples in a life which was, from beginning to end, one long exercise of that virtue. It will suffice to sum up all in a saying of Mary Teresa, which may serve as an encouragement and consolation to those whom fear of suffering keeps back on the threshold of perfection: 'The excess of my sorrow has caused peace and strength to descend into my broken heart; for whenever one accepts the chalice to the dregs, one finds Jesus Christ and His all-powerful help.... It is the first portion of the chalice which is bitter, and not that sediment which we so much fear.'

We have enumerated the characteristics which complete the portrait of Mary Teresa; we have now only to say a few words concerning her way of understanding her institute.

The history of the foundation has made known the primitive thought whence issued the Institute of the 'Adoration Réparatrice.' It was a thought of zeal for the outraged honour of God in the Holy Eucharist, and for the salvation of sinners. To attract pure souls to the presence of the Blessed Sacrament exposed on the altar; to associate them by prayer and penance with the reparation of Jesus Christ,—such was the design which first united in one common effort the founders of the Perpetual Adoration, and the pious instigator of a devotion which was to terminate in the formation of a new religious family. But if zeal were the motive power, and the Eucharist the means, what was the form, the particular characteristic of the institute? Here is revealed what we might call the *special genius* of Mary Teresa, if it were not better to reserve to that inspiration of a great soul the true name which is suited to it—*her divine mission.* It is natural for those who know the different forms of life which a variety of religious rules has introduced into the Church to suppose that a new institute, specially devoted to Reparation for sin, would borrow from the old Orders what was most austere in exterior appearance, most rigid in spirit, and most painful in practice. Such, however, was not Mary Teresa's idea; and if we wish to know the reason, it is that her future foundation was from the very beginning revealed to her entire, with its spirit, its proceedings, and its maxims; and that if more than once she found it necessary to defend her primitive idea against alterations which threatened it from without, yet, to carry out its details, she had only to place herself before her model, and continue to reproduce it in all simplicity.

Now this type of the Institute of Reparation is easily to be recognised: a single word suffices to describe it, the word which Mary Teresa had made the motto of her institute—*Nazareth.* In the life of Nazareth she found the finished model of the Reparation, a model more sublime and inimitable than any other; a model perpetuated under our very eyes, and communicated to our souls in the Sacrament of the Eucharist. Let us hear her own account of the perfections which she discovered in it.

'This hidden life of Nazareth appears to me to be the life of predilection of the Incarnate Word: to it He gave thirty out of the thirty-three years that He was to remain visible on this earth. The Divine Word appears to me there to be more annihilated than in all His other mysteries, especially on account of the kind of life that He there embraced. In these days, as at all times, we are struck by extreme poverty; we pity and compassionate it. The poor man in the hospital is cared for; but what is thought of the workman who earns his bread? No particular interest attaches itself to him; there is no poetry in his life or in the thoughts of him; his is looked upon as a vulgar commonplace existence. For this very reason Jesus became an artisan, and obeyed an artisan. Such is the life that I desire for myself, for my daughters, for our brothers, if God gives us any..... Labour is a divine precept, the first reparation demanded by God of the sinner. Labour regenerates man; it strengthens his faculties without satisfying his evil tendencies; it extinguishes concupiscence without ruining the body; it mortifies corrupt instincts without exalting self-love. A life of labour, to accomplish the precept of penance, appears to me to be far preferable to the austerities invented by fervour. O, how much better I love to see my sisters washing the linen, or scraping off the mud from the feet of passers-by, than if they had lay-sisters to serve them, so that they might occupy themselves in doing penance!.... How I love to say to those who ask me, "How do you live?" "We live exactly like poor workwomen!" This life agrees with all healths, all characters, and all educations. Jesus made Himself all to all; His daily life should be imitated by great numbers, and yet that life is contemned by even the good; ... and I have loved it, as I consider it the most efficacious means of bringing men back to the belief that evangelical simplicity is not a mere fable.'

We should have to quote all the letters and meditations of Mary Teresa before we should exhaust the reflections with which the interior of Nazareth inspired her. In it she found all things, both the common basis of a life of perfection and the especial food of the vocation of Reparation.

'The most excellent Reparation,' she said, 'is the love of God and one's neighbour, because the revolt of creatures against these two commandments is the cause of every sin without exception. Now Jesus practised charity in a divine manner at Nazareth: He loved all men in Mary and in Joseph, and, in loving them, He acted as a Reparation for them; and Mary and Joseph, by their charity to Jesus, repaired the indifference of all creatures for their God; and by uniting themselves to the adoration of the Saviour for His Father, they glorified the Creator in a perfect and all-sufficient manner.... I see Nazareth as a sanctuary in which the Divine Love fully exercises His power.'

She one day replied to some one who questioned her respecting the progress of her institute: 'Remember that the Réparatrice work advances like a tortoise, but this does not mean that it is not zealous. Jesus, who desired so greatly to eat the Pasch with His disciples, remained for thirty years without seeing His disciples or instructing them; and what important work then was He doing which so greatly retarded His mission? He was sawing wood and working as a common carpenter, in order to make reparation for human presumption and over-eagerness.'

How, then, can we be astonished at hearing her cry out, 'I have often begged God to let me die before my work shall be much known or talked of?' How can we be astonished to find her resisting eager friends, who offered her considerable advantages at the cost of a deviation, insignificant in appearance, but which would have gradually drawn away her institute from the simple and hidden path she had chosen both for herself and her children?'

And if, whilst seeking to bury herself and them in the obscurity of Nazareth, she also wished to see her Saviour issue from the shadow of the Tabernacle, it was in order to make the great lesson of the hidden life still more striking. It is in vain to expose the Eucharist; the veil cannot be withdrawn: the Living Bread will always remain a mystery; and it is well to contemplate it closely, in order to conform oneself to Its great example. The Blessed Sacrament exposed thus becomes the school of the life of Nazareth.

The following is the burning language in which Mary Teresa speaks of it. The reader will kindly excuse some exaggerated expressions, and remember the pure and passionate love which inspired them:

'This bread, become the body of the Man-God, is nevertheless left, abandoned, despised. His Eucharistic veils did not then suffice to hide Him? It seems as if men wished to weaken their faith by creating a fresh prison for Jesus; and the priests, who should be the seraphim of earth, have become His gaolers. O Jesus! was it not Thyself who inspired me with these thoughts when Thy love, piercing the gates of the Tabernacle, sent a burning dart into my heart? Like the disciples of Emmaüs, I can say that I always feel my soul burning when I converse with Jesus after the breaking of bread. And never, never have I been able to restrain my indignation at seeing Emmanuel shut up and deserted. I say to myself: There are societies of every kind, but the part of Mary and the work of Magdalen has not been undertaken. Thou art a King, O Jesus, and Thou hast no guards. Thou art God, and Thou hast no adorers. Thou art Bread, and yet the Food of none! . . . No watch is kept by the Eucharistic Bread! heretics and infidels profit by this indifference, and say, "What, then, has become of the God of the Eucharist?" . . . . Doctors and theologians preserve the faith of the Scriptures, and yet there is no special institution to preserve the Eucharistic life!'

Such is truly the language of love; it sees only its object; whatever may have been accomplished, it considers that nothing has been effected if there still remain something to be done. Let her not be accused of severity or injustice; if she perceived that she were accusing any one, she would instantly retract; for charity is humble and mild—*Charitas non cogitat malum.* But when there is a question of God, she forgets all, and only remembers the creature to invite him to immolation and adoration.

It was in those times, when she felt herself pressed to form a Court for Jesus, that her work appeared to her so incomplete, and that she longed to confide it to priestly hands, by giving her daughters both fathers and brothers.

"My God, my God,' she exclaimed, 'Thou knowest how insufficient poor women are to uphold this sublime vocation! . . . Others will come whose shoes we are not worthy to loose; for our Saviour has confided His adorable Body to those alone who consecrate It. O, I blush when I think that the royal priesthood of Christ leaves to poor girls the honour of guarding the person of the King. . . . I wander, perhaps. . . . Pardon me, Divine Master! But I have too often shared the sadness of Thy heart in Thine abandonment not to feel profoundly that Thou desirest and wilt call souls whom Thy love hath reserved to rekindle faith in this century. Thou hast shown me the splendour of these souls amid the stars of Thy Church, and Thou wilt not deceive the faith of Thy poor servant: she will see before her death her children provided with fathers.'

God hears the prayers of the saints in His own way; and that manner is not always such as they had dreamed. Mary Teresa died without seeing the fathers she so ardently desired. Others, however, had commenced the execution of the project. But, whilst leaving to God the secret of His counsels, who can fail to admire the elevated views, the ardent desires, and impetuous flights of zeal of this ardent soul?

In order to complete her idea of a foundation, there is a third name which must be added to Nazareth and the Eucharist, viz. Carmel. Mary Teresa was not ambitious, neither was she an innovator. If she saw the opportunity of, in some degree, restoring to youth the old forms of the devotion of Reparation, she felt still more keenly the necessity of grafting the new institute on the old stem, which was still vigorous and full of the sap of Christ; and this venerable stem she found in Carmel. The vocation which had first attracted her to the cloister, which had led her to hope to find repose among the daughters of St. Teresa, had been but a preparation for her real vocation. God had conducted her to the spring, not that she might quench her own thirst alone, but that she might thence draw living water to dispense to her children. Let us listen to her exposition of her doctrine on this point:

'The graces given to the Church receive a divine fecundity by the instruments organised for the aim which our Saviour—the sole founder and legislator—proposes. Now there is not a single work, constituted and approved of by the Church, which has not certain springs from whence it draws its sap; and there is not a single one of these springs that has not fully received the Spirit of Jesus Christ. These springs, my beloved sisters, are but few in number. Many religious families have had founders who appear to have been their springs; but, on studying their origin, it will be seen that they are really but off-shoots, receiving their substance from the great Parent-tree, already loaded with numerous branches. I declare to you honestly, that I should regard as a sterile branch, and one that would deserve to be cut off by the Church, a religious family which does not drink of the old source laid down by the Saints. Well, sisters, God has given you the grace to point out to you Himself, by a rare manifestation of Divine Providence, who was to be your real Mother. It was in the womb of St. Teresa—my dear patroness —that you were conceived; you came forth from her; the fire of her heart has animated you; the strength and sweetness of the milk of her doctrine have nourished your childhood.'

The feast of St. Teresa was never allowed to pass without the Réparatrice sisters receiving from their Mother some great lesson. We can read her correspondence with her communities year by year; and as the 15th October comes round we are sure to find a letter, breathing the spirit of St. Teresa, burning with the desire to spread it, and impregnated with the doctrine of Carmel.

'All the fundamental virtues of your religious and Réparatrice life,' she wrote, 'are the distinctive seals of the soul of St. Teresa and her institute. Your manner of life, though apparently different, is really conformable to that which the heart of your holy patroness studied and conceived.'

She placed even the minor points of her institute under the protection of the name of St. Teresa, being thoroughly persuaded that, whilst deviating materially from a few of her rules, she still conformed to her spirit. One day, when a mother importunately pleaded for an exception to be made in favour of her daughter, she replied, 'I am thought severe; those who come after me will perhaps make concessions; and when such concessions have given rise to abuses we shall be cloistered. Grilles are more convenient. People murmur less against a superior force than against the firmness of a Founder. . . . But I am wrong in saying this. Sometimes I am anxious about the future, when I see how apt this century is to ally nature with the Evangelical Counsels; but I am ungrateful to my children, in supposing that they will not be faithful children of St. Teresa.'

The tie which attached her to this Mother formed her

greatest consolation and strength amid the crosses of her vocation. 'O my Mother and mistress,' she exclaimed, 'great and worthy spouse of the Incarnate Word, how good and useful it is to glorify myself with the Holy Church in the beatitude of your sanctity, in the fecundity of your apostolate! What would have become of me, under the load that weighs me down, had I not the privilege of taking shelter under that mantle of Elias, transmitted through centuries to the reformer of Carmel ?'

A few weeks before her death, the last time that she took up her pen to write to her children, it was to draw up for them a kind of will. 'I leave you,' she said, 'a magnificent inheritance—the perpetual adoration of the Blessed Sacrament Exposed.' Then, after developing in a few words the excellence of this privilege, she added, 'I leave you another property, which is inestimable. I bequeath you St. Teresa of Jesus. . . . She is a Mother who will never die.'

Such was her conception of the Institute of Reparation, modelled on Nazareth, consecrated to the Eucharist, vivified by the spirit of Carmel. Thus did Mary Teresa understand it; thus did she realise it during her lifetime; thus do her children continue to maintain and spread it under the posthumous influence of her blessing and her tenderness.

Our task is ended. We have endeavoured to make our readers acquainted with a soul who, in our opinion, belongs to the family of the Saints. If this work reveals to some few the supernatural action of God in the world and the power of His grace; if it breathes an atmosphere of faith; if the pious reader derives some profit from his intercourse with a great heart; if, finally, after reading this life, some understand better the place occupied in the life of the Church by the Eucharistic mystery, —we shall esteem ourselves well rewarded for a work which we wish were less imperfect, but which could not be more sincere.

THE END.

BURNS AND OATES'S LIST.

LIBRARY OF RELIGIOUS BIOGRAPHY.
Edited by EDWARD HEALY THOMPSON, M.A.

Vol. I. *Life of St. Aloysius Gonzaga, S.J.* 5s. Second edition.
   II. *Life of Marie-Eustelle Harpain, the Angel of the Eucharist.* 5s. Second edition.
  III. *Life of St. Stanislas Kostka, S.J.* 5s.
   IV. *Life of the Baron de Renty; or Perfection in the World exemplified.* 6s.
    V. *Life of the Venerable Anna Maria Taigi, the Roman Matron* (1769-1837). With Portrait. Cloth, 6s.
   VI. *Life and Revelations of Marie Lataste, Lay Sister of the Congregation of the Sacred Heart.*
Others in preparation.

Louise Lateau of Bois d'Haine: her Life, her Ecstasies, and her Stigmata. A Medical Study. By Dr. F. LEFEBVRE, Professor of General Pathology and Therapeutics in the Catholic University of Louvain, &c. Translated from the French. Edited by Rev. J. SPENCER NORTHCOTE, D.D. Full and complete edition. 3s. 6d.

Mental Prayer. By Père COURBON, S.J. Translated from the French, with Preface, by the Very Rev. Fr. GORDON, of the Oratory. Cloth, 2s. 6d.

Ecclesiastical Antiquities of London and its Suburbs. By ALEXANDER WOOD, M.A. Oxon., of the Somerset Archæological Society. 5s.

'O, who the ruins sees, whom wonder doth not fill
With our great fathers' pompe, devotion, and their skill.'

'Very seldom have we read a book entirely devoted to the metropolis with such pleasure. He has produced a book which from beginning to end is full of Catholic religious local lore of the highest interest.'—*Catholic Times.*
'Written by a very able and competent author, one who thoroughly appreciates his subject, and who treats it with the discrimination of a critic and the sound common sense of a practised writer.'—*Church Herald.*

The Early Martyrs. By Mrs. HOPE. New edition. 2s. 6d. and 3s.

Homeward: a Tale of Redemption. By the Rev. Fr. RAWES, O.S.C. Second edition. 3s. 6d.
'Full of holy thoughts and exquisite poetry.'—*Dublin Review.*

---o---

BURNS & OATES, 17 & 18 PORTMAN STREET, W.

The Prophet of Carmel: a Series of Practical Considerations upon the History of Elias in the Old Testament. With a supplementary Dissertation. By the Rev. CHARLES B. GARSIDE. Dedicated to the Very Rev. Dr. NEWMAN. 5s.

Contents: Chap. I. Introduction. II. The King and the Prophet. III. The Drought. IV. Sarephta. V. Mourning and Joy. VI. The Message of Mercy. VII. Troubling Israel. VIII. Necessary Antagonism. IX. Carmel. X. The Torrent of Cison. XI. Watching for Rain. XII. Fear and Flight. XIII. The Vision at Horeb. XIV. Breaking of the Clouds. XV. The Prophet's Mantle. XVI. The coveted Vineyard. XVII. The iniquitous Plot. XVIII. The unexpected Meeting. XIX. The Man of God. XX. The Parting and Ascension.

A Dissertation upon the following Questions: 1. The Condition and Abode of Elias after his Translation. 2. His Appearance on the Mount of Transfiguration. 3. His Return at the End of the World. 4. The Meaning of Luke i. 17; John i. 21, 25; Luke ix. 7, 8, 54-56; Matt. xxvii. 49.

'There is not a page in these sermons but commands our respect. They are Corban in the best sense; they belong to the sanctuary, and are marked as Divine property by a special cachet. Except the discourses of him to whom they are dedicated, Dr. Newman, we know of no better sermons in the language. They are simple without being trite, and poetical without being pretentious.'—*Westminster Gazette*.

Mary Magnifying God: May Sermons. By Rev. Fr. HUMPHREY, O.S.C. Cloth, 2s. 6d.

'Each sermon is a complete thesis, eminent for the strength of its logic, the soundness of its theology, the lucidness of its expression, and the force and beauty of its language.'—*Tablet*.

The Divine Teacher. By the same. 2s. 6d.

'The most excellent treatise we have ever read. It could not be clearer, and while really deep is perfectly intelligible to any person of the most ordinary education.'—*Tablet*.

'We cannot speak in terms too high of the matter contained in this most excellent and able pamphlet.'—*Westminster Gazette*.

God in His Works. A Course of Five Sermons. By the Rev. Fr. RAWES, O.S.C. Cloth, 2s. 6d.

Subjects: 1. God in Creation. 2. God in the Incarnation. 3. God in the Holy See. 4. God in the Heart. 5. God in the Resurrection.

'Full of striking imagery; and the beauty of the language cannot fail to make it valuable for spiritual reading.'—*Catholic Times*.

Fénélon's Reflections for every Day in the Month. Translated by the Rev. Dr. FLETCHER. Cloth, 1s.

Thoughts on some Passages of Holy Scripture. By a Layman. Translated from the French. Edited by JOHN EDWARD BOWDEN, Priest of the Oratory of St. Philip Neri. 2s. 6d.

'Contains some very devotional thoughts, and will be useful as a help to meditation.'—*Tablet*.

———o———

BURNS & OATES, 63 PATERNOSTER ROW, E.C.

Jesuits in Conflict; or Historic Facts illustrative of the Labours and Sufferings of the English Mission and Province of the Society of Jesus in the Times of Queen Elizabeth and her Successors. First Series. By a Member of the Society of Jesus. With illustrations in Photographed Etching. 1 vol. crown 8vo, 5s.

Life of Blessed Alphonsus Rodriguez, Lay Brother of the Society of Jesus. By the same. With Engraved Portrait. 1 vol. crown 8vo, 5s.

Lectures on certain Portions of the earlier Old Testament History. By PHILIP G. MUNRO. 3s. 6d.

'Sound, sober, and practical, and will be found extremely valuable.'— *Weekly Register.*

The Ritual of the New Testament: an Essay on the Principles and Origin of Catholic Ritual. By Rev. T. E. BRIDGETT, C.SS.R. Being the Second Edition of 'In Spirit and in Truth.' 5s.

'Written with singular force and simplicity. It goes to the root of the whole matter, discussing all the principles involved in a most exhaustive manner.'—*Tablet.*

The Question of Anglican Ordinations Discussed. By E. E. ESTCOURT, M.A. F.A.S., Canon of St. Chad's Cathedral, Birmingham. With an Appendix of Original Documents and Photographic Facsimiles. 14s.

'A valuable contribution to the theology of the sacrament of order.'—*Month.*

'Marks a very important epoch in the history of that question, and virtually disposes of it.'—*Messenger.*

'Will henceforth be an indispensable portion of every priest's library.'— *Tablet.*

'A work of very great value.'—*Catholic Opinion.*

'Superior both in literary method, tone, and mode of reasoning to the usual controversial books on this subject.'—*Church Herald.*

Count de Montalembert's Letters to a Schoolfellow: 1827-1830. Translated from the French by C. F. AUDLEY. With Portrait. 5s.

'Simple, easy, and unaffected in a degree, these letters form a really charming volume. The observations on men and manners, on books and politics, are simply wonderful, considering that when he wrote them he was only seventeen or eighteen years of age.'—*Weekly Register.*

Meditations for the Use of the Clergy for every Day in the Year, on the Gospels for the Sundays. From the Italian of Mgr. SCOTTI, Archbishop of Thessalonica. Revised and edited by the Oblates of St. Charles. Vols. i. ii. and iii., 4s. each.

'It is a sufficient recommendation to this book of meditations that our Archbishop has given them his own warm approval. . . . They are full of the language of the Scriptures, and are rich with unction of their Divine sense.'— *Weekly Register.*

'A manual of meditations for priests, to which we have seen nothing comparable.'—*Catholic World.*

'There is great beauty in the thoughts, the illustrations are striking, the learning shown in patristic quotation considerable, and the special applications to priests are very powerful. It is entirely a priest's book.'—*Church Review.*

———o———

BURNS AND OATES, 17 & 18 PORTMAN STREET, W.

Geology and Revelation ; or the Ancient History of the Earth considered in the light of Geological Facts and Revealed Religion. With Illustrations. By the Rev. GERALD MOLLOY, D.D. Second edition, much enlarged and improved. 6s. 6d.

Art of always Rejoicing. By SARASA, S.J. 2s. 6d.

Bible History. By REEVE and CHALLONER. New and improved edition, 2s. Questions on ditto, 4d. Set of Illustrations for ditto, coloured, 12s.; larger size, 16s.

Manual of Church History. For Families and Schools. Compiled from the best sources. 12mo, cloth, 3s. (School edition, 2s.)

The Day Sanctified. Select Meditations and Spiritual Readings from Approved Writers. 3s. 6d.; red edges, 4s.

Sister Emmerich on the Passion. Full edition. 3s. 6d.

Fander : Catechism of the Christian Religion. Cloth, 2s.

Liguori (St. Alphonso). New and improved Translation of the Complete Works of St. Alphonso, edited by Father COFFIN:

Vol. I. The Christian Virtues, and the means for obtaining them. Cloth elegant, 4s. Or separately: 1. The Love of our Lord Jesus Christ, 1s. 4d. 2. Treatise on Prayer, 1s. 4d. (in the ordinary editions a great part of this work is omitted). 3. A Christian's Rule of Life, 1s.

Vol. II. The Mysteries of the Faith—the Incarnation; containing Meditations and Devotions on the Birth and Infancy of Jesus Christ, &c.; suited for Advent and Christmas. 3s. 6d.; cheap edition, 2s.

Vol. III. The Mysteries of the Faith—the Blessed Sacrament. 3s. 6d.; cheap edition, 2s.

Vol. IV. Eternal Truths—Preparation for Death. 3s. 6d.; cheap edition, 2s.

Vol. V. Treatises on the Passion : containing 'Jesus hath loved us,' &c. 3s.; cheap edition, 2s.

Vol. VI. Glories of Mary. New edition. 2s. 6d.; cloth, 3s. 6d.; with Frontispiece, cloth elegant, 4s. 6d.; also in better bindings.

'Jesus hath loved us,' separately, new and correct edition, 9d. cloth.

Visits to the Blessed Sacrament and to the Blessed Virgin Mary. An entirely new translation by the Redemptorist Fathers. 1s. cloth; bound roan, 1s. 6d.; French morocco, 2s. 6d.; calf, 4s. 6d.; morocco plain, 5s.; morocco gilt, 6s.

Month of Mary. 1s.; cloth, 1s. 6d.

Devotions to St. Joseph. 3d.; cloth, 4d.

Hymns and Verses on Spiritual Subjects. Cloth elegant, 1s.; cheap edition, 6d. Music, 1s.

Reflections on Spiritual Subjects, and on the Passion of our Lord. With Memoir and Frontispiece. Cloth, 2s. 6d.

BURNS AND OATES, 63 PATERNOSTER ROW, E.C.

THE THREE MISSION BOOKS,

Comprising all that is required for general use; the cheapest books ever issued.

1. *Complete Book of Devotions and Hymns: Path to Heaven*, 1000 pages, 2s. This Volume forms the Cheapest and most Complete Book of Devotions for Public or Private use ever issued. (33d Thousand.) Cloth, Two Shillings. Also in various bindings.
2. *Complete Choir Manual (Latin) for the Year*, 230 pieces. 10s. 6d.
3. *Complete Popular Hymn and Tune Book (English)*, 250 pieces. 10s. 6d. Melodies alone, 1s. Words, 3d.; cloth, 5d.

Prayers of SS. Gertrude and Mechtilde. Neat cloth, lettered, 1s. 6d.; Fr. morocco, red edges, 2s.; best calf, red edges, 4s. 6d.; best morocco, plain, 5s.; gilt, 6s. Also in various extra bindings. On thin *vellum paper* at the same prices.

Devotions for the 'Quarant' Ore,' or New Visits to the Blessed Sacrament. Edited by Cardinal Wiseman. 1s. 6d., or in cloth, gilt edges, 2s.; morocco, 5s.

Imitation of the Sacred Heart. By the Rev. Father ARNOLD, S.J. 12mo, 4s. 6d.; or in handsome cloth, red edges, 5s.; also in calf, 8s. 6d.; morocco, 9s. 6d.

Manual of the Sacred Heart. New edition, 2s.; red edges, 2s. 6d.; calf, 5s. 6d.; morocco, 6s. 6d.

The Spirit of St. Teresa. 2s.; red edges, with picture, 2s. 6d.

The Spirit of the Curé d'Ars. 2s. Ditto, ditto. 2s. 6d.

The Spirit of St. Gertrude. 2s. 6d.

Manna of the New Covenant: Devotions for Communion. Cloth, 2s.; bound, with red edges, 2s. 6d.

A'Kempis. The Following of Christ, in four books; a new translation, with borders, and illustrative engravings. Fcap. 8vo, cloth, 3s. 6d.; calf, 7s.; morocco, 8s. 6d.; gilt, 11s. The same, pocket edition. Cloth, 1s.; bound, roan, 1s. 6d.; calf, 4s. 6d.; morocco, 5s.

Spiritual Combat; a new translation. 18mo, cloth, 3s.; calf, 6s. 6d.; morocco, 7s. 6d. The same, pocket size. Cloth, 1s.; calf, neat, 4s. 6d.; morocco, 5s.

BURNS AND OATES, 17 & 18 PORTMAN STREET, W.

Missal. New and Complete Pocket Missal, in Latin and English, with all the new Offices and the Proper of Ireland, Scotland, and the Jesuits. Roan, embossed gilt edges, 5*s.*; calf flexible, red edges, 8*s.* 6*d.*; morocco, gilt edges, 9*s.* 6*d.*; ditto, gilt, 11*s.*

Epistles and Gospels for the whole Year. 1*s.* 6*d.*

Vesper Book for the Laity. This Volume contains the Office of Vespers (including Compline and Benediction), complete for *every day in the year.* Roan, 3*s.* 6*d.*; calf, 6*s.*; morocco, 7*s.*; gilt, 8*s.*

The Golden Manual; or Complete Guide to Devotion, Public or Private. New edition, enlarged and improved, 800 pp. Embossed, gilt edges, 6*s.*; calf flexible back, very neat and durable, 8*s.* 6*d.*; morocco plain, 9*s.* 6*d.*; gilt, 11*s.* Also bound for presents in elegant bindings, with antique boards and edges, clasps, corners, &c., 21*s.* and upwards; ivory, beautifully ornamented, 42*s.*; velvet rims and clasp, very elegant, 24*s.*

Also an edition on fine thin satin paper, *one inch thick.* Calf, 8*s.* 6*d.*; morocco, 9*s.* 6*d.*; gilt, 11*s.*; limp morocco, edges turned over, 12*s.*

The same, with *Epistles and Gospels,* 1*s.* extra.

Golden Manual and Missal in one. Calf, 15*s.*; morocco plain, 17*s.*; gilt, 18*s.* Also in various antique bindings.

Holy Communion, Books on the, &c.:
  Sacramental Companion. [Manna of the New Covenant.] New edition, 2*s.* 6*d.*
  Eucharistic Month. 6*d.*; cloth, 1*s.*
  Père Boone on Frequent Communion. Cloth, 3*d.*
  Devotions for Confession and Communion (Oratory). Covers, 6*d.*
  Liguori, St., on the Holy Eucharist. 3*s.* 6*d.*; cheap edition, 2*s.*
  „ Visits to the Most Blessed Sacrament. 1*s.*
  New Visits. Preface by Cardinal WISEMAN. 1*s.* 6*d.*; cloth, 2*s.*
  First Communion, Letters on. 1*s.*
  Reflections and Prayers for Holy Communion. From the French. Cloth, 4*s.* 6*d.*; do., red edges, 5*s.*; calf, 9*s.*; morocco, 10*s.*

Considerations for a Three Days' Preparation for Communion. Taken chiefly from the French of St. JURE, S.J. By CECILIE MARIE CADDELL. 8*d.*

Day Hours of the Church. Cloth, 1*s.* Also, separately, The Offices of Prime and Compline, 8*d.*; The Offices of Tierce, Sext, and None, 3*d.*

———o———

BURNS AND OATES, 63 PATERNOSTER ROW, E.C.

The Words of Jesus. Edited by the Rev. F. CASWALL. Cloth, 2s.

Lyra Liturgica: Verses for the Ecclesiastical Seasons. By Canon OAKELEY. 3s. 6d.

Select Sacred Poetry. 1s.

Instructions in Christian Doctrine. 3s.

New Testament Narrative for Schools and Families. 2s. 6d.

Letters on First Communion. 1s.

Flowers of St. Francis of Assisi. 3s.

Manual of Practical Piety. By St. FRANCIS DE SALES. 3s. 6d.

Manresa; or the Spiritual Exercises of St. Ignatius. 3s.

The Christian Virtues. By St. ALPHONSUS. 4s.

Eternal Truths. By the same. 3s. 6d.

On the Passion. By the same. 3s.

Jesus hath loved us. By the same. 9d.

Reflections on Spiritual Subjects. By the same. 2s. 6d.

Glories of Mary. By the same. New edition. 3s. 6d.

The Raccolta of Indulgenced Prayers. 3s.

Rodriguez on Christian Perfection. Two vols. 6s.

Stolberg's Little Book of the Love of God. 2s.

The Hidden Life of Jesus: a Lesson and Model to Christians. Translated from the French of HENRI-MARIE BOUDON, Archdeacon of Evreux, by EDWARD HEALY THOMPSON, M.A. 3s.

Devotion to the Nine Choirs of Holy Angels, and especially to the Angel-Guardians. Translated from the French of HENRI-MARIE BOUDON, Archdeacon of Evreux, by EDWARD HEALY THOMPSON, M.A. 3s.

Family Devotions for every Day in the Week, with occasional Prayers. Selected from Catholic Manuals, ancient and modern. Foolscap, limp cloth, red edges, very neat, 2s.

Aids to Choirmasters in the Performance of Solemn Mass, Vespers, Compline, and the various Popular Services in General Use. 2d.

P.S. Messrs. B. & O. will be happy to send any of the above Books on inspection.

A large allowance to the Clergy.

———o———

BURNS & OATES, 17 & 18 PORTMAN STREET, W.

RELIGIOUS BIOGRAPHY AND HISTORY.

St. Aloysius Gonzaga. 5s.
St. Stanislas Kostka. 5s.
St. Paula. 2s.
Marie-Eustelle Harpain. 5s.
St. Charles Borromeo. 3s. 6d.
St. Vincent de Paul. 3s.
St. Francis de Sales. 3s.
The Curé d'Ars. 4s.
St. Thomas of Canterbury. 4s. 6d.
Wykeham, Waynflete, & More. 4s.
The Blessed Henry Suso. 4s.
M. Olier of Saint Sulpice. 4s.
The Early Martyrs. 2s. 6d.
St. Dominic and the Dominican Order. 8s. 6d.
Madame Swetchine. 7s. 6d.
The Sainted Queens. 3s.
Blessed John Berchmans. 2s.
St. Francis Xavier. 2s.
St. Philip Neri. 3s.
St. Frances of Rome. 2s. 6d.
Heroines of Charity. 2s. 6d.
Saints of the Working Classes. 1s. 4d.
Sœur Rosalie and Mdlle. Lamourous. 1s.
St. Francis and St. Clare. 1s.
Lives of Pious Youth. 2s.
Modern Missions in the East and West. 3s.
Missions in Japan and Paraguay. 3s.
The Knights of St. John. 3s. 6d.
Anecdotes and Incidents. 2s. 6d.
Remarkable Conversions. 2s. 6d.
Pictures of Christian Heroism. 8s.
Lives of the Roman Pontiffs. By DE MONTOR. 2 vols. 58s. (cash, 48s.).
Darras' History of the Church. 4 vols. 2l. 8s. (cash. 2l.).
Mary Ana of Jesus, the Lily of Quito. 3s. 6d.
A Noble Lady. 2s. 6d.
Mme. de Soyrcourt. 3s.
St. Ignatius. By BARTOLI. 2 vols. 14s.—Ditto, small size, 2s.

St. Ignatius and his Companions. 4s.
Abulchar Bisciarah. 2 vols. 3s. 6d.
St. Angela Merici. 3s. 6d.
St. Margaret of Cortona. 3s. 6d.
Princess Borghese. 2s.
F. Maria Ephraim. 5s.
Mrs. Seton. 8s. 6d.
Mme. de la Peltrie. 2s.
F. Felix d'Andreis. 4s. 6d.
St. Philomena. 2s. 6d.
St. Cecilia. By GUERANGER. 6s.
Fathers of the Desert. 4s. 6d.
Pius VI. 3s.
St. Bridget. 2s. 6d.
St. Mary Magdalen. 2s. 6d.
St. Zita. 3s.
St. Francis of Assisi. 2s.
St. Catherine of Sienna. 5s.
Bishop Flaget. 4s. 6d.
Dr. Maginn. 4s. 6d.
Cath. M'Auley, Foundress of the Sisters of Mercy. 10s. 6d.

EDITED BY LADY G. FULLERTON.
Mary Fitzgerald, a Child of the Sacred Heart. 2s.
The Honourable E. Dormer, late of the 60th Rifles. 2s.

The Apostle of Abyssinia. By Lady HERBERT of Lea. Post 8vo, cloth, 6s.; cheap edition, 3s.

The Corean Martyrs. 2s.

FOREIGN MISSIONARY SERIES.
1. *Henry Dorié, Martyr.* Translated by Lady HERBERT. Cloth, 2s.
2. *Théophane Vénard, Martyr in Tonquin.* Cloth. 3s.
3. *Bishop Bruté.* Cloth, 3s.
4. *Monseigneur Berneux, Bishop and Martyr.* Cloth, 3s.

BURNS & OATES, 63 PATERNOSTER ROW, E.C.

www.ingramcontent.com/pod-product-compliance
Lightning Source LLC
Chambersburg PA
CBHW032042230426
43672CB00009B/1430